PUER PAPERS

James Hillman
Henry A. Murray
Thomas Moore
James Baird
Thomas Cowan
Randolph Severson

Edited by James Hillman

SPRING PUBLICATIONS
THOMPSON, CONN.

Published by Spring Publications
Thompson, Conn.
www.springpublications.com

Third, revised edition 2025 (3.0)
First published in 1979

Library of Congress Control Number: 978-0-88214-184-8
ISBN: 978-0-88214-183-1

A Note for the Reader
(1979)

The preparation of *Puer Papers* has seemed at times a particularly trying task. The apparently straightforward project of assembling a few articles for publication has proved instead to be a prolonged and dusky contest with thousands of slippery words, each apparently eager to escape being bound up in a conventional and accessible package. As a member of the printer's staff said in frustration, after weeks of trying to coax recalcitrant copy through rebellious machines: "This thing doesn't want to be a book."

Perhaps this elusiveness speaks most convincingly of the way in which the essays collected here touch the essence of the puer. Like the divine boy himself, they have resisted the imposition of order, the confinement of materiality, the insult of an ordinary fate. Although the puer wants to be seen, he does not want to be known, for to be known is to be caught, he will not willingly relinquish his cherished arcana in a book any more than in therapy. So each of the writers represented in this gathering has caught no more than a glimpse—the flash of a wing, the flank of a horse, the gape of a wound.

Yet, however cleverly the puer may escape our senex nets, we chase him still. The patients, characters, lovers, friends whose lives are organized by the puer pattern frustrate and fascinate us; our own lives are tugged by puer longings, ruffled by spirit breezes. We need to know him, for he is in us all, somewhere.

Between these needs—the puer's need to avoid death by exposure, our need to penetrate his pathologies and uncover the springs of spirit—this book emerges. It is cast within that destructive/creative tension that has always vibrated between earth and heaven, intellect and inspiration. Thus. it is a psychological book in the most fundamental sense. But it should not be mistaken for a "psychology" book; it is an evocation, rather than an explanation of the puer, and it is meant for artist, analyst, and scholar alike.

CYNTHIA GILES

CONTENTS

I

ARCHETYPAL PHENOMENOLOGY

II

PUER PATHOLOGIES

III

PUER IN MYTH AND LITERATURE

Abbreviations

CW= *Collected Works of C. G. Jung,* edited and translated by Gerhard Adler and R.F.C. Hull, 20 vols. (Princeton, N.J.: Princeton University Press, 1953–79), cited by paragraph number

UE = *Uniform Edition of the Writings of James Hillman,* edited by Klaus Ottmann, 12 vols. (Putnam and Thompson, Conn.: Spring Publications, 2004–)

I

ARCHETYPAL PHENOMENOLOGY

First presented at Eranos and published in *Eranos Yearbook* 35 (1967). Reprinted in 1979 in *Puer Papers* and revised in 2005 for inclusion in *UE*3: *Senex & Puer*.

Senex and Puer:
An Aspect of the Historical and Psychological Present

JAMES HILLMAN

"But it is rather time," saith she, "to apply remedies, than to make complaintes."
—Boethius, *The Consolation of Philosophy*

We are living in what the Greeks called the kairos—the right moment—for a "metamorphosis of the gods," of the fundamental principles and symbols. This peculiarity of our time, which is certainly not of our conscious choosing, is the expression of the unconscious man within us who is changing. Coming generations will have to take account of this momentous transformation if humanity is not to destroy itself through the might of its own technology and science.
—C.G. Jung, *The Undiscovered Self*

Our special problem today is just this: we are essentially primitive creatures struggling desperately to adjust ourselves to a way of life that is alien to almost the whole past history of our species…the transition from primitive to sophisticated technology must be made swiftly—the resource problem demands that this be so. Today we are living at a unique moment, neither in the long primitive era nor in the better adjusted prosperous future. It is our century, our millennium, that must perforce take the maximum strain, for it is our fate to live during the transitional phase. And because we live in this special phase we find social difficulties, pressures, situations that defy even the simplest logical processes. We find ourselves in no real contact with the forces that are shaping the future.
—Fred Hoyle, *Of Men and Galaxies*

To have "no real contact with the forces that are shaping the future" (Hoyle)[1] would be to fail the *kairos* of transition. To come to terms with this *kairos* would mean discovering a connection between past and future. For us, individuals, makeweights that may tip the scales of history, our task is to discover the psychic connection between past and future, otherwise the unconscious figures within us who are as well the archaic past will shape the historical future perhaps disastrously. Thus the *kairos*, this unique moment of transition in world history, becomes a transition within the microcosm, within us each individually, as we struggle with the psychological connections between past and future, old and new, expressed archetypally as the polarity of senex and puer.

Psychology and History. A polar division between senex and puer is all about us outside in the historical field. We find good example of this in demography that has reached back to an archaic system: peoples are again divided along lines of age and youth. The principle categories of social structure—race, region, religion, class, occupation, economics, sex—are insufficient. Modern urban society emphasizes again the division according to age levels. There are communities in the United States—new communities, not just the derelict hamlets from which youth has always fled where only "oldsters" live, entire cities of the retired, the "home for the aged" now extended over square miles. There are new suburbs in France where the average age of population is less than twenty-one. In Sweden, in Britain, in the United States, there are communities the size of towns where only young married couples live; and settlements, apartment houses, resorts for only the young or only the old. Two new fields of psychotherapy have been invented—geriatrics and juvenile delinquency—and we have specialists for the psyche of the old and of the adolescent. In this crowded world of our future, the division is between age and youth: on one side the established nations with slower, controlled birth rates and aging population; on the other, the so-called newer, younger, and needy nations with high birth rates and the proliferation of children reflected in a low median age.

---

1. Fred Hoyle, *Of Men and Galaxies* (London: Heinemann, 1965), 65.

The division is in the family as the conflict of generations, some-times no longer a conflict of misunderstandings but a silence. There is a division of communication systems between age and youth: the latter learns today not through traditional forms and printed words but from altogether other media in our urban collective. Youth forms a social class, self-enclosed and uninitiated by its elders, and thus largely with-out communication outside of itself.

The division is in the political world with its aging leaders and sys-tems attempting to maintain "law and order," and the rebellions of youth in the name of "rights and freedom." As one legal philosopher has put it: never in the history of the United States have we had so many laws, so much science of law and its enforcement, and never have we had so much disorder and violence.

> The falcon cannot hear the falconer;
> Things fall apart; the centre cannot hold;
> Mere anarchy is loosed upon the world,
> The blood-dimmed tide is loosed...
> The best lack all conviction, while the worst
> Are full of passionate intensity.
> Surely some revelation is at hand;
> Surely the Second Coming is at hand,[2]

said William Butler Yeats in his poem, "The Second Coming."

And theology, also riven by the senex-puer problem, having found God dead, both Father and Son, awaits some revelation. For when it is announced: "The King is dead," immediately follows: "Long live the King." At the same moment, the King dies and the Prince becomes King. If God is dead, what princely power is succeeding? Why the silence, and where the succession?

The polar division between senex and puer, falcon split from fal-coner, that is all about us is of course our historical concern. But it is not only historical and for the historian only. The psyche is not iso-lated from history, and psychology takes place not only in a small room between two people in two chairs walled off from the historical scene. History is in the room. And just as the psyche is situated in an historical

---

2. W.B. Yeats, "The Second Coming," *Collected Poems* (London: Macmillan, 1952).

present that trails behind it the roots of a thousand ancestral trees, so too does history have psychological existence. Mircea Eliade has shown that historical events, those accumulations of irreversible time, are not the primary facts of existence.[3] Historical facts are secondary; they are incomplete and imperfect actions calling for a before and after, historical consequences built on historical antecedents, and are, as such, only accumulations of sins and sufferings that are senseless unless they point inward to central meanings. The historical "facts" may be but fantasies attached to and sprouting from central archetypal cores. Below the tangled pattern of events are experiences, psychological realities of passionate importance, a mythological substrate that gives the soul a feeling of destiny, an eschatological sense that *what happens matters.* And it matters to someone, to a person. Without the person, without the individual's sense of personal soul (that makeweight in the scales) we are simply pre-historic revenants with only collective destiny. Without the sense of soul, we have no sense of history. We never enter it. This core of soul that weaves events together into the meaningful patterns of tales and stories recounted by reminiscing creates history. History is story first and fact later.

The fantasy we call "current events," that which is taking place outside in the historical field, is a reflection of an eternal mythological experience. An historical analysis of these events—old Mao and the Red Guard, the hippie flower youth, the sociology of ageing—will not lead to their meaning. We can no more grasp the soul of the times through the TV news than we can understand the soul of a person only through the events of his case history. (Twenty-two volumes of a Warren Report can never settle or explain the living ferment of a myth.) Nothing can be revealed by a newspaper, by the world's *chronique scandaleuse,* unless the essence is grasped from within through an archetypal pattern. The archetype provides the basis for uniting those incommensurables, fact and meaning. Outer historical facts are archetypally colored, so as to disclose essential psychological meanings. Historical facts disclose the

---

3. Mircea Eliade, *The Myth of the Eternal Return,* translated by Willard R. Trask (New York: Pantheon, 1954); *Images and Symbols: Studies in Religious Symbolism,* translated by Philip Mairet (London: Harvill Press, 1961); *Myth and Reality,* translated by Willard R. Trask (New York and Evanston: Harper & Row, 1963); *The Two and the One,* translated by J. M. Cohen (London: Harvill Press, 1965).

eternally recurring mythemes of history and of our individual souls. History is but the stage on which we enact the mythemes of the soul.

The experiencing that makes history possible and is its *a priori* has been called Clio. And Clio, as first daughter, has a special relation to the mother of muses, Remembering. Clio's name signifies *gloria*, honor, celebration, and she remembers best the actions of heroes. Her interest is hardly in the daily news of the world's case history, or what Mircea Eliade calls "profane time." Rather her interest lies in those unique nuclear moments, the heroic moments through which the archetype at the soul's core is revealed, redeeming events from the blindness of mere fact. As we individuals are fastened to the facts of our personal case histories by what we remember of our personal lives, so is our culture addicted to the history of profane time. An addiction demands more and more, faster and faster. Much of our inventiveness serves merely making, gathering, and reproducing events. As the time of the millennium runs out, events speed up. We need more "information," we have less time to wait. We have even achieved "instant history," which Arthur Schlesinger defends by calling, "Contemporary History," where everything that happens to everyone on the public scene must be recorded and what is recorded must be published—and fast.[4] The profane *chroniques scandaleuse*—the profanities—of the heroes replace the *gloria* of Clio.

In analytical practice we have learned that an archetypal understanding of events can cure the compulsive fascination with one's case history. *The facts do not change, but their order is given another dimension through another myth.* They are experienced differently; they gain another meaning because they are told through another tale. So redemption from the addiction to profane history might come in the same way. This way would show another archetypal organization of the events from which we suffer. But this reorganization first requires a change in memory itself, so that one asks each day not "what happened?" but "what happened to the soul?" For this way of remembering events, memory needs to return again to its reminiscence of primordial ideas, to its original association with the root metaphors of human expe-

---

4. Arthur Schlesinger, "On the Writing of Contemporary History," *Atlantic Monthly* 219 (1967), sec. 3.

rience. Memory thus transformed would register first the experiences of the soul and only secondarily the accidents of events. Or rather, it could take up the events psychologically, ritually, no longer only their victim.

This archetypal understanding could regenerate history in the sense of reversing it or cleansing it. Such work is immensely difficult, demanding that heroic intensity that Clio celebrates. For this reason, analytical work on the collective levels of the soul is so "heroic." Psychological changes—changes of attitude, changes of personality, those fundamental lustrations of the soul—are also regenerations of history. Transforming my family's attitudes by uncovering patterns in the entwined ancestral roots is not merely a personal analytical problem. It is an historical step towards freeing a generation from a collective pattern. By changing that collective, there is a change in history itself. And each one, anyone, who makes a clearing in his bit of the forest of the past is the hero who redeems time and is the scapegoat who by taking on the sins undoes time. Thus are we makeweights in the historical transition and what we do with our psychological life is of historical import, not merely on the inner plane of salvation of the individual soul from history. More, it is the way in which history, as that which goes on collectively outside us, itself may be washed and healed.

Our polarities—senex and puer—provide the archetype for the psychological foundation of the problem of history. First, in the conventional sense, puer and senex are history as sequence and transition, as a process through time from beginning to end. And second, history as a problem in which I am caught, for which I suffer and from which I long to be redeemed, is given by the same pair as Father Time and Eternal Youth, temporality and eternity, and the puzzling paradoxes of their connection. To be involved with these figures is to be drawn into history. To be identified with either is to be dominated by an archetypal attitude towards history: the puer who transcends history and leaps out of time, and is as such ahistorical, or antihistorical in protest and revolt; or the senex who is an image of history itself and of the permanent truth revealed through history.

Our concern with the archetype of senex-puer is determined by the transition of millennia and it indicates the late stage of our culture. Curtius has amassed evidence enough from classical Latin literature to support his statements that the term "*puer senilis* or *puer senex* is a coinage of late pagan antiquity" and that where early cultures may extol youth and honor age, "late periods develop a human ideal in which the polarity youth-age works towards a balance."[5] Thus our concern is itself a reflection of the archetype now manifested symbolically in the culture around us and in the complexes of our inner world. And the constellation of this polarity *as a split* demonstrates the gravity of our historical crisis. Therefore our engagement with this archetype may restore a balance and have an effect on the historical lysis.

We are not concerned with the case history of our times and its anarchy, with the psychology of aging, of revolt and tradition, of youth, of fathers and sons, of stages of life, and such "timely topics." These are diversions. The soul is neither young nor old—or it is both. Our contemporary obsession with age and youth reflects the fall of the soul into the time and measurement system of historical materialism. Behind it all is an archetypal split. Therefore, our concern must be with archetypal therapy or therapy of an archetype. And our approach must be radical if we would put history back into the psyche. Thus we take historical problems as psychological symptoms in order to contain the speeding and spreading of these events. We shall try to hold them as psychological problems, regarding the splits in which we are caught as manifestations of an archetypal split within our individual souls.

Furthermore, because of its special relation with time as process, *this specific archetype will be involved with the process character of any complex*, with the youth and age, the temporality and eternity conundrums of any psychological attitude or part of personality. Senex and puer are bound up with the very nature of development. Any attitude as it comes into being can take on the wings of the puer and streak skyward; any attitude as it passes its ripeness can lose touch with revelation, cling to its power, and be out of Tao. Lao Tzu says: "After things reach their prime, they begin to grow old, which means being contrary to Tao."[6] Our puer attitudes are not bound to youth, nor are our senex qualities reserved for age. The complete coincidence of psychological development and the biological course of life is yet to be established. The psyche seems to have its own

---

5. E.R. Curtius, *European Literature and the Latin Middle Ages* (New York: Pantheon, 1953), 98–101.

6. Wing-tsit Chan, *The Way of Lao Tzu (Tao-te ching)* (Indianapolis: Bobbs-Merrill, 1963), sec. 55.

course, its own timing. The senex as well as the puer may appear at many phases and may influence any complex. So we cannot fit psychological life into the historical conditions or the narrowly biological frames of a "first half/second half." To do so would be an early indication that we have ourselves too easily succumbed to the faulted thinking of the split archetype.

If we look about us we see too well that the first-half/second-half scheme simply does not fit. Can the generation that is now to make the transition of the millennium put off until "some time later" the issues of meaning, of religion, of selfhood, meanwhile adapting to sociological and biological norms that have been handed them by another age and have lost their inherent value? A young person today is pressed to take up the problems of the second half in the first half. He has been born into a second half, into the end of an age (as those of us who are older are forced to live a first half of the wholly new spirit of the next age which is now beginning). We have not only our own problems; we have by historical necessity the collective problem of individuation loaded onto us. We carry a pack of history on our backs and are expected to meet the requirements of an old culture. Thus we start out as a *puer senilis*, both older than our age and struggling heroically against our oldness.

The "puer problem" of today is not only a collective neurosis; it is a psychic expression of an historical claim, and as such is a call. If psychic energy is not able to flow through the usual external channels of tradition, it falls inward and activates the unconscious. The unconscious as "mother" makes it then appear as if all a young person's questioning and maladaptation were his own personal mother complex. But it is a reflection of the transition and, as Jung says, "not of our conscious choosing." It reflects "the unconscious man within us who is changing." Can this unconscious man be put off until the second-half?

The second half is with us from the beginning, as is Saturn in our birth charts, just as the little boy and his question "why," the child Eros, and the winged angel are with us to the last. The puer inspires the blossoming of things; the senex presides over the harvest. But flowering and harvest go on intermittently throughout life. And do we know finally who takes charge at death—greybeard with his scythe or the young angel?

Polarities in Analytical Psychology. Since it will be in the form of a polar split that we shall encounter the archetype puer-senex, we need first to regard polarities, in general, in analytical psychology. Analytical psychology as a structured field depends for this structure upon polar descriptions. Jung's life and thought makes more use of polarities than does any other major psychological vision.[7] The polar model is basic in all his major psychological ideas.[8]

In all of this, the primary poles are conscious and unconscious, whether conceived as topological areas, as modalities of being, or as adjectival descriptions of mental contents and behavior. For psychology, all polarities are subjected to this primary division. This primary polarity, however, is given only as a potential within the archetype, which theoretically is not divided into poles. The archetype per se is ambivalent and paradoxical, embracing both spirit and nature, psyche and matter, consciousness and unconsciousness; in it the yea and nay are

---

7. Jung does, of course, use other explanatory models for psychic structure, such as: 1) *Schichtentheorie* and a hierarchical schema when describing levels of the psyche or when describing the process of individuation. 2) He uses a situational condition-alism—a major model of thought for the existentialists—when discussing therapeutics and interpretation. 3) He uses as well an organismic functional model when he accounts for the evolutionary, developmental, or transformative aspects of the psyche as a whole. 4) And, further, we find in Jung an atomist-molecular model when describing the associations and constellations of the psyche. These are each but one metaphor for seizing the ungraspable nature of psychic realities. The one which he favored most is that of polar opposites.

8. The main features of Jung's polar model are as follows: 1) The psyche is primarily divided into conscious and unconscious, the relation between which is compensatory. 2) The energy of the psyche flows between two poles that can be variously qualified by opposites. 3) The attitudes of the psyche (introversion and extraversion) and the four psychological functions are described in polar pairs. 4) Instinctual pattern of behavior and archetypal image are polar ends of a spectrum-continuum. 5) There are recurrent themes of polarities such as: logos and eros, power and love, ego and shadow, spirit and nature, sexuality and religion, rational and irrational, individual and collective, container and contained, as well as the notions of two kinds of thinking, first-half and second-half, les *extrêmes se touchent*, etc. 6) Polarity is fundamental to Jung's writings on practice as a dialectic and his writings about himself, e.g., personality number one and personality number two. 7) Finally, the major theme of his later years: the male-female polarity and union in its various alchemical forms. (*Eranos Yearbooks* 2: 379–81; 3:248–53; 4: 298–329; and 20: 408–10).

one. There is neither day nor night, but rather a continual dawning. The inherent opposition within the archetype splits into poles when it enters ego-consciousness. Day breaks with the ego; night is left behind. Our usual daily consciousness grasps only one part and makes it into a pole. *For psychology, the ontological basis of polarity is ego-consciousness.*

For every bit of light that we grasp out of archetypal ambivalence, illumining with the candle of our ego a bright circle of awareness, we also darken the remainder of the room. At the same moment that we light the candle we create "outer darkness," as if the light were a theft from the penumbra of dawn and twilight, of paradoxical archetypal light. Consciousness and the unconscious are created into a polarity at the same moment out of original twilight states; and they are continually being created at the same moment. The process of making conscious thereby also makes unconscious, or as Jung put this awkward truth: "So we come to the paradoxical conclusion that there is no conscious content which is not in some other respect unconscious. Maybe, too, there is no unconscious psychism which is not at the same time conscious."[9] We may not speak therefore of an evolutionary process of light emerging from darkness, an extension of light at the expense of darkness. The light is not stolen from the dark where there is privation of light; rather the ego concentrates into one pole the divine primordial half-light, thereby also darkening the divine. Snuff the candle and the twilight dawns again at the outer edges of the room which just before were impenetrable recesses of shadow. In other words, for psychology the phenomenon of polarity is not archetypally primary, but is a consequent of the ego's affinity for light, just as the term *polarity* entered Western language with the Cartesian ego and the Enlightenment.[10]

As long as we remain within metaphors of light and vision, it does not matter which comes first or which is best. The metaphors of vision, of intuition, require neither logic nor value. Clarity is enough. Both poles of the archetype are necessary and equal. On this plane of vision, of intuition, one is beyond the opposites, beyond good and evil. But consciousness and unconsciousness require other metaphors, especially

---

9. C.G. Jung, "The Spirit of Psychology," in *Spirit and Nature: Papers from the Eranos Yearbooks*, edited by Joseph Campbell (Princeton, N.J.: Princeton University Press, 1982), 399.

10. Owen Barfield, *History in English Words* (London: Faber, 1962).

those of value. So we find that the basic yea and nay as positive and negative values in all their modes interfere and complicate a simple co-existing polarity. The Bible's God, in the first value judgment of the universe, declares light to be good, and by calling it Day and by separating it from the darkness of Night implies that the latter is not good. Thus are plus and minus signs attached to the primary poles of conscious and unconscious. Thus does the human world begin when feeling values add complexity to perception, and we *feel* the polarities and recognize moral choice.

So when we speak of consciousness we still tend to say good or bad consciousness, attributing at the same time the opposite sign to the unconscious. This tendency works for every pair of opposites. The view and value we have of one pair of a polarity is taken from within the standpoint of the other. Owing to the nature of consciousness as a polarity with the unconscious, we can never be wholly outside our own unconsciousness. Thus, too, the so-called objective standpoint of the conscious observer is actually from within the same archetype but from the opposite pole of it. Does not the most penetrating revelation of the negative senex come from his own son? Is not the most objective critic of the negative puer his own father?

Puer and senex are therefore each both positive and negative. Because these figures are in special relation forming, if you will, a two-headed archetype, or a *Janus Gestalt*, we shall find it impossible to say good of one without saying bad of the other as long as the two remain in polar opposition, as long as the ego wears only one face.

Nevertheless, though polarities may split into contradictories and even strive against each other as in all the classic puer-senex struggles, they may also be re-approximated. This rapprochement in order to heal a fundamental split is the main work of psychoanalysis. *Our attempt at rapprochement shall go by way of returning to the original condition of the archetype before it has been broken apart and turned against itself.*

May I insist here that we cannot over-estimate the importance of this rapprochement. It is worth every attempt, not for the success or cure that it might bring, but because each attempt makes us aware of the split and thereby begins healing. The division into mutually indifferent or repugnant polarities is tearing the soul apart. The soul itself stands amidst all sorts of opposites as the "third factor." It has always existed half-way between Heaven and Hell, spirit and flesh, inner and outer, individual and collective—or, these opposites have been held together within its unfathomed reaches. From the lyre of Heraclitus to the spectrum of Jung, the soul holds polarities in harmony. It is the psychic connection. But now the ego, having replaced the soul as the center of the conscious personality, cannot hold the tension. With its disjunctive rationalism it makes divisions where the soul gives feeling connections and mythic unities. So the soul has come unstrung; its suffering and illness reflect the torn condition of the split archetype.

As an early sign of this reunion we may expect a new experience of ambivalence. Psychology usually gives to ambivalence a major pejorative judgment. It is associated with schizophrenia. Like the term "twilight state," "ambivalence" tends to be reserved only for a faulty ego. But *ambivalence is natural,* as the necessary concomitant to the ambiguity of psychic wholeness whose light is in a twilight state. Neither ambivalence nor twilight consciousness is per se a pathological condition even though, as with anything psychological, they may present pathological forms. Living in ambivalence is living where yea and nay, light and darkness, right action and wrong, are held closely together and are difficult to distinguish. Psychology usually attempts to meet this condition through reaffirming consciousness by decision and differentiation: solidify and strengthen the ego; turn against the mixture of feelings and the indistinct soft light of the first-half or of old age. But ambivalence, rather than being overcome in this manner, may be developed within its own principle. It is a way in itself.

As there is a way of decision, there is also a way of ambivalence; and this way can comprehend the archetype in its wholeness, leading one down even to the psychoid[11] level. Ambivalence rather than corrected may be encouraged towards encompassing ever more profound paradoxes and symbols, which always release ambivalent feelings that hinder clarity and decisiveness. Paradox and symbol express the coexistence of polarity, the fundamental two-headed duality that is both logically absurd and symbolically true. *Ambivalence is the adequate reaction of the whole psyche* to these whole truths. To cure away ambiva-

---

11. Jung introduced the term "psychoid" in 1946 (*CW*8). It refers to that aspect of archetypal reality that suggests an overlap of psyche and matter.

lence removes the eye with which we can perceive the paradox, whereas bearing ambivalence places us within symbolic reality where we perceive both faces at once, even exist as two realities at once. That which is not split does not have to be rejoined; thus going by way of ambivalence circumvents *coniunctio* efforts of the ego because by bearing ambivalence one is in the *coniunctio* itself as the tension of opposites. This way works at wholeness not in halves but through wholeness from the start. The way is slower, action is hindered, and one fumbles foolishly in the half-light and the symbolic. The way finds echo in many familiar phrases from Lao Tzu, but especially: "Soften the light, become one with the dusty world."[12]

The Senex. Let us begin with a prayer to Saturn, an Arabic one from the *Picatrix* of the tenth century, which circulated widely in the late Middle Ages of Western Europe:

> O Master of sublime name and great power, supreme Master; O Master Saturn: Thou, the Cold, the Sterile, the Mournful, the Pernicious; Thou, whose life is sincere and whose word sure; Thou, the Sage and Solitary, the Impenetrable; Thou, whose promises are kept; Thou who art weak and weary; Thou who hast cares greater than any other, who knowest neither pleasure nor joy; Thou, the old and cunning, master of all artifice, deceitful, wise, and judicious; Thou who bringest prosperity or ruin and makest men to be happy or unhappy! I conjure Thee, O Supreme Father, by Thy great benevolence and Thy generous bounty, to do for me what I ask.[13]

Appropriately, our starting point is duplex. Cronus-Saturn is on one hand:

> ...a benevolent God of agriculture...the ruler of the Golden Age when men had abundance of all things...the lord of the Islands of the Blessed...and the building of cities...On the other hand he was the gloomy, dethroned, and solitary god conceived as "dwell-

---

12. *Tao-te ching*, 20, 55.

13. Jean Seznec, *The Survival of the Pagan Gods* translated by Barbara F. Sessions (New York: Pantheon, 1953), 53.

ing at the uttermost end of land and sea," "exiled...ruler of the nether gods"...prisoner or bondsman in...Tartarus...the god of death and the dead. On the one hand he was the father of gods and men, on the other hand the devourer of children, eater of raw flesh, the consumer of all, who "swallowed up all the gods."[14]

According to the Warburg Institute's authoritative study of Saturn, in no Greek god-figure is the dual aspect so real, so fundamental, as in the figure of Cronus, so that even with the later additions of the Roman Saturn who "was originally not ambivalent but definitely good," the compounded image remains at core bipolar. Saturn is at once archetypal image for wise old man, solitary sage, the *lapis* as rock of ages with all its positive moral and intellectual virtues, *and* for the Old King,[15] that castrating castrated ogre. He is the world as builder of cities *and* the not-world of exile. At the same time that he is father of all he consumes all; by living on and from his fatherhood he feeds himself insatiably from the bounty of his own paternalism. *Saturn is image for both positive and negative senex.*

We turned to the *Picatrix*,[16] a popular astro-magical text for a first description of the senex because astrology provides the best descriptions of character qualities. More than any other field, astrology gives background for the psychology of personality when personality is conceived as a collection of stable traits. This fixed characterological view, personality conceived through heredity, disposition, virtues and vices, is less to be found in personality theory and psychopathology today. Personality theory and psychopathology tend to favor psycho-dynamics, learning theory, conditioning and behaviorism, and at times so extremely that even endogenic and structural disorders have been considered not as inherent traits but as reaction formations.[17] The astrological view of personality is saturnine, and Saturn is the "ruler" of

---

14. Raymond Klibansky, Erwin Panofsky, and Fritz Saxl, *Saturn and Melancholy: Studies in the History of Natural Philosophy, Religion, and Art* (Montreal: McGill-Queen's University Press, 2019), 134–35.

15. Philipp Wolff-Windegg, *Die Gekrönten* (Stuttgart: Klett, 1958).

16. *Picatrix*, translated into German from the Arabic by Hellmut Ritter and Martin Plessner (London: Warburg Institute, 1962).

17. Recent bio-genetic determinism is returning to Saturnian physiological fatalism: e.g., we are our inheritance.

astrology. The psycho-dynamic view is mercurial: nothing is given and everything can be transformed; all limits may be overcome and conditions may be altered through re-learning, behavior therapy, drive reinforcement, and psycho-dynamics. The impetus behind therapy itself owes more to mercurial optimism and less to the saturnine attitude of fateful limits set by character traits where psychic disposition is congenital. Congenital means synchronous with birth, that is, astrological.

But the pessimism of Saturn has deeper implications. Although the virtues and vices of character may be modified, they do not disappear through cure because they belong to one's nature as the original gift of sin. Congenital structure is karma; character is fate. Thus personality descriptions of the senex given by astrology will be statements of the senex by the senex. It is a description from the inside, a self-description of the bound and fettered condition of human nature set within the privation of its characterological limits and whose wisdom comes through suffering these limits.

From astrology, then, from the medicine of the humors, from lore and iconography, from the collections of the mythographers, we can piece together the major characteristics of Cronus-Saturn as archetypal image of the senex.[18] His duality we have already mentioned. In astrology, this duality was traditionally handled by the examination of Saturn's place in the birth-chart. In this way, the good and bad poles inherent to his nature could be kept distinct. His temperament is *cold*. Coldness can be expressed also as *distance*; the lonely wanderer set apart, out-cast. Coldness is also cold reality, things just as they are; and yet Saturn is at the far-out edge of reality. As lord of the nethermost, he views the world from the outside, from such depths of distance that he sees it, so to speak, all upside down, yet structurally and abstractly. The concern with structure and abstraction makes him the principle of *order*, whether through time, or hierarchy, or exact science and system, or limits and borders, or power, or inwardness and reflection, or earth and the forms it gives. The cold is also *slow*, heavy, leaden, and dry or rheumy moist, but always the *coagulator* through denseness, slowness,

---

18. My condensation of traditional traits derives from: Saturn and Melancholy, especially 127–214; Erwin Panofsky, "Father Time," in *Studies in Iconography* (New York: Harper Torchbooks, 1965); *Picatrix*, 117, 209, 213ff., 333–35, 360.

and weight expressed by the mood of sadness, depression, or melan-
cholia. Thus he is black, winter, and the night, yet heralds through his
day, Saturday, the return of the holy Sunday light. His relation to *sexuality* is again dual: on the one hand he is patron of eunuchs and celi-
bates, being dry and impotent; on the other hand he is represented by
the dog and the lecherous goat, and is a fertility god as inventor of agri-
culture, a god of earth and peasant, the harvest and Saturnalia, a ruler
of fruit and seed. But the harvest is a *hoard*; the ripened end product
and in-gathering again can be dual. Under the aegis of Saturn it can
show qualities of greed and tyranny, where in-gathering means holding
and the purse of miserliness, making things last through all time. (Saturn governs coins, minting, and wealth.) Here we find the characteristics of avarice, gluttony, and such rapaciousness that Saturn is *bhoga*
(Hindu), "eating the world," and identified with Moloch[19]—which again
on its positive side demands the extreme *sacrifice* and can be understood as Abraham and Moses, the patriarchal mentor who demands
the extreme.

His relationship to the *feminine* has been put in a few words: those born
under Saturn "do not like to walk with women and pass the time." "They
are never in favor with woman or wife." So Saturn is in association with
widowhood, childlessness, orphanhood, child exposure, and he attends
childbirth so as to be able to eat the newborn, as everything new coming
to life can become food to the senex. Old attitudes and habits assimilate
each new content; everlastingly changeless, it eats its own possibilities
of change.

His *moral aspects* are two-sided. He presides over honesty in speech—
and deceit; over secrets, silence—and loquaciousness and slander; over
loyalty and friendship—and selfishness, cruelty, cunning, thievery
and murder. He makes both honest reckoning and fraud. He is god of
manure, privies, dirty linen, bad wind, and is also cleanser of souls. His
intellectual qualities include the inspired genius of the brooding melancholic, creativity through contemplation, deliberation in the exact sci-
ences and mathematics, as well as the highest occult secrets such as
angelology, theology, and prophetic furor. He is the aged Indian on the
elephant,[20] the wise old man and "creator of wise men," as Augustine

19. *Saturn and Melancholy*, 135n and 208.
20. Ibid., 204.

ironically called him in his antipagan polemic, which used Saturn for whipping-boy.[21]

This amplification may give a phenomenological description of an archetype, but it is not psychology. Psychology may be based on archetypal themata, but psychology proper begins only when these dominants, experienced as emotional realities through and within our complexes, are felt to pull and shape our lives. The senex is at the core of *any complex* or governs *any attitude* when these psychological processes pass to end phase. We expect it to correspond to biological senescence, just as many of its images: dryness, night, coldness, winter, harvest, are taken from the processes of time and of nature. To speak accurately, however, the senex archetype transcends mere biological senescence and is given from the beginning as a potential of order, meaning, and teleological fulfillment—and death—within all the psyche and all its parts. So the death that the senex brings is not only biophysical. It is the death that comes through perfection and order. It is the death of accomplishment and fulfillment, a death which grows in power within any complex or attitude as that psychological process matures through consciousness into order, becoming habitual and dominant—and therefore unconscious again. Paradoxically, we are least conscious where we are most conscious. Where we are in our ego-efficiency, habitual, feeling most certain, ruling from within that which we know best, we are the least reflectively aware. Close to the light our sight is shortest. Our destructivity is felt in the closest neighborhood and is the result of the shadow that issues from the very ego-center of our light. Out of its own light, the ego makes shadow; the ego is its own shadow; perhaps the ego is shadow. So the senex represents just this force of death that is carried by the glittering hardness of our own ego-certainty, the ego-concentricity that can say "I know"—for it does know, and this knowledge is power. It is also dry and cold, and its boundaries are set as if by its own precision instruments.

The hardening process of consciousness has been represented by the symbol of the Old King.[22] The Old King with his sickness is an alchemical image for the negative *lapis*, the *lapis* as petrifaction. This

---

21. Ibid., 161–64.
22. *CW* 14, sec. IV (Rex et Regina).

end-phase has also been formulated mainly as a consequent of the absent feminine, resulting in dryness and coldness. Consciousness is out of touch with life. The elixir does not flow and the negative tincture stains the surrounding with blight. The main blame for this condition of the senex has been laid upon the ego, which often gets a moralistic-pedagogical rap over the knuckles for "wrong attitudes." It is the ego's fault that consciousness is ingathered to itself. It is the power-greed of the ego that makes its point of view tyrannical and its consciousness deaf. It is the one-sidedness or the over-rationality of the ego that cuts it off from the living.

Let us reconsider the relation between the ego and the senex. We have just seen from our amplification that it is the senex that in-gathers and hoards. It is the senex that *a priori* is the archetypal principle of coldness, hardness, and exile from life. As principle of coagulation and of geometrical order, it dries and orders, "builds cities" and "mints money," makes solid and square and profitable, overcoming the dissolving wetness of soulful emotionality. It is the senex as certainty principle that directs the ego away from the uncertainty principle, the doubts and provisional confusions of dawn and twilight. No, it is not the ego that gives the senex its authority and ultimate tyranny, but the brief authority in which the ego is dressed depends upon its relation with the senex archetype. Even the ego's notion of itself as authoritative dominant of consciousness results from the archetypal senex. The Old Wise Man and the Old King are there from the beginning, before the ego is born, governing the mysterious ordering aspect of ego-formation by meaningfully structuring contents into knowledge and extending the area of the will's control. As Jung pointed out in discussing the "Stages of Life," knowledge is the hallmark of consciousness and is at the beginning of ego-formation in the child.[23] This knowing precedes the ego that says "I know." The cognitive capacity precedes cognition, which, in turn, precedes ego-subjectivity. The ego does not come *ex nihilo* onto the scene, cognizing the world into existence by turning its attention like a spotlight upon its surround. Rather, the ego is gradually formed "like a chain of islands or an archipelago," from pre-existent fragments of cognitive consciousness.[24] Something prior to the ego cognizes, gives

---

23. *CW* 8: 754–55.
24. *CW* 8: 387.

meaning, and patterns into order this fragmentary twilight conscious-ness. This "something" has been called the Self, which is another name for the archetype of meaning,[25] or the Old Wise Man.

Thus we conclude *that the senex is there at the beginning as an arche-typal root of ego-formation.* It makes consolidation of the ego possible, giving its rule as an identity within fixed borders, its tendency to omniv-orous rapacious aggrandizement ("swallowing all the gods" and their ambivalent natural light) through the principle of association with con-sciousness, and its perpetuation through habit, memory, repetition, and time. These qualities—identity of borders, association with conscious-ness, continuity—we use to describe the ego, and these qualities are each properties of Cronus-Saturn, the senex. The senex as *spiritus rec-tor* bestows the certainty of the spirit, so that one is led to state that ego-development is a phenomenon of the senex spirit that works at ordering and hardening within the ego with such compulsion that it must be—as well as the Promethean thrust of the Hero—an instinctual source of ego energy. Here we approach Freud's notion of Thanatos.

Because the negative senex is not an ego fault it cannot be altered by the ego. The negative senex problem is not merely a matter of moral attitude (as if the ego should do better, be more modest or humble or "conscious"). Nor is it a problem of outdated ideas (as if the ego should keep up with the times), nor of biological vitality (as if the ego should keep fit and active), nor even of the absent feminine. *These ego problems are consequents rather than causes; they reflect a prior disorder in the archetypal ground of the ego.* This ground is *senex-et-puer*, briefly con-ceived as its order on the one hand, its impetus on the other. Together they give the ego what has been called its *Gestaltungskraft* or intention-ality, or meaningfulness of the spirit. When the duality of this ground is split into polarity, then we have not only the alternating plus and minus valences given to one half or the other, but we have a more fundamental negativity, that of the split archetype, and its corollary: ego-conscious-ness split from archetypal reality, the gods.

We must further conclude that the negative senex is the senex split from its own puer aspect. He has lost his "child." The archetypal core of the complex, now split, loses its inherent tension, its ambivalence, and

---

25. *CW* 9.1: 66ff.

is just dead in the midst of its brightness, which is its own eclipse, as a negative *Sol Niger*. Without the enthusiasm and eros of the son, authority loses its idealism. It aspires to nothing but its own perpetuation, leading but to tyranny and cynicism; *for meaning cannot be sustained by structure and order alone*. Such spirit is one-sided, and one-sidedness is crippling. Being is static, a pleroma that cannot become. Time—called euphemistically "experience" but more often just the crusted accretions of profane history—becomes a moral virtue and even witness of truth, "*veritas filia temporis* (truth is the daughter of time)." The old is always preferred to the new. Sexuality without young eros becomes goaty; weakness becomes complaints; creative isolation, only paranoid loneliness. Because the complex is unable to catch on and sow seed, it feeds on the growth of other complexes or of other people, as for instance the growth of one's own children, or the developmental process going on in one's analysands. Cut off from its own child and fool, the complex no longer has anything to tell us.[26] Folly and immaturity are projected onto others. Without folly it has no wisdom, only knowledge—serious, depressing, hoarded in an academic vault or used as power. The feminine may be kept imprisoned in secret, or may be Dame Melancholy, a moody consort, as an atmosphere emanating from the moribund complex, giving it the stench of Saturn. The integration of personality becomes the subjugation of personality, a unification through dominance, and integrity only a selfsame repetition of firm principle. Or, to reawaken the puer side again there may be a complex-compelled falling-in-love. (Venus is born from imaginal froth—i.e. the repressed fantasies—of dissociated sexuality cut off through Saturn.)

To sum up then with the senex: It is there from the beginning as are all archetypal dominants and is found in the small child who knows and says "I know" and "mine" with the full intensity of its being, the small child who is the last to pity and first to tyrannize, destroys what it has built, and in its weakness lives in oral omnipotence fantasies, defending its borders and testing the limits set by others. But although the senex is there in the child, the senex spirit nevertheless appears most evidently when any function we use, attitude we have, or complex of the psyche

---

26. Cf. Adolf Guggenbühl-Craig, *The Old Fool and the Corruption of Myth* (Putnam, Conn.: Spring Publications, 2006 [1991]).

begins to coagulate past its prime. It is the Saturn within the complex that makes it hard to shed, dense and slow and maddeningly depressing—the madness of lead-poison—that feeling of the everlasting indestructibility of the complex. It cuts off the complex from life and the feminine, inhibiting it and introverting it into an isolation. Thus it stands behind the fastness of our habits and the ability we have of making a virtue of any vice by merely keeping it in order or attributing it to fate.

The senex as complex appears in dreams long before a person has himself put on his *toga senilis* (*aet.* 60 in Rome). It manifests as the dream father, mentor, old wise man, to which the dreamer's consciousness is pupil. When accentuated it seems to have drawn all power to itself, paralyzing elsewhere, and a person is unable to make a decision without first taking counsel with the unconscious to await an advising voice from an oracle or vision. Though this counsel may come from a dream or revelation, it may be as collective as that which comes from the standard canons of the culture. For statements of sagacity and meaning, even spiritual truths, can be bad advice. These representations—father, elders, mentors, and old wise men—provide an authority and wisdom that is beyond the experience of the dreamer. Therefore it tends to have him rather than he it, so that he is driven by an unconscious certainty, making him wise beyond his years, ambitious for recognition by his seniors and intolerant of his own youthfulness.

The senex spirit also affects any attitude or complex when the creative contemplation of its ultimate meaning, its relation to fate, its deepest "why," become constellated. Then the husk of any habitual attitude deprived of all outward power shrinks to a grain, but imprisoned in the little limits of this seed is all the *vis* of the original complex. Turned thus in on itself almost to the point of disappearing altogether, leaving only a melancholy mood of *mortificatio* or *putrefactio*, in the black cold night of deprivation it holds a sort of lonely communion in itself with the future; and then with the prophetic genius of the senex spirit reveals that which is beyond the edge of its own destructive harvesting scythe, that which will sprout green from the grain it has itself slain.

This duality within the senex itself that is imaged by the positive-negative Cronus-Saturn figure gives each of us those intensely difficult problems in our lives. How does the Old King in my attitudes change? How can my knowledge become wisdom? How do I admit uncertainty, disorder, and nonsense within my borders? How we work out these issues affects the historical transition since we are each a makeweight in the scales.

We might easily believe that the difference between the negative and positive senex is mainly a matter of the difference between the Old King of power and extraversion as a profane end stage of the Puer-Hero, and the Old Wise One of knowledge and introversion as the sacred end-stage of the Puer-Messiah. But this simplification will not hold because we are involved with an archetypal structure that is not only dual as is the image of Cronus-Saturn, reflected by the universal duality of the senex dominants Chief and Medicine Man. (These figures stand for the inner polarity of the senex, the two ways of order and meaning, neither of which is positive or negative *per se*.) The simplification will not hold because *the duality of the senex rests upon an even more basic archetypal polarity: the senex-puer archetype.*

Thus the crucial psychological problem expressed by the terms "negative senex" and "positive senex," ogre and wisdom, which concerns our individual lives and "how to be," and which is determining the symptoms of the ageing millennium, arises from a fundamental split between senex and puer within the same archetype. Negative senex attitudes and behavior result from this split archetype, while positive senex attitudes and behavior reflect its unity; so that the term "positive senex" or "old wise man" refers merely to a transformed continuation of the puer. Here the first part of our thesis reaches its issue: *the difference between the negative and positive senex qualities reflects the split or connection within the senex-puer archetype.*

The Puer. Unlike the term senex, analytical psychology uses the concept of *puer eternus* widely and freely. It appears early in Jung's work (1912)[27] and has been elaborated in various aspects by him and by many

---

27. C.G. Jung, *Wandlungen und Symbole der Libido* (Leipzig/Vienna: Deuticke, 1912); *CW*5: 194, 392, 526; *CW*9.2 ("Psychological Aspects of the Mother Archetype," "The Psychology of the Child Archetype," "On the Psychology of the Trickster Figure"); *CW*16: 336; *CW*13 ("The Spirit Mercurius"); *CW*11: 742.

since then.[28] We are especially indebted to Marie-Louise von Franz for her work on this figure and the problem.[29] The single archetype tends to merge in one: the Hero, the Divine Child, the figures of Eros, the King's Son, the Son of the Great Mother, the Psychopompos, Mercurius-Hermes,[30] Trickster, and the Messiah. In him, we see a mercurial range of these "personalities": narcissistic, inspired, effeminate, phallic, inquisitive, inventive, pensive, passive, fiery, and capricious. Furthermore, a description of the puer will be complicated because archetypal background and neurotic foreground, positive and negative, are not clearly distinguished. Let us nevertheless sketch some main lines of a psychological phenomenology.

The concept puer eternus refers to that archetypal dominant, which personifies or is in special relation with transcendent spiritual powers. Puer figures can be regarded as avatars of the psyche's spiritual aspect, and puer impulses as messages from the spirit or as calls to the spirit. When the collective unconscious in an individual life is represented mainly by parental figures, then puer attitudes and impulses will show personal taints of the mother's boy or *fils du papa*, the perennial adolescence of the provisional life. Then the neurotic foreground obscures the archetypal background. One assumes that the negative and irksome adolescence, the lack of progress and reality, is all a puer problem, whereas it is the personal and parental in the neurotic foreground that is distorting the necessary connection to the spirit. Then the transcendent call is lived within the family complex, distorted into a transcendent function of the family problem, as an attempt to redeem the parents or be their Messiah. The true call does not come through, or is

---

28. "The Provisional Life," in H.G. Baynes, *Analytical Psychology and the English Mind* (London: Kegan Paul, 1950); Margit Van Leight Frank, "Adoration of the Complex," in *The Archetype*, edited by Adolf Guggenbühl-Craig (Basel: Karger, 1964); H. Binswanger, *Vol de Nuit von A. de St.-Exupéry: Versuch einer Interpretation*, Diss., C.G. Jung Institut, n.d.; Henry A. Murray, "American Icarus," in this volume.

29. Marie-Louise von Franz, *The Problem of the Puer Aeternus* (New York: Spring Publications, 1970); Commentary to *Das Reich ohne Raum* by Bruno Goetz (Zurich: Origo, 1962); "Über religiose Hintergründe des Puer-Aeternus Problems," in *The Archetype*, op. cit.

30. Karl Kerényi, *Hermes: Guide of Souls*, translated by Murray Stein (Thompson, Conn.: Spring Publications, 2020 [1976]).

possible only through technical breakthroughs: drugs or death-defying adventure.

The parental complex, however, is not solely responsible for the crippling, laming, or castration of the archetypal puer figures. This laming refers to the especial weakness and helplessness at the beginning of any enterprise. Inherent in the one-sided vertical direction is the Icarus-Ganymede propensity of flying and falling. It must be weak on earth, because it is not at home on earth. The beginnings of things are *Einfälle*; they fall in on one from above as gifts of the puer, or sprout up out of the ground as daktyls, as flowers. But there is difficulty at the beginning; the child is in danger, easily gives up. The horizontal world, the space-time continuum, which we call "reality," is not its world. So the new dies easily because it is not born in the *Diesseits*, and this death confirms it in eternity. Death does not matter because the puer gives the feeling that it can come again another time, make another start. Mortality points to immortality; danger only heightens the unreality of "reality" and intensifies the vertical connection.

Because of this vertical *direct* access to the spirit, this immediacy where vision of goal and goal itself are one, winged speed, haste—even the short cut—are imperative. The puer cannot do with indirection, with timing and patience. It knows little of the seasons and of waiting. And when it must rest or withdraw from the scene, then it seems to be stuck in a timeless state, innocent of the passing years, out of tune with time. Its wandering is as the spirit wanders, without attachment and not as an odyssey of experience. It wanders to spend or to capture, and to ignite, to try its luck, but not with the aim of going home. No wife waits; it has no son in Ithaca. Like the senex, it cannot hear, does not learn. The puer therefore understands little of what is gained by repetition and consistency, that is, by work, or of the moving back and forth, left and right, in and out, which makes for subtlety in proceeding step by step through the labyrinthine complexity of the horizontal world. These teachings but cripple its winged heels, for there, from below and behind, it is particularly vulnerable. It is anyway not meant to walk, but to fly.

The direct connection to the spirit can be misdirected through or by the Great Mother. Puer figures often have a special relationship with the Great Mother, who is in love with them as carriers of the spirit; incest with them inspires her—and them—to ecstatic excess and destruction.

She feeds their fire with animal desire and fans their flame with promise of scope and conquest over the horizontal world, her world of matter. Whether as her hero-lover or hero-slayer, the puer impulse is reinforced by this entanglement with the Great Mother archetype, leading to those spiritual exaggerations we call neurotic. Primary among these exaggerations is the labile mood and the dependency of the spirit upon moods. Again, they are described in vertical language (heights and depths, glory and despair) and we hear echoes of the festivals for Attis called *tristia* and *hilaria*.[31]

The eternal spirit is sufficient unto itself and contains all possibilities. As the senex is perfected through time, the puer is primordially perfect. Therefore there is no development; development means devolution, a loss and fall and restriction of possibilities. So for all its changeability the puer, like the senex, at core resists development. This self-perfection, this aura of knowing all and needing nothing, is the true background of the self-containment and isolation of any complex, reflected for instance in the ego's narcissistic attitudes, that angelic hermaphroditic quality where masculine and feminine are so perfectly joined that nothing else is needed. There is therefore no need for relationship or woman, unless it be some magical puella or some mother-figure who can admiringly reflect and not disturb this exclusive hermaphroditic unity of oneself with one's archetypal essence. The feeling of distance and coldness, of impermanence, of Don Juan's ithyphallic sexuality, of homosexuality, can all be seen as derivatives of this privileged archetypal connection with the spirit, which may burn with a blue and ideal fire, but in a human relationship it may show the icy penis and chilling seed of a satanic incubus.

Because eternity is changeless, that which is governed only by the puer does not age. So, too, it has no maturing organic face that shows the bite of time. Its face is universal, given by the archetype, and so it cannot be faced, confronted in personal confrontation. It has a pose—phallic cavalier, pensive poet, messenger—but not a persona of adaptation. The revelations of the spirit have no personal locus in personality; they are eternally valid statements, good forever.

---

31. M. J. Vermaseren, *The Legend of Attis in Greek and Roman Art* (Leiden: Brill, 1966).

Yet, in this faceless form it captures psyche.[32] It is to the puer that psyche succumbs, and just because it is psyche's opposite; the puer spirit is the least psychological, has the least soul. Its "sensitive soulfulness" is rather pseudopsychological, and a derivative of the hermaphroditic effeminacy. It can search and risk; it has insight, aesthetic intuition, spiritual ambition—all but not psychology, for psychology requires time, femininity of soul, and the entanglement of relationships. Instead of psychology, the puer attitude displays an aesthetic point of view: the world as beautiful images or as vast scenario. Life becomes literature, an adventure of intellect or science, or of religion or action, but always unreflected and unrelated and therefore unpsychological. It is the puer in a complex that "unrelates" it, that volatilizes it out of the vessel—that would act it out, call it off and away from the psychological—and thus is the principle that uncoagulates and disintegrates. What is unreflected tends to become compulsive, or greedy. The puer in any complex gives it drive and drivenness, makes it move too fast, want too much, go too far, not only because of the oral hunger and omnipotence fantasies of the childish, but archetypally because the world can never satisfy the demands of the spirit or match its ideal beauty. Hungering for eternal experience makes one a consumer of profane events. When the puer spirit falls into the public arena, it hurries history along.

And finally, as Henry Corbin has often pointed out, the puer eternus figure is the vision of our own first nature, our primordial golden shadow, our affinity to beauty, our angelic essence as messenger of the divine, as divine message.[33] From the puer we are given our sense of destiny and mission, of having a message and being meant as eternal cup-bearer to the divine, that our sap and overflow, our enthusiastic wetness of soul, is in service to the gods, bringing eternal refreshment to the archetypal background of the universe.

So the puer personifies that moist spark within any complex or attitude that is the original dynamic seed of spirit. It is the call of a thing to the perfection of itself, the call of a person to his or her daimon, to be true to itself. The puer offers direct connection with spirit. Break this vertical connection and it falls with broken wings. When it falls we lose

32. Erich Neumann, *Amor and Psyche* (New York: Bollingen, 1956).
33. Cf. Henry Corbin in *Eranos Yearbooks* 17 (1949), 19 (1950), 25 (1956), and 27 (1958).

the urgent burning purpose and instead commence the long proces-
sional march through the halls of power towards the heart-hardened
sick old king who is often cloaked and indistinguishable from the sick
wise old man or woman.

The spark extinguished by this "heroic overcoming" leaves behind
sad regrets, bitterness and cynicism, the very emotions of the negative senex. By conquering the parental complexes in the neurotic foreground, we smother the archetypal background. The puer suffers an
enantiodromia into senex; he switches Janus faces. Thus are we led to
realize *that there is no basic difference between the negative puer and
negative senex,* except for their difference in biological age. The critical time in this process that is represented by the midpoint of biological life is as well the midpoint of any attitude or psychological function
that ages but does not change. The eros and idealism of the beginning
succumb to success and power, to be refound, as we have seen from
our examination of the senex, only at the end when power and success fail, when Saturn is in exile from the world—then eros as loyalty
and friendship, and idealism as prophetic insight and contemplation of
truth return.

In all this, the greatest damage is done to meaning, distorted from
idealism into cynicism. As the spirit becomes meaning through senex
order, so the puer is meaning's other face. As archetypal structure, the
puer is the inspiration of meaning and brings meaning as vision wherever he appears. A beginning is always meaningful and filled with the
excitement of eros. Meaning expresses the invisible coincidence of the
positive puer with the positive senex. The puer aspect of meaning is in
the *search,* as the dynamus of the child's eternal "why?"; the quest, or
questioning, seeking, adventuring, which grips personality from behind
and compels it forward. All things are uncertain, provisional, subject to
question, thereby opening the way and leading the soul toward further
questioning.

However, if persuaded into the temporal world by the negative senex,
the puer loses connection with its own aspect of meaning and becomes
the negative puer. Then it goes dead, and there is passivity, withdrawal,
even physical death. These pueri are only flower people like Hyacinthus,
Narcissus, Crocus, whose tears are but wind-flowers, anemones of the
goddess, and whose blood gives only Adonis roses and Attis violets of

regret. They are flower-people who are unable to carry their own meaning through to the end, and as flowers they must fade before fruit and seed. Eternal Becoming never realized in Being; possibility and promise only. Or the negative puer may become hyperactive and we find all the traits accentuated and materialized, but without inherent meaning. When the falcon cannot hear the falconer, wingedness becomes mere haste and fanaticism, an unguided missile. A person is caught in the puer activities of social rebellion, intellectual technology, or physical adventure with redoubled energy and loss of goal. Everything new is worshipped because it gives promise of the original, while the historical is discarded because it is of the senex who is now enemy. Personal revelation is preferred to objective knowledge so that minor epiphanies weigh more than the classics of culture. Eventually meaning declines into a philosophy of the absurd, action into the *acte gratuite* or violence, or intoxication, or flight into the future; and the chaos returns, which the puer as archetype is itself called to oppose. By refusing history, by pushing it all down into the unconscious in order to fly above it, one is forced to repeat history unconsciously. In the unconscious the senex position builds up with a compulsive vengeance until with all the force of historical necessity it takes over in its turn, reducing new truths to old cliches again, switching the only-puer into an only-senex, split from the next generation.

The puer gives us connection to the spirit and is always concerned with the eternal aspect of ourselves and the world. However, *when this concern becomes only puer, exclusive and negative, the world is itself in danger of dissolution into the otherworldly.* This danger is especially present in the psyche and history of this fraction of our era. Therefore it is of immense importance that the puer be recognized and valued, for it carries our future—positive or negative—not necessarily as the next step in time, but as the futurity within every complex, its prospective meaning, its way out and way forward, as a possibility of renewal through eros and as a call to meaning built on the eternities of spirit. Therefore it is of immense importance that we attempt the healing of the archetypal split, which divides puer from senex, turning them into a negative antithesis, hardening the heart against one's own puer imagination, thereby demonizing one's angel so that the new, which comes into being through the puer, is demonic. When the archetype is split, the dynamus works independently of the patterns of order. Then we have a too-familiar pattern: action that does not know and knowledge that does not act, fanatic versus cynic, commonly formulated as youth and age. This negative turn happens not only in young people or in the first half of life or in new movements.

We must therefore deny again the usual separation into first and second halves of life, as presented for example by Jacobi, Fordham, and Dunn.[34] It dangerously divides puer and senex. Always the puer is described from within the senex-puer duality and therefore comes out negatively, which also implies a positive senex view of itself.

Let us look at the usual recommendations for the "first half" of life, or "how to cure a puer": analyze the unconscious, reduce the fantasies, dry the hysterics, confront the intuitions, bring down to earth and reality, turn the poetry into prose. The will is to direct sexuality into relationship; the crippling is to be overcome through the exercise of work; practicality, sacrifice, limits, hardening. The face is to be set, positions defended, the provisional overcome through the panacea of commitment. Concentration, responsibility, roots, historical continuity and identity: in a word, ego-strengthening. Note well: all these images are Saturnian.

Commitment as duty clips the wings and binds the feet, as Saturn is chained through his commitments. Ego-strengthening fosters a revolutionary unattached shadow that would smash all fetters, for the strong ego has the strong shadow, the brilliance makes its own blackness. This path of worldly commitment aims to sever the puer from its own vertical axis; it reflects a senex personality, which has not itself separated the parental from the archetypal and is thus threatened by its own child, its own phallus, and its own poetry.

However we conceive the tasks of youth, or of the beginning of things, they cannot be accomplished without the meaning given by the spiritual connection. Initiation into reality is not to take away the initiant's relation with the primordial origins but only to separate these origins

34. Jolande Jacobi, *Der Weg zur Individuation* (Zurich: Rascher, 1965); Michael Fordham, "Individuation and Ego Development," *Journal of Analytical Psychology* 3, no. 2 (1958); I.J. Dunn, "Analysis of Patients Who Meet the Problems of the First Half of Life in the Second," *Journal of Analytical Psychology* 6, no. 1 (1961); also M. Esther Harding, *The Parental Image* (New York: Putnam, 1965).

from the confusions of the personal and parental. Initiation is not a demythologizing into "hard" reality, but an affirmation of the mythical meaning within all reality. Initiation "softens" reality by filling in its background with layers of mythological perspective, providing the fantasy, which makes the "hardness" of reality meaningful and tolerable, and at the same time truly indestructible. The puer figure—Baldur, Tammuz, Jesus, Krishna—brings myth into reality, presents in himself the reality of myth that transcends history. His message is mythical, stating that he, the myth—so easily wounded, easily slain, yet always reborn—is the seminal substructure of all enterprise. Traditional initiation of the puer by the positive senex confirms this relation to the archetype. Some substitutes for initiation—and analysis can be one—may instead sever this relation.

Relation with any archetype involves the danger of possession, usually marked by inflation. This is particularly true of the puer because of its high-flights and mythical behavior. Of course, possession through the senex brings an equally dangerous set of moods and actions: depression, pessimism, and hardness of heart. Even a minimum of psychological awareness—that I am just what I am as I am—can spare complete archetypal possession. This awareness is made possible through the reflective, echoing function of the psyche. This function is the human psyche's contribution to spirit and to meaning, which noble as they may be can also be, without psyche, runaway destructive possessions. So the main puer problem is not lack of worldly reality but *lack of psychic reality*. Rather than commitment to the order of the world the puer needs to be wedded to psyche, to which the puer is anyway naturally drawn. Rather than historical continuity and roots in the horizontal, he needs devotion to the anima. First psyche, then world; or through the psyche to the world. The anima has the thread and knows the step-by-step dance that can lead through the labyrinth, and can teach the puer the subtleties of left hand/right hand, opening and closing, accustoming and refining vision to the half light of ambivalence.

Let us not mistakenly take this as *Lebensphilosophie* or a psychological prescription for "cure"—i.e., only involvement with a real woman leads a man out of his mother-bound adolescent compulsions. We are discussing rather an archetypal structure, not "how to be." Each "hot idea," at whatever time of life in whomever, wherever, requires psychization. It needs first to be contained within the relationship to psyche, given the soul connection. Each complex needs realization and connection within the psyche, taming the puer's hot compulsions with the common salt of the soul. This salt makes things last and brings out their true flavor. The young and burning sulphur needs union with the elusive quicksilver of psychic reality before it becomes fixed and weighty.

This turning to the soul means *taking in our complexes out of the world,* out of the realm of senex power and system. Only this can slow the speed of history and technology and the acceleration of particle-men into bits of information without souls. It means that the search and questing be a psychological search and questing, a psychological adventure. It means that the messianic and revolutionary impulse connect first with the soul and be concerned first with its redemption. This alone makes human the puer's message, at the same time reddening the soul into life. It is in this realm of the soul that the gifts of the puer are first needed.

The Union of Sames. With the phenomenology of the senex and the puer behind us, we now see that we have actually been describing a secret identity of two halves—two halves not of life, but of a single archetype. This secret identity should not astonish us, since a corresponding feminine union of sames (the Mother-Daughter mysteries) has been placed at the center of feminine personality. Archetypal representations of this single figure with double aspects are: Tages, the Etruscan God who was a grey-haired boy appearing out of the furrows of a plowed field; the Islamic Chidr, a beauteous youth with a white beard; and Lao Tzu, whose name means senex-puer, i.e., "Lao"="old" and "Tzu"=both "master" and "child." (Other literary and hagiographic descriptions of the puer-senex polarity in the same figure are given in detail by Curtius.[35]) Through Jung's work we also know of this union of sames: *a)* first, on a dangerous and primitive level in the figure of Wotan, both youthful and Cronus,[36] *b)* in the figures of Mercurius,[37] Dionysus,[38] and Christ,

---

35. Curtius, *European Literature and the Latin Middle Ages,* loc. cit.
36. *CW*10: 375, 393ff.
37. *CW*13 ("The Spirit Mercurius").
38. *CW*5: 184; Karl Kerényi, *Dionysos: Archetypal Image of Indestructible Life,* trans-

each as *senex-et-puer, c*) in Asclepius, *senex-et-puer* who heals, and d) in the alchemical King and King's Son as two faces of the same dominant. These mythological figures, representing the union of sames that energize (Wotan), transform (Mercurius, Dionysus), heal (Asclepius), renew (King-*cum*-King's Son), and redeem (Christ), each state the psychological axiom that the archetype is timeless. It seems utterly unconcerned with aging, with historical accumulations; there is no conflict of generations since it is all generations at any moment. Ego-consciousness as the self-divisive instrument of the Self, its "father" or its "son" and thus its "enemy," instigates the factions and the differences. Thus does the ego act as the shadow of the Self.

We are also used to finding a secret identity in those we call in our offhand psychological jargon "typically puer" or "typically senex": the same self-willed petulance and resistance to change, the same ego-centricity and coldness of feeling, the same destructive effect on the middleground values of life, regarding them with scurrility, bitterness, and contempt. "Typically puer" or "typically senex" therefore means a possession through one face only. Again, because of the secret identity, it does not matter by which face one is possessed since they are the same. "Typical" therefore means "only," and the typical puer is identical with the typical senex; each is only puer or senex, not *puer-et-senex*. They are the same in a negative identification because they have lost the ambivalent consciousness of the union of sames. That tragedy of changelessness, of being "stuck," of being "unmoved" (expressed symbolically in "deafness," "heart disease," and "feet troubles"), is also accounted for by this negative identification. If the senex will not change and the puer cannot change (change requires listening, feeling, and going step-by-step), it is because the alpha-omega polarity has been negatively identified and thus obliterated. Without this polarity, which is at the essence of the archetype and holds its meaning together, there is perfection but no process, no movement from here to there, from past to future. A tension of ambivalent opposites is the structural pre-condition for change.

lated by Ralph Manheim (Princeton, N.J.: Princeton University Press, 1976); Walter F. Otto, *Dionysos: Myth and Cult,* translated by Robert B. Palmer (Bloomington: Indiana University Press, 1965).

The critical age of change in an individual life is, as Jung noted, around its midpoint in the fourth decade. Then the archetype of the process of life—and life for the psyche is a symbol—can break into two halves, sometimes killing the physical life of the individual who is broken by this symbolic crisis. That critical midpoint, when the puer impulse so often "dies" or becomes converted to senex values, is less a biological fact than a psychic symbol. As such it is governed less by the physiology of life processes than by the archetype of the process of life. This archetype of puer and senex is therefore particularly constellated at the midpoint, when the two faces are so close to each other and yet seem to look in opposite directions. It can be of utmost therapeutic value for the individual to realize (not that one is "getting old" but) that one is in the midst of a symbolic situation characterized by ambivalence of feeling and attitude, and that fears and confusions are appropriate. This realization that one's psyche is now being governed mainly by a union of sames may save one from an only ego view of necessary oppositions and choices. The therapeutic key to the midpoint would lie in the secret identity of the two faces of the same archetype. By continuing true to one's past puer spirit and consciously affirming it, one has already assumed the senex virtue of responsibility and order.

We are able to establish this identity of the two faces not only through psychological observations. It can be confirmed as well through mythographical amplification. A review of the main characteristics of each half shows parallels in symbolic forms with the other:

The Holy Old Man as Attis[39] is concealed and as Saturn has his head covered or cloaked; Harpocrates, the boy, is hooded, faceless or covered; so, too, are Attis[40] and Telesphorus. Saturn has a sparse beard; Mercurius wears his first downy beard or a small beard. Saturn is taciturn and guards secrets; Harpocrates has his fingers to his lips. As Mercurius is winged, so can Cronus-Saturn, as Aion, or on tombstones, be winged. Both are related to the dead, to time and eternity, and to the Golden Age. On a tomb in the Vatican "Saturn appears sadly reflecting, like Attis on other tombs." Both are concerned with truth—and with

---

39. Gershom Scholem, "Die mystische Gestalt der Gottheit in der Kabbala," *Eranos Yearbook* 29 (1960): 175.

40. *The Legend of Attis in Greek and Roman Art*, 54n.

deceit, craftiness, and thieving. Their animals are the same breed: Goat and Kid, and sometimes Dog. Both show abnormality of the feet: Saturn is lamed and crippled; the feet of Attis are bound, and Mercurius has winged foot-gear and Achilles the vulnerable heel of heroic illusion. One cannot walk, the other can only fly. The deformity points to their each being only half of a whole reality. As Jung says, "they are separated by deformity." Both Attis and Saturn show the castration motif and cold, cutoff satanic sexuality. For some, Mercurius is the principle of reason, governing astrology, mathematics, geometry, writing, knowledge, wisdom; for others, all these areas belong to Saturn. Both can be cold and dry. Saturn is lord of melancholy, yet Mercurius gives depression and worry. Harpocrates wears a wolfskin, and Mercurius, patron of merchants, shows the greed for gain; yet Saturn is the greedy one, miserly at home and rapacious abroad. Both are wanderers, both outcasts, and Saturn, who governs "magic and revels" (which could as well be said of the puer), is also against the bourgeois canons of society. As the puer is suicidal, Saturn presides over self-destruction. Both show an absence of the feminine, and both may have the ithyphallic attribute. The remoteness of Saturn at the *imum coeli* is matched at the other pole by the ascending puer Icarus-Ganymede. Yet Ganymede the cup bearer is also Saturn as Aquarian Water Carrier, the sign of our new age; and in reverse, the alchemical mercurial spirit is buried deep in the bowels of the earth, in exile and stench, in the lowest of low. The vertical axis, which connects them, gives them the spiritual point of view: both see the world *sub specie aeternitatis.* The one sees through it from below, as criminal or peasant, having suffered it with the privative vision given of melancholy. The other looks down upon it from above and from within as the divine seed-spark that knows the true *eidos* of all things.[41]

We seek this merger in our own lives. We seek a transformation of the conflict of extremes into a union of sames. Our time and its longing to be healed asks that the two ends be held together, that our other half so near to us, so like us as the shadow we cast, enter the circle of our light. Our other half is not only of another sex. The union of opposites— male with female—is not the only union for which we long and is not the

---

41. *Saturn and Melancholy,* 196–97; 213; 131–34; 157, 177–79; 203; 266n.; *The Survival of the Pagan Gods,* 294ff.

only union that redeems. There is also the union of sames, the re-union of the vertical axis, which would heal the split spirit. Adam must re-unite with Eve, but there still remains his re-union with God. Still remains the union of the first Adam at the beginning with the second Adam at the end of history. This division, experienced as the chasm between consciousness and the unconscious, is in us each at the unhealed heart of the process of individuation. No wonder that our theme is so charged, that we cannot take hold of the senex-puer problem anywhere without getting burnt; no wonder that it cannot be fully circumscribed and contained. It cannot become clarified, for we stand in the midst of its smoke. Its split is our pain.

This split of spirit is reflected in the senescence and renewal of God and of civilization. It is behind the fascination with *Lebensphilosophie* and the comforting aphorisms of stages of life, which by taking the polarity as its starting point can offer no healing.[42] This split gives us the aches of the father-son problem and the silent distance between generations, the search of the son for his father and the longing of the father for his son, which is the search and longing for one's own meaning; and the theological riddles of the Father and the Son. It tells us that we are split from our own likeness and have turned our sameness with this likeness into difference. And the same split is in the feminine as the spirit is represented in her by the animus, its poles that divide her and cause her to divide others, leading her into the either/or clarifications of the animus that but further new divisions such as love versus loyalty, principle versus abandon, or find her mothering the inspired puer or being the inspired daughter of the senex. The same split gives the frustrations of homosexual eros, the search for angelic beauty, the fear of ageing, the longing for the union of sames. We find it too in the insoluble difficulties of the master-pupil transference, the senex-teacher who must have a disciple and the puer-pupil who must have his image of the old wise man carried for him.[43] This is the traditional way the spirit is transferred. Yet, just this outer constellation reflects the inner division within each. Owing to the split archetype, a negative polarity is inevi-

---

42. Mircea Eliade, "Dimensions réligieuses du renouvellement cosmique," *Eranos Yearbook* 28 (1959): 251.

43. Panofsky, "Father Time," in *Studies in Iconography*, 75, 78.

tably constellated.[44] This leads to the curse between generations, the betrayals, to kings and powers not sages and wisdom, and the inability of the master to recognize his pupil and give him blessing. The pupil then "slays the Old King" in order to come into his own kingdom, only to become an Old King himself in the course of time.

What might this union of sames feel like? How would it be were the polarity healed? We have only hints: some in concepts, some in images.

A primary image of the union of sames is given in that "most widely cherished Renaissance maxim" *festina lente* (make haste slowly). Holding the opposites together in a balanced tension was represented in countless emblematic variations summarized by Wind. The puer-senex or *paedogeron* was one major example of *festina lente*. Maturity in this ideal was not a negation of the puer aspect since the puer was an essential face of "two-fold truth."[45]

Festina lente, in other words, presents an ego-ideal based on the two-faced archetype. It is an ideal that may be achieved, however, only by remaining consequently true to the puer aspect. To be true to one's puer nature means to admit one's puer past—all its gambols and gestures and sun-struck aspirations. From this history we draw consequences. By standing for these consequences, we let history catch up with us and thus is our haste slowed. History is the senex shadow of the puer, giving him substance. Through our individual histories, puer merges with senex, the eternal comes back into time, the falcon returns to the falconer's arm.

The dynamus of one combines with the order of the other. The bipolar spirit becomes ambivalent, logically incoherent but symbolically cohesive, as we see in the paradoxes of mysticism. There will be a curious intermingling of time and eternity, as in nature. Temporal continuity, that causal chain of history, the basis of order and the basis of ego, is broken up or broken through by the eternal. The world of Saturn is pierced through with Mercurius; the silver-quick flow coagulated into solid moments: quantum jumps, spontaneous events, forgetting and foolishness, uselessness in the world of power yet full knowledge,

---

44. *CW* 5: 184.

45. Edgar Wind, *Pagan Mysteries in the Renaissance* (Harmondsworth: Peregrine, 1967), 98ff.

unpredictable—"discontinuity," as Erich Neumann called it.[46] Yet, this is not chaos nor random destruction. Rather, these ordered happenings within limits are vividly meaningful, happenings having their own meaning, a sense or non-sense that is not dependent upon before or after from which it may be discrete, discontinuous, or only in the same "topological space." So the sense is given wholly by the experience itself as a gift of soul. And one feels through such experiences that there is meaning, that one is in meaning, that one is personally, individually meant. Let us call it meaningful discontinuity or the order of chance governed by fate, or call it living from the principle that Jung circumscribed as synchronicity.

Another hint comes from the paradoxes of knowing and not-knowing, the archetypal mystery, which is behind the phenomenon of dialogue. For dialogue does not rest only on the people who are involved, nor does their involvement rest on some existential para-concept. Dialogue, the union-forming effect of dialectic, the press within us to enter into dialectic to find knowledge and to discover meaning, is already embedded within the archetype of senex-puer relationship—that question "why" and that answer "I know." For meaning is as much in the questioning as in the knowing, or as Jung put it in his autobiography: The meaning of my existence is that life has addressed a question to me. Or, conversely, I myself am a question which is addressed to the world, and I must communicate my answer…I also think of the possibility that through the achievement of an individual a question enters the world, to which he must provide some kind of answer.[47]

In answering one's own question one is *puer-et-senex*. In questioning one's own answer one is *senex-et-puer*. The two faces turned toward each other in dialogue. This unending dialogue with oneself and between oneself and the world is that which holds one in meaning.

Alchemy gives a further hint in one of the paradoxes of the *lapis*. The stone is not only hard as the senex face might view it, not only a jade of longevity, a diamond body of immortality. The lapis, as Erwin Rous-

46. Erich Neumann, "Das Bild des Menschen in Krise und Erneuerung," *Eranos Yearbook* 28 (1959): 42ff.

47. C.G. Jung, *Memories, Dreams, Reflections*, edited by Aniela Jaffé; translated by Richard and Clara Winston (New York: Random House, 1961), 318.

selle[48] and Henry Corbin[49] have carefully elaborated, is the puer eternus. The end of the *via longissima* is the child. But the child begins in
the realm of Saturn, in lead or rock, ashes or blackness, and it is there
the child is realized. It is warmed to life in a bath of cinders, for only
when a problem is finally worn to nothing, wasted and dry, can it reveal
a wholly unexpected essence. Out of the darkest, coldest, most remote
burnt-out state of the complex the phoenix arises. *Petra genetrix*; out of
the stone a child is born, laughing, tender, unable. The stone, says Sir
George Ripley, is "of so tender and oily a substance that it is apt to dissolve in every moist place."[50] So it must be kept as sugar in a dry place.
The *ceratio* makes it soft to the touch; lead, Mercurius, and gold have a
kindred softness. Because it is wax-like and malleable, it takes the "type"
easily, impressions can be struck and then wiped out, forgotten, history
leaving no marks. At the human touch, at body temperature, the stone
relaxes its form. Oily and fat, it anoints that which it touches, spreads
blessing: *Christos, Messias,* anointed; the oily nature which "walks on
water" and heals wounds. This stone of changeless substance nevertheless has discontinuity of form and face, of defensive borders. It is easily persuaded into positions and dissuaded out of them again. Though
receptive to any imprint, it is not committed to any *eidos* but its own
substance. So, of *purus actus,* it is also purely acted upon and is thus a
spirit indistinguishable from matter. Highly impressionable yet leaving
no trace, it may take on any shape for a little while yet through warmth
be ready to dissolve again. The coagulation is always subject to renewed
dissolution, the senex certainty always provisionally puer.

These are hints of our healing. To get there where the spirit is whole,
where meaning holds together, we have begun on a way of mythical
images. There is an advantage in going this way towards archetypal
healing, for myth is the language of ambivalence; nothing is only this
or that; the gods and dancers will not stand still. They allow no sharp
pictures of themselves, only visions. Besides, as Kluckhohn has para-
phrased Lévi-Strauss: "...mythical thought always works from aware-

48. Erwin Rousselle, "Seelische Führung im lebenden Taoismus," *Eranos Yearbook*
1 (1933).

49. Henry Corbin, *Temple and Contemplation,* translated by Philip and Liadain Sher-
rard (London and New York: Routledge, 2009), 169.

50. George Ripley, "The Bosom Book" in *Collectanea Chemica* (London: Stuart, 1963),
141.

ness of binary oppositions toward their progressive mediation. That is, the contribution of mythology is that of providing a logical model capable of over-coming contradictions."[51]

Do we truly have a choice of ways? The binary oppositions, the polar coordinates, cannot be healed through an effort of mind and will, since the willful mind is the splitting instrument. We are incapable, as Hoyle said,[52] of solving the problems of the day with even the simplest logical processes. Any solution originating from the usual mind would be one-sided; it would be a solution imposed by either the senex or puer components of the ego. Thus the ego must first undergo an archetypal therapy of its split root.

The ego today is a "mind at the end of its tether." All it can do is leave itself open to the possibility of grace and to a renewal that might then take place in its absence. In the *absence of ego* and into its emptiness an imaginal stream can flow, providing mythical solutions for the psychic connection or "progressive mediation" between the senex/puer contradictions. These mythical solutions will be unclear, ambivalent, foolish. Ego-absence will feel first like ego-weakness; the solutions will seem to regress rather than to advance the problem into new terrain. But at this moment of transition we cannot advance until we have first retreated enough inward and backward so that the unconscious figures within can catch up with us. We cannot bring healing to the split without their cooperation since it is from them that we are split. To elicit their cooperation we must go part of the way, into the penumbral world.

---

51. Clyde Kluckhohn, "Recurrent Themes in Myths and Mythmaking" in *Myth and Mythmaking*, edited by Henry A. Murray (New York: Braziller, 1960), 58.

52. Fred Hoyle, *Of Men and Galaxies*, 65.

Originally delivered as a lecture in 1975 at the University of California Medical Center, San Francisco, and first published in *On the Way to Self-Knowledge*, edited by Jacob Needleman and Dennis Lewis (New York: Knopf, 1976). Reprinted in 1979 in *Puer Papers* and revised in 2005 for inclusion in *UE*3: *Senex & Puer*.

Peaks and Vales:
The Soul/Spirit Distinction as Basis for the Differences
between Psychotherapy and Spiritual Discipline

JAMES HILLMAN

The way through the world
Is more difficult to find than the way beyond it.
—Wallace Stevens, "Reply to Papini"

Search of Soul. Long ago and far away from California and its action, its
concern, its engagement, there took place in Byzantium, in the city of
Constantinople, in the year 869, a Council of the Principals of the Holy
Catholic Church,[1] and because of their session then and another one
of their sessions a hundred years prior (Nicaea, 787), we are all in this
room tonight.

Because at that Council in Constantinople the soul lost its dominion. Our anthropology, our idea of human nature, devolved from a tripartite cosmos of spirit, soul, and body (or matter), to a dualism of spirit
(or mind) and body (or matter). And this because at that other Council, the one in Nicaea in 787, images were deprived of their inherent
authenticity.

We are in this room this evening because we are moderns in search
of a soul, as Jung once put it. We are still in search of reconstituting that
third place, the intermediate realm of psyche—that is also the realm
of images and the power of imagination—from which we were exiled
by theological, spiritual men more than a thousand years ago: long
before Descartes and the dichotomies attributed to him, long before the
Enlightenment and modern positivism and scientism. These ancient
historical events are responsible for the malnourished root of our Western psychological culture and of the culture of each of our souls.

What the Constantinople Council did to soul only culminated a long process beginning with Paul (the saint) of substituting and disguising and forever after confusing, soul with spirit. Paul uses *psyche* only four times in his Epistles. *Psyche* appears in the entire New Testament only fifty-seven times compared with two hundred seventy-four occurrences of *pneuma*.[1] Quite a score! Of these fifty-seven occurrences of the word *psyche*, more than half are in the Gospels and Acts. The Epistles, the presentation of doctrine, the teachings of the school, could expose its theology and psychology without too much need for the word *soul*. For Paul four times was enough.

Much the same is true in regard to dreams and myths.[2] The word *to dream* does not appear in the New Testament; *dream* (*onar*) occurs only in three chapters of Matthew (1, 2, and 27). *Mythos* occurs only five times, pejoratively. Instead, there is stress on spirit phenomena: miracles, speaking in tongues, visions, revelations, ecstasy, prophecy, truth, faith.

Because our tradition has systematically turned against soul, we are each unaware of the distinctions between soul and spirit—therefore confusing psychotherapy with spiritual disciplines, obfuscating where they conflate and where they differ. This traditional denial of soul continues within the attitudes of each of us whether Christian or not, for we are each unconsciously affected by our culture's tradition, the unconscious aspect of our collective life. Ever since Tertullian declared that the soul (anima) is naturally Christian, there has been a latent Christianity, an antisoul spirituality, in our Western soul. This has led eventually to a psychological disorientation, and we have had to turn to the Orient. We place, displace, or project into the Orient our Occidental disorientation. And my task in this lecture is to do what I can for soul. Part of this task, because it is ritualistically appropriate, is to point out C.G. Jung's part in prying loose the dead fingers of those dignitaries in old

---

1. David L. Miller, "Achelous and the Butterfly," *Spring: An Annual of Archetypal Psychology and Jungian Thought* (1973): 14.

2. Cf. Morton T. Kelsey, *God, Dreams, and Revelation* (Minneapolis: Augsburg Publishing House, 1974), 80–84; Amos N. Wilder, "Myth and Dream in Christian Scripture," in *Myths, Dreams and Religion*, edited by Joseph Campbell (New York: Dutton, 1970). Hans Schär, "Bemerkungen zu Träumen in der Bibel," in *Traum und Symbol*, edited by C.A. Meier (Zurich: Rascher, 1963), 171–79.

Turkey, both by restoring the soul as a primary experience and field of work and by showing us ways—particularly through images—of realizing that soul.

Psyche and Image. The three hundred bishops assembled at Nicaea in 787 upheld the importance of images against the enemies of images, mainly the Imperial Byzantine army. Images were venerated and adored all through the antique world—statues, icons, paintings, and clay figures formed part of the local cults and were the focus of the conflict between Christianity and the old polytheistic religions. At the time of the Nicaean Council there had been another of those long battles between spirit and soul, between abstractions and images, between iconoclasts and idolaters, such as occur in the Bible and in the life of Mohammed, and such as those which took place in the Renaissance and in the Reformation when Cromwell's men broke the statues of Christ and Mary in the churches in England because they were the Devil's work and not Christian.

The hatred of the image, the fear of its power, and of the imagination is very old and very deep in our culture.

At Nicaea, a subtle and devastating differentiation was made. Neither the imagists nor the iconoclasts got their way entirely. A distinction was drawn between the *adoration* of images and the free formulation of them on the one hand, and the *veneration* of images and the authorized control over them on the other.[3] Church Councils split hairs, but the roots of these hairs are in our heads, and the split goes deep indeed. At Nicaea, a distinction was made between the image as such, its power, its full divine or archetypal reality, and what the image represents, points to, means. Thus, images became allegories.

When images become allegories, the iconoclasts have won. The image itself has become subtly depotentiated. Yes, images are allowed, but only if they are officially approved images illustrative of theological doctrine. One's spontaneous imagery is spurious, demonic, devilish, pagan, heathen. Yes, the image is allowed, but only to be venerated for what it represents: the abstract ideas, configurations, transcendencies

---

3. Hefele, *A History of the Councils of the Church,* 5:399–400.

behind the image. Images became ways of perceiving doctrine, helps in focusing fantasy. They become representations, no longer presentations, no longer presences of divine power.

The year 787 marks another victory in our tradition of spirit over soul. Jung's resuscitation of images was a return to soul and what he calls its spontaneous symbol formation, its life of fantasy (which, as he notes, is inherently tied with polytheism).[4] By turning to the image, Jung returned to the soul, reversing the historical process that in 787 had depotentiated images and in 869 had reduced soul to the rational intellectual spirit.

This is history, yet not only history. For each time you or I treat images as representations of something else—Penis, or Great Mother, or Power Drive, or Instinct, or whatever general, abstract concept we prefer—we have smashed the image in favor of the idea behind it. To give to imagination interpretative meanings is to think allegorically and to depotentiate the power of the imagination.

Here I want to remind you of Jung's position, from which I have developed mine. Jung's psychology is based on soul. It is a tripartite psychology. It is based neither on matter and the brain nor on the mind, intellect, spirit, mathematics, logic, metaphysics. He uses neither the methods of natural science and the psychology of perception nor the methods of metaphysical science and the logic of mentation. He says his base is in a third place between: *esse in anima*, "being in soul."[5] And he found this position by turning directly to the images in his insane patients and in himself during his breakdown years.

The soul and its images, having been alienated so long from our conscious culture, could be recognized only by the alienist. (Or by the artist, for whom imagination and madness have long been kissing cousins in our culture's anthropology.) So, Jung said, if you are in search of soul, go first to your fantasy images, for that is how the psyche presents itself directly.[6] All consciousness depends upon fantasy images. All we know about the world, about the mind, the body, about anything whatsoever, *including the spirit* and the nature of the divine, comes through images and is organized by fantasies into one pattern or another. This holds

---

4. *CW*8:92.
5. *CW*6:66.
6. *CW*8:618, 623; *CW*11:769.

true also for such spiritual states as pure light, or the void, or absence, or merging bliss, each of which is captured or structured in soul according to one or another archetypal fantasy pattern.[7] Because these patterns are archetypal, we are always in one or another archetypal configuration, one or another fantasy, including the fantasy of soul and the fantasy of spirit. The "collective unconscious," which embraces the archetypes, means our unconsciousness of the collective fantasy that is dominating by means of the archetypes our viewpoints, ideas, behaviors.

Let me continue for just a moment with Jung—though we are almost through the abstract, thinky part of this lecture—who says, "Every psychic process is an image and an imagining."[8] The only knowledge we have that is immediate and direct is knowledge of these psychic images. And further, when Jung uses the word image, he does not mean the reflection of an object or a perception; that is, he does not mean a memory or after-image. Instead he says his term is derived "from poetic usage, namely, a figure of fancy or fantasy image."[9] I have spelled all this out because I want you to know what I am doing. I am showing how soul looks at spirit, how peaks look from the vale, from within the fantasy world that is the shifting structure of our consciousness and its formulations, which are always shaped by archetypal images. We are always in one or another root-metaphor, archetypal fantasy, mythic perspective. From the soul's point of view we can never get out of the vale of our psychic reality.

———

Soul and Spirit. I have called this talk "Peaks and Vales," and I have been aiming to draw apart these images in order to contrast them as vividly as I can. Part of separating and drawing apart is the emotion of hatred. So I shall be speaking with hatred and urging strife, or *eris,* or *polemos,* which Heraclitus, the first ancestor of psychology, has said is the father of all.

The contemporary meaning of "peak" was developed by Abraham Maslow, who in turn was resonating an archetypal image, for peaks have belonged to the spirit ever since Mount Sinai and Mount Olympus,

———

7. *CW* 8: 746.
8. *CW* 11: 889.
9. *CW* 6: 743.

Mount Patmos and the Mount of Olives, and Mount Moriah of the first patriarchal Abraham. And you will easily name a dozen other mountains of the spirit. It does not require much explication to realize that the peak experience is a way of describing pneumatic experience, and that the clamber up the peaks in search of spirit is the drive of the spirit in search of itself. The language Maslow uses about the peak experience—"self-validating, self-justifying and carries its own intrinsic value with it"—the God-likeness and God-nearness, the absolutism and intensity, is a traditional way of describing spiritual experiences. Maslow deserves our gratitude for having reintroduced *pneuma* into psychology, even if his move has been compounded by the old confusion of *pneuma* with psyche. But what about the *psyche* of psychology?

Vales do indeed need more exposition, just as everything to do with soul needs to be carefully imagined as accurately as we can. "Vale" comes from the Romantics: Keats uses the term in a letter, and I have taken this passage from Keats as a psychological motto: "Call the world, if you please, 'The vale of Soul-making.' Then you will find out the use of the world."

Vale in the usual religious language of our culture is a depressed emotional place—the vale of tears; Jesus walked this lonesome valley, the valley of the shadow of death. The very first definition of "valley" in the Oxford English Dictionary is a "long depression or hollow." The meanings of vale and valley include entire subcategories referring to such sad things as the decline of years and old age, the world regarded as a place of troubles, sorrow and weeping, and the world regarded as the scene of the mortal, the earthly, the lowly.

There is also a feminine association with vales. We find this in the *Tao Te Ching*; in Freudian morphological metaphors, where the wooded river valley teeming with animal life is an equivalent for the vagina; and also we find a feminine connotation of the valley in mythology. For valleys are the places of the nymphs. One of the etymological explanations of the word *nymph* takes these figures to be personifications of the wisps and clouds of mist clinging to valleys, mountainsides, and water sources.[10] Nymphs veil our vision, keep us shortsighted, myopic,

---

10. *Ausführliches Lexikon der griechischen und römischen Mythologie,* edited by

caught—no long-range distancing, no projections or prophecies as from the peak.

This peak/vale pairing is also used by the fourteenth Dalai Lama of Tibet. In a letter (to Peter Goullart) he writes:

> The relation of height to spirituality is not merely metaphorical. It is physical reality. The most spiritual people on this planet live in the highest places. So do the most spiritual flowers…
>
> I call the high and light aspects of my being *spirit* and the dark and heavy aspect *soul.*
>
> Soul is at home in the deep, shaded valleys. Heavy torpid flowers saturated with black grow there. The rivers flow like warm syrup. They empty into huge oceans of soul.
>
> Spirit is a land of high, white peaks and glittering jewel-like lakes and flowers. Life is sparse and sounds travel great distances.
>
> There is soul music, soul food, soul dancing, and soul love…
>
> When the soul triumphed, the herdsmen came to the lamaseries, for soul is communal and loves humming in unison. But the creative soul craves spirit. Out of the jungles of the lamasery, the most beautiful monks one day bid farewell to their comrades and go to make their solitary journey toward the peaks, there to mate with the cosmos…
>
> [N]o spirit broods over lofty desolation; for desolation is of the depths, as is brooding. At these heights, spirit leaves soul far behind…people need to climb the mountain not simply because it is there but because the soulful divinity needs to be mated with the spirit…[11]

May I point out one or two little curiosities in this letter? They may help us to see further the contrast between soul and spirit. First, did you notice how important it is to be *literal* and not "merely metaphorical" when one takes the spiritual viewpoint? Also, this viewpoint requires the physical sensation of height, of "highs." Then, did you see that it is the most *beautiful* monks who leave their brothers, and that their mating is with the *cosmos,* a mating that is compared with snow? (Once in

W.H. Roscher (Leipzig: B.G. Teubner, 1884), III: "Pan."

11. "The Dalai Lama of Flowers," in Pierre Delattre, *Tales of a Dalai Lama* (Boston: Houghton Mifflin, 1971), 32–34.

our witch-hunting Western tradition, a time obsessively concerned with protecting soul from wrong spirits—and vice versa—the devil was identified by his icy penis and cold sperm.) And finally, have you noticed the two sorts of anima symbolism: the dark, heavy, torpid flowers by the rivers of warm syrup and the virginal petaled flowers of the glaciers?

I am trying to let the *images* of language draw our distinction. This is the soul's way of proceeding, for it is the way of dreams, reflections, fantasies, reveries, poems, and paintings. We can recognize what is spiritual by its style of imagery and language; so with soul. To give *definitions* of spirit and soul—the one abstract, unified, concentrated; the other concrete, multiple, immanent—puts the distinction and the problem into the language of spirit. We would already have left the valley. We would be making differences like a surveyor, laying out what belongs to whom according to logic and law rather than according to imagination. Let us turn to another culture a little closer to home even if far away in time: the early desert saints in Egypt, whom we might call the founders of our Western ascetic tradition, our discipline of the spirit.

We must first recall that these men were Egyptians, and as Violet MacDermott has shown,[12] their spiritual moves need to be understood against their Egyptian religious background. As the inheritor of an enduring polytheistic religion, the desert saint attempted to "reverse the psychological effects of the ancient religion." His discipline aimed to separate the monk from his human community and also from nature, both of which were of vital importance to the polytheistic religion in which divine and human interpenetrated everywhere (that is, in the valley, not only at the peak or the desert). By living in a cave—the burial place of the old religion—the desert saint performed a mimesis of death: the rigors of his spiritual discipline, its peculiar postures, fasting, insomnia, darkness, etc. These rigors helped him withstand the assault of the demons or ancestral influences of the dead, as well as his personal and cultural history:

> The world of the gods was, in Egypt, also the world of the dead. Through dreams, the dead communicated with the living...

---

12. Violet MacDermott, *The Cult of the Seer in the Ancient Middle East* (Berkeley and Los Angeles: University of California Press, 1971). See Henri Frankfort, *Ancient Egyptian Religion* (New York: Harper Torchbook, 1961), chap. 1, for an excellent summary of Egyptian polytheistic psychology.

therefore sleep represented a time when his soul was subject to his body and to those influences which derived from his old religion…his ideal was to sleep as little as possible.[13]

Again you will have noticed the turn away from sleep and dreams, away from nature and community, away from personal and ancestral history and polytheistic complexity. These factors from which the spiritual discipline works to be free give specific indications about the nature of the soul.

We find another contrast between soul and spirit, couched in different terms from the spiritual ones we have been examining. E.M. Forster's little volume *Aspects of the Novel* lays out the basic components of the art of the novel. He makes a distinction between fantasy and prophecy. He says that both involve mythology, gods. Then he calls up fantasy with these words:

> …let us now invoke all beings who inhabit the lower air, the shallow water, and the smaller hills, all Fauns and Dryads and slips of the memory, all verbal coincidences, Pans and puns, all that is medieval this side of the grave [by which I guess him to mean the coarse, common, and humorous, the daily, the grotesque and freakish, even bestial, but also festive].[14]

When Forster comes to prophecy we gain yet more images of spirit, for prophecy in the novel pertains to:

> …whatever transcends our abilities, even when it is human passion that transcends them, to the deities of India, Greece, Scandinavia, and Judea, to all that is medieval beyond the grave and to Lucifer son of the morning [by which last I take him to mean the "problem of good and evil"]. By their mythologies we shall distinguish these two sorts of novels.[15]

By their mythologies we shall also distinguish our therapies.

Forster goes on with the comparison, but we shall break off, taking only a few scattered observations. Spirit (or the prophetic style) is humble but humorless. "It may imply any of the faiths that have haunted humanity—Christianity, Buddhism, dualism, Satanism, or the mere

---

13. Ibid., 46.
14. E.M. Forster, *Aspects of the Novel* (Harmondsworth: Pelican, 1971), 115.
15. Ibid.

raising of human love and hatred to such a power that their normal receptacles no longer contain them."[16] (You recall the lama mating with the cosmos, the desert saint alone.) Prophecy (or spirit) is mainly a tone of voice, an accent, such as we find in the novels of D.H. Lawrence and Dostoevsky. Fantasy (or soul, in my terms) is a wondrous quality in daily life. "The power of fantasy penetrates into every corner of the universe, but not into the forces that govern it—the stars that are the brain of heaven, the army of unalterable law, remain untouched—and novels of this type have an improvised air."[17] Here I think of the free associations of Freud as a *method* in psychology, or of Jung's mode of writing where a paragraph may not logically follow the one preceding, or of Lévi-Strauss's figure, the *bricoleur*, the handyman and his ragtag putting together of collages, and how different this psychological style is from that of intensely focused transcendental meditation, the turning away, the emptying out.

And finally for our purposes Forster says about fantasy novels, or soul-writing, "If one god must be invoked specially, let us call upon Hermes—messenger, thief, and conductor of Souls."[18]

Forster points to something else about soul (by means of his notion of fantasy), and this something else is history. The soul involves us in history—our individual case history, the history of our therapy, our culture as history. (We have seen the Coptic ascetics attempting to overcome ancestral history through spiritual practices.) Here I, too, am speaking soul language in going back all the time to historical examples, such as old E.M. Forster, little fussy man in his room in Cambridge, now dead, and dead Freud and Jung, back to old myths and their scholarship, to etymologies and the history in words, and down to specific geographical localities, the actual vales of the world. For this is the way the soul proceeds. This is psychological method, and psychological method remains within this valley world, through which history passes and leaves its traces, our "ancestors."

The peaks wipe out history. History is to be overcome. History is bunk, said Henry Ford, prophetic manufacturer of obsolescence, and

16. Ibid., 129.
17. Ibid., 116.
18. Ibid.

the past is a bucket of ashes, said Carl Sandburg, prophetic singer. So the spirit workers and spirit seekers first of all must climb over the debris of history, or prophesy its end or its unreality, time as illusion, as well as the history of their individual and particular localities, their particular ethnic and religious roots (Jung's ill-favored earlier term "racial unconscious"). Thus, from the spirit point of view, it can make no difference if our teacher be a Zaddik from a Polish *shtetl,* an Indian from under a Mexican cactus, or a Japanese master in a garden of stones, these differences are but conditionings of history, personalistic hangups. The spirit is impersonal, rooted not in local soul, but timeless.

I shall ride this horse of history until it drops, for I submit that history has become the Great Repressed. If in Freud's time sexuality was the Great Repressed and the creator of the internal ferment of the psychoneuroses, today the one thing we will not tolerate is history. No; we are each Promethean with a bag of possibilities, Pandoran hopes, open, unencumbered, the future before us, so various, so beautiful, so new— new and liberated men and women living forward into a science fiction. So history rumbles below, continuing to work in our psychic complexes.

Our complexes are history at work in the soul: father's socialism, his father's fundamentalism, and my reaction against them like Hefner to Methodism, Kinsey to Boy-Scoutism, Nixon to Quakerism. It is so much easier to transcend history by climbing the mountain and let come what may than it is to work on history within us, our reactions, habits, moralities, opinions, symptoms that prevent true psychic change. Change in the valley requires recognition of history, an archaeology of the soul, a digging in the ruins, a recollecting. And—a planting in specific geographical and historical soil with its own smell and savor, in connection with the spirits of the dead, the *po*-soul sunk in the ground below.

From the viewpoint of soul and life in the vale, going up the mountain feels like a desertion. The lamas and saints "bid farewell to their comrades." As I'm here as an advocate of soul, I have to present its viewpoint. Its viewpoint appears in the long hollow depression of the valley, the inner and closed dejection that accompanies the exaltation of ascension. The soul feels left behind, and we see this soul reacting with anima resentments. Spiritual teachings warn the initiate so often about introspective broodings, about jealousy, spite, and pettiness, about attachments to sensations and memories. These cautions present an accurate phenomenology of how the soul feels when the spirit bids farewell.

If a person is concurrently in therapy and in a spiritual discipline—Vedanta, breathing exercises, transcendental meditation, etc.—the spiritual teacher may well regard the analysis as a waste of time with trivia and illusions. The analyst may regard the spiritual exercises as a leak in the psychic vessel, or an escape into either physicality (somatizing, a sort of sophisticated hysterical conversion) or into metaphysicality. These are conditions that grow in the same hedgerow: both physicalize, substantiate, hypostasize, taking their concepts as things. They both lose the "as if," the metaphorical Hermes approach, forgetting that metaphysics, too, is a fantasy system, even if one that must unfortunately take itself as literally real.

Besides these mutual accusations of triviality, there is a more essential question that we in our analytical armchairs ask: *Who* is making the trip? Here it is not a discussion about the relative value of doctrines or goals; nor is it an analysis of the visions seen and experiences felt. The essential issue is not the analysis of content of spiritual experiences, for we have seen similar experiences in the county hospital, in dreams, in drug trips. Having visions is easy. The mind never stops oozing and spurting the sap and juice of fantasy, and then congealing this play into paranoid monuments of eternal truth. And then are not these seemingly mind-blowing events of light, of synchronicity, of spiritual sight in an LSD trip often trivial—seeing the universe revealed in a buttonhole stitch or linoleum pattern—at least as trivial as what takes place in a usual therapy session that picks apart the tangles of the daily domestic scene?

The question of what is trivial and what is meaningful depends on the archetype that gives meaning, and this, says Jung, is the self. Once the self is constellated, *meaning* comes with it. But as with any archetypal event, it has its undifferentiated foolish side. So one can be overwhelmed by displaced, inferior, paranoid meaningfulness, just as one can be overwhelmed by eros and one's soul (anima) put through the throes of desperate, ridiculous love. The disproportion between the trivial content of a synchronistic event on the one hand, and on the other, the giant sense of meaning that comes with it, shows what I mean. Like a person who has fallen into love, so a person who has fallen into meaning begins that process of self-validation and self-justification of trivia that belong to the experience of the archetype within any complex and form part of its defense. It therefore makes little difference, psychodynamically, whether we fall into the shadow and justify our disorders of morality, or the anima and our disorders of beauty, or the self and our disorders of meaning. Paranoia has been defined as a disorder of meaning—that is, it can be referred to the influence of an undifferentiated self-archetype. Part of this disorder is the very systematization that would, by defensive means of the doctrine of synchronicity, give profound meaningful order to a trivial coincidence.

Here we return to Mr. Forster, who reminded us that the spirit's voice is humble and the soul's humorful.[19] Humility is awed and wowed by meaning; the soul takes the same events more as the puns and pranks of Pan.[20] Humility and humor are two ways of coming down to *humus*, to the human condition. Humility would have us bow down to the world and pay our due to its reality. Render unto Caesar. Humor brings us down with a pratfall. Heavy meaningful reality becomes suspect, seen through, the world laughable—paranoia dissolved, as synchronicity becomes spontaneity.

Thus the relation of the soul analyst to the spiritual event is not in terms of the doctrines or of the contents. Our concern is with the person, the Who, going up the mountain. Also we ask, Who is already up there, calling?

This question is not so different from one put in spiritual disciplines, and it is crucial. For it is not the trip and its stations and path, not the rate of ascent and the rung of the ladder, or the peak and its experience, nor even the return—it is the person in the person prompting the whole endeavor. And here we fall back into history, the historical ego, our Western-Northern willpower, the very willpower that brought the missionaries and trappers, the cattlemen and ranchers and planters, the Okies and Arkies, the orange-growers, wine-growers, and sectarians, and the gold-rushers arid railroaders to California to begin with. Can this be left at the door like a dusty pair of outworn

---

19. On the relation of humor and psyche, see Miller's "Achelous and the Butterfly."
20. On synchronicity and Pan, see "An Essay on Pan" in my *Pan and the Nightmare* (with W. H. Roscher) (New York and Zurich: Spring Publications, 1972), lvi–lix.

shoes when one goes into the sweet-smelling pad of the meditation room? Can one close the door on the person who brought one to the threshold in the first place?

The movement from one side of the brain to the other, from tedious daily life in the supermarket to supra-consciousness, from trash to transcendence, the "altered state of consciousness" approach—to put it all it in a nutshell—denies this historical ego. It is an approach going back to Saul who became Paul, conversion into the opposite, knocked off one's ass in a flash.

So you see the archetypal question is neither *how* does the soul/ spirit conflict happen, nor *why*, but *who* among the variety of figures of which we are each composed, which archetypal figure or person is in this happening? What God is at work in calling us up the mountain or in holding us to the vales? For archetypal psychology, there is a god in every perspective, in every position. All things are determined by psychic images, including our formulations of the spirit. All things present themselves to consciousness in the shapings of one or another divine perspective. Our vision is mimetic to one or another of the gods.

Who is going up the mountain: is it the unconscious do-gooder Christian in us, he who has lost his historical Christianity and is an unconscious crusader, knight, missionary, savior? (I tend to see the latent "Christian Soldier" of our unconscious Christianity as more of a social danger than so-called latent psychosis, latent homosexuality, or masked, latent depression.)

Who is going up the mountain: is it the Climber, a man who would become the mountain himself, I on Mount Rushmore—humble now, but just you wait and see...

Is it the heroic ego? Is it Hercules, still at the same labors: cleaning up the stables of pollution, killing the swamp creatures, clubbing his animals, refusing the call of women, progressing through twelve stages (all in the end to go mad and marry Hebe, who is Hera, Mom, in her younger, sweeter, smilingly hebephrenic form)?

Or is the one ascending the spiritual impetus of the *puer aeternus*, the winged godlike imago in us each, the beautiful boy of the spirit— Icarus on the way to the sun, then plummeting with waxen wings; Phaethon driving the sun's chariot out of control, burning up the world; Bellerophon, ascending on his white winged horse, then falling onto the

plains of wandering, limping ever after? These are the puer high climb-
ers, the heaven stormers, whose eros reflects the torch and ladder of
Eros and his searching arrow, a longing for higher and further and more
and purer and better. Without this archetypal component affecting our
lives, there would be no spiritual drive, no new sparks, no going beyond
the given, no grandeur and sense of personal destiny.

So, psychologically, and perhaps spiritually as well, the issue is one
of finding connections between the puer's drive upward and the soul's
clouded, encumbering embrace. My notion of this connection would
avoid two side tracks. The first would take the soul up too, "liberate
it" from its vale—the transcendentalist's demand. The second would
reduce the spirit to a complex and would thus deny the puer's legitimate
ambition and art of flying—the psychoanalyst's demand. Let's remember here that he who cannot fly cannot imagine, as Gaston Bachelard
said, and also Mohammed Ali. To imagine in a true high-flying, free-
falling way, to walk on air and put on airs, to experience pneumatic reality and its concomitant inflation, one must imagine out of the valley,
above the grainfields and the daily bread. Sometimes this is too much
for professional analysts, and by not recognizing the archetypal claims
of the puer, they thwart imagination.

Let us now turn to the puer-psyche connection without forcing the
claims of either figure upon the other.

———

The Puer-Psyche Marriage. The accommodation between the high-driv-
ing spirit on the one hand and the nymph, the valley, or the soul on
the other can be imagined as the puer-psyche marriage. It has been
recounted in many ways—for instance, in Jung's *Mysterium Coniunctionis* as an alchemical conjunction of personified substances, or in Apuleius's tale of Eros and Psyche.[21] In the same manner as these models, let us imagine in a personified style. Then we can feel the different

———

21. There are many Jungian interpretative attempts on this tale. Cf. Marie-Louise
von Franz, *A Psychological Interpretation of the Golden Ass of Apuleius* (New York and
Zurich: Spring Publications, 1970); Erich Neumann, *Amor and Psyche* (New York:
Pantheon, 1956); and my *The Myth of Analysis* (Evanston: Northwestern University
Press, 1972), 55ff.

needs within us as volitions of distinct persons, where puer is the Who in our spirit flight, and anima (or psyche) is the Who in our soul.

Now the main thing about the anima[22] is just what has always been said about the psyche: it is unfathomable, ungraspable. For the anima, "the archetype of life," as Jung has called her, is that function of the psyche that is its actual life, the present mess it is in, its discontent, dishonesties, and thrilling illusions, together with the whitewashing hopes for a better outcome. The issues she presents are as endless as the soul is deep, and perhaps these very endless labyrinthine "problems" *are* its depth. The anima embroils and twists and screws us to the breaking point, performing the "function of relationship," another of Jung's definitions, a definition that becomes convincing only when we realize that relationship means perplexity.

This mess of psyche is what puer consciousness needs to marry so as to undertake "the battle of the sexes." The opponents of the spirit are first of all the hassles under its own skin: the morning moods, the symptoms, the prevarications in which it gets entangled, and the vanity. The puer needs to battle the irritability of this inner "woman," her passive laziness, her fancies for sweets and flatteries—all that which analysis calls "autoeroticism." This fighting is a fighting *with*, rather than a fighting off or fighting against, the anima, a close, tense, devoted embracing in many positions of intercourse. Where puer madness is met with psychic confusion and deviation, and where this madness is reflected in that distorted mirror. It is not straight and not clear. We do not even know what weapons to use or where the enemy is, since the enemy seems to be my own soul and heart and most dear passions. The puer is left only with his craziness, which, through the battle, he has resort to so often that he learns to care for it as precious, as the one thing that he truly is, his uniqueness and limitation. Reflection in the mirror of the soul lets one see the madness of one's spiritual drive, and the importance of this madness.

------

22. For a full exploration of anima, relevant literature, and citations from Jung, see my two papers "Anima" in *Spring: An Annual of Archetypal Psychology and Jungian Thought* (1973), 97–132, and *Spring: An Annual of Archetypal Psychology and Jungian Thought* (1974), 113–46. Later published as *Anima: An Anatomy of a Personified Notion* (Dallas: Spring Publications, 1985).

Precisely this is what the struggle with the anima, and what psycho-therapy as the place of this struggle, is all about: to discover one's mad-ness, one's unique spirit, and to see the relationship between one's spirit and one's madness, that there is madness in one's spirit, and there is spirit in one's madness.

The spirit needs witness to this madness. Or to put it another way, the puer takes its drive and goal literally unless there is reflection, which makes possible a metaphorical understanding of its drive and goal. By bearing witness as the receptive experiencer and imager of the spirit's actions, the soul can contain, nourish, and elaborate in fantasy the puer impulse, bring it sensuousness and depth, involve it in life's delusions, care for it for better or for worse. Then the individual in whom these two components are marrying begins to carry with him his own reflective mirror and echo. He becomes aware of what his spiritual actions mean in terms of psyche. The spirit turned toward psyche, rather than desert-ing it for high places and cosmic love, finds ever further possibilities of seeing through the opacities and obfuscations in the valley. Sunlight enters the vale. The Word participates in gossip and chatter.

The spirit asks that the psyche help it, not break it or yoke it or put it away as a peculiarity or insanity. And it asks the analysts who act in psyche's name not to turn the soul against the puer adventure but rather to prepare the desire of both for each other.

Unfortunately a good deal of the psychotherapeutic cosmos is dom-inated by the perspective of Hera's social adaptation (and her favorite minion, the strong ego of coping Hercules). Hera is out to get the ren-egade puer spirit and "do" something sensible with it. The puer spirit is not seen for its authentic archetypal value. Hera's priests and priest-esses of psychological counseling attempt to make problems clearer, give therapeutic support, by trying to understand what upsets a person. Psychological counseling then literalizes problems and, by killing the possibility of seeing through to their madness, kills the spirit.

Psychologists who do not attend enough to spirit forget that it is one of the essential components of the conjunction and cannot be dis-missed as a head trip, as intellect, as just theology or metaphysics or a puer flight. Spirit neglected comes into psychology through the back door, disguised as synchronicity, magic, oracles, science fiction, self-symbolism, mandalas, tarot, astrology, and other indiscriminations, equally prophetic, ahistorical, and humorless. For it requires spirit to discern among the spirits.

Diakrisis (discernment) itself is a gift of the spirit, and psychologists who refuse the puer chug along empowered by doctrinal mechanisms of dead masters, their own imaginative sails decayed or never even hoisted, circling in the doldrums of low-profile, low-horizon humility: the practice of psychotherapy.

Once the spirit has turned toward the soul, the soul can regard its own needs in a new way. Then these needs are no longer attempts to adapt to Hera's civilizational requirements, or to Venus's insistence that love is God, or to Apollo's medical cures, or even Psyche's work of soul-making. Not for the sake of learning love only, or for community, or for better marriages and better families, or for independence does the psyche present its symptoms and neurotic claims. Rather these demands are asking also for inspiration, for long-distance vision, for ascending eros, for vivification and intensification (*not* relaxation), for radicality, transcendence, and meaning—in short, the psyche has spiritual needs, which the puer part of us can fulfill. Soul asks that its preoccupations be not dismissed as trivia but seen through in terms of higher and deeper perspectives, the verticalities of the spirit. When we realize that our psychic malaise points to a spiritual hunger beyond what psychology offers and that our spiritual dryness points to a need for psychic waters beyond what spiritual discipline offers, then we are beginning to move both therapy and discipline.

The puer-psyche marriage results first of all in increased interiority. It constructs a walled space, the thalamus or bridal chamber, neither peak nor vale, but rather a place where both can be looked at through glass windows or be closed off with doors. This increased interiority means that each new puer inspiration, each hot idea at whatever time of life in whomever, be given psychization. It will first be drawn through the labyrinthine ways of the soul, which wind it and slow it and nourish it from many sides (the "many" nurses and "many" maenads), developing the spirit from a one-way mania for "ups" to *polytropos,* the many-sidedness of the Hermetic old hero, Odysseus. The soul performs the service of indirection to the puer arrow, bringing to the sulphuric compulsions of the spirit the lasting salt of soul.

Likewise, for soul: the bridal chamber intensifies the brooding, gives it heat and pressure, building soul from amorphous clouds into driving needs. And these, by benefit of puer, become formulated into language. There is a sense of process, direction, continuity within one's interior life of dreams and wishes. Suffering begins to make sense. Instead of the repetitious and usual youth-nymph pairings of virginal innocence coupled with seed spilled everywhere foolishly, psychic conception takes place and the opus of one's life begins to form.

The puer-psyche marriage finally implies taking our complexes both out of the world and out of the realm of spiritual systems. It means that the search and questing go through a psychological search and questing, an exploration of soul by spirit for psychic fecundation. The messianic, liberating, transcending movement connects first with soul and is concerned first with its movement: not "what does this mean?"—the question asked of spirit by spirit—but "what does this move in my soul?"—the interiorization of the question. This alone puts psychic body into the puer message and trip, adding to it psychic values, so that the puer message can touch soul and redden it into life. For it is especially in this realm of soul—so lost, emptied, and ignorant—that the gifts of the puer spirit are first needed. It is soul, psyche, and psychology that need the spirit's attention. Come down from the mountain, monks, and like beautiful John Keats, come into the vale of soul-making.

Four Points of Difference. At this point I am leaving the puer's enthusiastic perspective to return again to soul. I want to suggest now three fundamental qualities of soul-making in distinction to spirit disciplines. These three are: 1) *Pathologizing*[23]—an interest in the psychopathologies of our lives—that is, an attentive concern to the logos of the pathos of the psyche. By keeping an ear tuned to the soul's pathologizings, we maintain the close link of soul with mortality, limitation, and death. 2) *Anima*—a loyalty to the clouded moods of the water sources, to

----

23. Pathologizing points to the psyche's autonomous ability to create illness, morbidity, disorder, abnormality, and suffering in any aspect of its behavior and to experience and imagine life through this deformed and afflicted perspective; see "Pathologizing," Part 2 of my *Re-Visioning Psychology* (New York: Harper & Row, 1975).

the seductive twists and turns of the interior feminine figures who personify the labyrinthine path of psychic life, those nymphs, dark witches, lost Cinderellas and Persephones of destruction, and the elusive, illusional fantasies that anima creates, the images of soul in the soul. 3) *Polytheism*—single-minded commitment to discord and cacophony, to variety and not getting it all together, to falling apart, the multiplicity of the ten thousand things, to the peripheries and their tangents (rather than centers), to the episodic, occasional, wandering movement of the soul (like this lecture) and its compulsion to repeat in the valleys of its errors, and the necessity of errancy and error for discovering the many ways of many gods.

I am aware that these lectures have been organized in order to relate East and West, religious disciplines and psychotherapy, and so I must make a contribution to an issue that I believe is not the main one (the East-West pair). For I believe the true passion is between North and South, between the upper and lower regions, whether they be the repressive Northern Protestantism of Europe and America on the one hand, and on the other, Southland, the oppressed Mediterranean, the Latin darkness below the borders, across the rivers, under the Alps; whether this division be the manic industrial North and the depressive ritualistic South, or between San Francisco and Los Angeles.

But Professor Needleman says the line is blurred between the therapist and the spiritual guide, and he would draw that line spiritually—that is, vertically—creating East and West across the mountaintops, perhaps like the Continental Divide, whereas I would draw the line horizontally, as rivers flow, downward. The three qualifications I have just made—pathologizing, anima, polytheism—are my way of drawing the line more heavily and bluntly, thick with shadow.

Anyone who is engaged with these three factors, regarding them as important, as religious even, seems to me to be engaged in therapy and psychology. Anyone who tends to dismiss pathologizing for growth, or anima confusions for ego strength or spiritual illumination, or who neglects the differentiation of multiplicity and variety for the sake of unity is engaged in spiritual discipline.

The lines between the two labors I would draw in this way. But I would also suggest that they are drawn not by what a person preaches but according to the weight of importance he lays upon trivia, the little things in daily practice. There are, for instance, many who are called "psycho-therapists" and pretend its practice, but who, according to these criteria, are actually daily engaged in spirit. In the emphasis they give and in the values they select, their main concern is with ascension (growing *up*), strengthening, unity, and wholeness. Whereas I believe, though I am less familiar with the spiritual side of things (coming from Switzerland, where our main words are complex, schizophrenia, introvert-extrovert, Rorschach and Bleuler, and the spectrum of drugs from Ciba-Geigy, Sandoz, and Hoffmann-La Roche; that is, our fantasy is more psychiatric, more psychopathological than yours, which is more spiritually determined by your history and geography, this Golden State, its founding missions, its holy spiritual names—Eureka, Sacramento, Berkeley (the Bishop), Los Angeles, San Diego, Santa Cruz, Santa Monica, Carmel, Santa Barbara) I believe that the spiritual masters may, despite their doctrine, very often be engaged in psychotherapy when they follow the female inner figure as guide, the *paredros* or angel, when they allow vision and fantasy to flourish, when they let the multiple voices in the symptoms speak and turn the pathologizings into inner teachers, when they move from all generalities and abstractions to concrete immediacy and the multivalence of events.

In other words, the lines between therapy and discipline, between soul and spirit, do not depend on the kind of patient or the kind of teacher, or whether the patient or teacher was born in the Cascades or the Himalayas, but rather depend upon which archetypal dominant is working through one's viewpoint. The issue always returns to "Who" in an individual's subjectivity is asking the questions and giving the answers.

Pathologizing, anima, and polytheism are, moreover, intimately connected with one another. It would take us too far in this talk to attempt to show the internal logic of this connection, and I am not up to doing it swiftly and succinctly. Besides, this interconnection has been a main theme of many of my writings, because one soon discovers in work with oneself and others that each of these criteria of soul-making tends to imply the other. The varied anima figures, elfin inspirations, and moods that move a person, men and women alike (for it is nonsense to hold that women can have only animuses, no souls, as if an archetype or a goddess could be limited to the personal psychology of sexual gender), give a peculiar double feeling. There is a sense of me-ness, personal importance, soul sense, that is not an ego inflation, and at the same time there is an awareness of one's subjectivity being fluid, airy, fiery, earthy, made of many components, shifting, ungraspable, now close and intimate and helpful as Athene giving wise counsel, then wily and disappearing, naively pulling one into hopeless holes like Persephone, and at the next moment fantasizing Aphroditic whisperings in the inner ear, sea foam, pink vulvar bivalves, and then proud and tall Artemis, keeping everything at bay, oneself at a distance, at one only with nature, a virgin soul among brothers and sisters, only.

Anima makes us feel many parts. Anima, as Jung said, is an equivalent of and a personification of the polytheistic aspect of the psyche.[24] "Polytheism" is a theological or anthropological concept for the experience of a many-souled world.

This same experience of multiplicity can reach us as well through symptoms. They too make us aware that the soul has other voices and intentions than the one of the ego. Pathologizing bears witness to both the soul's inherent composite nature and to the many gods reflected in this composition. Here I take my cue from two passing remarks of Jung's: "The divine thing in us functions as neuroses of the stomach, or the colon, or the bladder, simply disturbances of the underworld. Our gods have gone to sleep, and they only stir in the bowels of the earth."[25] And again: "The gods have become diseases; Zeus no longer rules Olympus but rather the solar plexus, and produces curious specimens for the doctor's consulting room."[26]

Sometimes going up the mountain one seeks escape from this underworld, and so the gods appear from below bringing all sorts of physiological disorders. They will be heard, if only through intestinal rumblings and their fire burning in the bladder.

---

24. CW9.2: 427, and my discussion of this theme in "Psychology: Monotheistic or Polytheistic?" *Spring: An Annual of Archetypal Psychology and Jungian Thought* (1971), 193–208. Reprinted in *UE1: Archetypal Psychology.*

25. C.G. Jung, "Psychological Commentary on Kundalini Yoga" (from the Notes of Mary Foote, 1932), *Spring: An Annual of Archetypal Psychology and Jungian Thought* (1975): 22.

26. CW13: 54.

Similar to going up the mountain, but in the disguise of psychology, are the behavior therapies and release-relax therapies. Cure the symptom and lose the god. Had Jacob not grappled with the Daemon he would indeed have not been hurt, and he would not have been Jacob either. Lose the symptom and return the world back to the ego.

Here my point is that soul-making does not deny gods and the search for them. But it looks closer to hand, finding them more in the manner of the Greeks and Egyptians, for whom the gods take part in all things. All existence is filled with them, and human beings are always involved with them. This involvement is what myths are all about—the traditional stories of human and divine interactions. There is no place one can be, no act one can do, no thought one can think without it being mimetic to a god. Thus we study mythology to understand personality structure, psychodynamics, pathologizing. The gods are within, as Heinrich Zimmer used to say, and they are within our acts, thoughts, and feelings. We do not have to trek across the starry spaces, the brain of heaven, or blast them loose from concealment with mind-blowing chemicals. They are there in the very ways you feel and think and experience your moods and symptoms. Here is Apollo, right here, making us distant and wanting to form artful, clear, and distinct ideas; here is old Saturn, imprisoned in paranoid systems of judgment, defensive maneuvers, melancholic conclusions; here is Mars, having to turn red in the face and kill in order to make a point; and here too is the wood nymph Daphne-Diana, retreating into foliage, the camouflage of innocence, suicide through naturalness.

Finally, I would point to one more, a fourth, difference between peaks and vales, the difference that has to do with death.

If spirit would transcend death in any of several ways—unification so that one is not subject to dissolution; union with Self, where self is God; building the immortal body, or the jade-body; the moves toward timelessness and spacelessness and imagelessness and mindlessness; dying to the world as place of attachments—soul-making would instead hew and bevel the ship of death, the vessel of death, a container for holding the dying that goes on in the soul. It imagines that psychic life refers most fundamentally to the life of the *po*-soul, that which slips into the ground—not just at the moment of physical death but is always slipping into the ground, always descending, always going deeper into concrete realities and animating them.

So I cannot conclude with ultimates, positions, final words, wise statements from masters. There is no end to a wandering discourse, no summation, summit, for to make an end is to come to a stop. I'd rather leave unconcluded and cloudy, no abstracted spiritual message—not even a particular image. You have your own. The soul generates them ceaselessly.

II

PUER PATHOLOGIES

First published in *Clinical Studies of Personality: Volume II of Case Histories in Clinical and Abnormal Psychology*, edited by Arthur Burton and Robert E. Harris (New York: Harper & Brothers, 1955) and emended for this edition.

American Icarus

HENRY A. MURRAY

Grope, the hero of this story, was one of an aggregate of college students who volunteered to serve as subjects in a series of experiments and tests conducted at the Psychological Clinic, Department of Social Relations, Harvard University.

If it were not for a dream of flying through the air on a maid's rump and an impromptu story of a modern Pegasus fertilizing from the sky a poor farmer's barren fields (and his cow to boot)—if it were not for these two exploits of the imagination, a psychologist might never have been goaded to delve in celestial myths and, with a selection of these in mind, to brood over the episodes of Grope's terrestrial career and personality.

Could this short, dark-haired, loose-knit young man be a reincarnation of Tammuz, Attis, or Adonis? A fertility god or sky hero? Such questions would never have occurred to anyone who noticed him approaching on a campus path—collar open at the neck, unshaved most probably, and with a dazed look as if he had just got out of bed. "A typical adolescent," one might have thought in passing. There was little about him to impel a second glance.

As far as we could see, Grope's overt attitudes and behaviors were not far from commonplace. There is nothing unusual, surely, in an apathetic reaction to college courses, lectures, and required reading. Not rare, though less frequent, is withdrawal from competitive extracurricular activities. The only manifest attitude which seemed incongruent with the prevailing sociological portrait of today's American adolescent was Grope's reluctance to become engaged in any erotic ventures. An embarrassment in this sphere, however, is not so irregular as our magazines—*Life* and *Look*, say—might lead us to believe: in our files are numerous case records of college men who are Grope's match on this count. In short, when assessed in terms of overt reactions and pro-actions, our subject seems to belong to an unextraordinary class of college variants.

It is when weighed in the scales of imaginary activities that Grope stands out as an unduplicated wonder. For these he had an abundance of free hours. Having rejected most opportunities to participate in real endeavors, he had little to interfere with his enjoyment of countless private shows of his excelling fitness for irreal endeavors, mostly of heroic scope. So pure, so unmodulated, so archetypal, were the majority of these dramas—exhibited in his dreams, reveries, story constructions, and most highly valued goals—that we could not escape the supposition that they had come all the way from childhood in their present shapes, with but slight revisions by negating or by counteracting tendencies. At our disposal there were no facts that contradicted this hypothesis, a good many that supported it.

The conclusion to be tentatively submitted here is that one highly influential covert part of Grope's current personality consists of a compound infantile complex, or unity thema, which approximates an ideal type.[1]

PROCEDURES

1. *Autobiography and interviews.* Grope was given a brief outline of important topics to serve as guide in writing his autobiography; and then, after his autobiography had been delivered and read, he was interviewed three times (each for an hour), with items in this document serving as starting points for special lines of interrogation.

2. *Questionnaires and inventories.* Grope filled out the following forms (an asterisk *indicates a form that is not yet published): (a)* Inventory of Overt Behaviors; (b)* Inventory of Abilities; (c) Extraversion-Introversion Questionnaire (Gray after Jung); (d) Four Functions Questionnaire (Gray after Jung); (e) Ascendance-Submission Test (All-

---

1. An "ideal" unity thema, or "ideal" integrate of infantile complexes, is a convenient theoretical construct, or fiction, which may be defined as a constellation of clear-cut, interdependent themata (forms of dynamic interaction) coupled with evaluations, which is not adulterated or contaminated by irrelevant, inconsistent, or antithetical components.

port); (f) Study of Values (Allport and Vernon); (g)*Literary Knowledge and Interests (Wilson); (h) Psychosomatic Inventory (McFarland).

3. *Projective procedures.* The unhappily named "projective" tests administered to Grope included: (a) MAPS (Shneidman); (b) Four Pictures (van Lennep); (c) Tri-Dimensional (Twitchell-Allen); (d) Dramatic Productions (Erikson); (e) Standard TAT (Murray); (f)*TAT No. 2 (Murray); (g) Rorschach; (h)*Musical Reveries; (i) Sentence Completion (modified); (i)* Sentence Construction; (k)*Similes; (l) Draw-A-Family; (m) Szondi; (n)* Mind-Reading; (o)*Psychodramatic.

4. *Miscellaneous.* Grope also acted as a subject in three special research projects: (a) Happiness Study (Goldings); (b) Facial Asymmetry Study (Lindzey); and (c) Study of Autonomic Reactions to Film of a Primitive Initiation (Mutilation) Ceremony (Lindzey, Ax, and Aas). Data pertinent to the assessment of Grope's level of mental ability were obtained from the college office: ratings on entrance examinations and course grades.

Since there is no space here to report the results of all these procedures, I shall select from our total collection of findings only those which seem most relevant to the formulation of the historic course of Grope's manifest personality and the formulation of his covert personality, or "unity thema," as expressed in his imagination. Although this circumscription of aim necessitates the exclusion of certain less related aspects of Grope's personality, it may be reassuring to know that it has not entailed the omission of any significant facts reported in his autobiography. The following is a reconstructed transcript of that document written, for the most part, in his own words.

PAST HISTORY, AUTOBIOGRAPHY

1. *Family history.* Grope was born near Springfield, Illinois, of a middle-class family in comfortable circumstances. His father graduated from a state university, worked his way from salesman to buyer in the shoe department of a large store, and, in middle age, organized a wholesale shoe distributing company of his own. His mother also had a college education. After graduation she did promotional work for a department store and later engaged in various civic enterprises. She gave birth to three children: Grope, our subject, another son born two years later, and fourteen years after that a daughter. During Grope's youth,

the family lived mainly in two suburban homes, with a few summers spent in the country, near one of the Great Lakes.

2. *Infancy and childhood.* Grope was a fat baby with curly hair. He believes that he was breast fed but has no idea at what age he was weaned. Weighing six and a half pounds at birth, he quadrupled his weight in the first year. Despite his rolls of fat, he learned to walk when he was twelve months old.

Grope's earliest memory is of dumping his supper on the floor. Seated in a high chair, he was asked by his mother if he wanted some string beans and. being in a bad mood, repeatedly said no, even though he usually liked string beans. She finally put the plate in front of him, and it was at this point that he upset it and pushed the beans on the floor. This, he writes, "was my first feelings of grief that accompany a sort of 'martyr complex' or 'cut off your nose to spite your face complex.'" (In an interview he defined the complex as a willingness to reject or throw away something he wanted or to fail in an enterprise if, by so doing, he could thwart and condemn, and thus aggrieve his parents. It seems that in his mind a suffering remorseful mother was the acme of sweet revenge.)

Grope has always been somewhat finicky about food. During his later grade-school years this finickiness was, in fact, the root of his most tempestuous quarrels with his mother. When he came home for lunch, he would sometimes run out of the house and back to school if he saw that turnips and cauliflower were being served. (Thus in one act did he deprive himself and condemn his mother.)

Several memories between the ages of 2 and 4 are of food: a cookie shop, a cookie given him by a lady, his mother saying, "What do you say?"; noticing a large display of fruit in a railroad station and being told by his mother that they were dates; receiving a "great big beautiful lollypop" at school and having his mother cut away all but a tiny piece of it.

Grope wet his bed and his pants quite frequently until he was 11. It was a daily issue at first which necessitated his carrying an extra pair of pants to nursery school. (He started nursery school at 3.) When he wet he would cry so sorrowfully that the teacher would give him a cookie and then change his clothes. He tells us that his parents now believe that his enuresis persisted because he "didn't have enough affection." There may be some grains of truth in this, because both parents drove to work immediately after breakfast and were likely to be too tired when they returned in the evening to spend much time with their children. To their eldest, playing alone most of the day, the summers seemed "interminable." When night came he would not go to bed without a particular, highly valued knotted bundle of cloth, which he called "my Ewa." Today, he imagines that in a child's life such an object "takes the place of a doll, which in turn takes the place of a Deity or an omnipresent mother."

In his autobiography, Grope devoted an unusual amount of space to an account of the toys of his childhood and of the course of his attachment to them. Whenever he was made to wait for something he had asked his parents tor, his desire for that particular thing, and hence the value of it, in his mind's eye, would rise. But within a week or two of its arrival, the toy's appeal would begin to wane and before very long it was discarded, broken, or perhaps stolen. His Mechano set, his chemistry set, and his bricklaying set each had lost its luster by the end of the day it was presented to him. Only his painting set, his cap pistol, and his bicycle held his interest for any length of time. He tells of a toy auto he enjoyed until the day he sat his little brother in it and sent it rolling down a hill. Since the little fellow couldn't steer, the descent ended in a collision which bent the front axle. (There is no mention of the sibling's fate.) The auto was useless after that. Only once did Grope "very seriously" want something—a pocket watch, and his father, responsive as usual to his requests, bought him a good one which cost about five dollars. When last seen, it was lying in the snow with both hands broken and the crystal gone. "This sight of utter waste sorely disgusted me and the memory still makes me slightly angry." All of a piece with these experiences is Grope's summary statement: "Throughout my life I have found it very difficult to accept gifts properly. My appreciation is restrained and unenthusiastic." (This avowal was later confirmed by observing Grope's dead-pan response to an "experimental" gift.)

He learned to ride a bicycle when he was 7. His father would run behind him with his hand on the seat while he turned the pedals. One day he went thirty yards in one stretch but, on looking around and seeing that his father had stopped supporting him, fell off. ("Which shows what confidence will do.") He was quite proud that he was able to ride a bicycle when other boys his age could not. One night he left the bicycle outside and it was stolen.

Grope would sometimes "make up" knowledge and say something astonishing for a child of his years. Once, at the age of 6, at his grandfather's house he overheard a discussion about fire. He announced that "Fire is a yellow-orange gas from outer space." This utterance made such a hit that he was asked to repeat it over and over again until he got "sick of it." Between the ages of 3 and 10 Grope was in the care of a German maid who tried to teach him how to read the clock. Each time he got it wrong she would slap him in the face, which only made him more flustered and her more frustrated." But the maid appealed to him despite this treatment, or perhaps because of it.

3. *School experiences.* Since he had gone to nursery school when he was 3, Grope did not have to attend kindergarten. He has few memories of his early years at primary school, except that he showed talent for drawing in second grade, and at home read and reread the Oz books (by L. F. Baum). In the third grade he overheard his teacher telling his mother that he was bright.

He acquired no athletic abilities until he moved to another school, just before entering fifth grade. Near his new home there were real woods which he enjoyed tremendously. He liked to climb birch trees and swing down again to earth, over and over again. He "shinnied up" practically every tree he could find. He developed a lot of strength this way, and one day after school he threw down, one by one, every boy in the class. He states that he soon became the best athlete in the school, the best football player, the best drawer, the smartest (with the highest mark on an achievement test), the first person to be elected president of the sixth-grade class, and the only person to be elected twice. The teacher kept telling him in front of the class that he was most likely to succeed. Besides, he was commander-in-chief of a club he formed, and "half a dozen girls" had a crush on him. He tells us that outwardly he was very modest, but inwardly he was convinced that no one surpassed him in all-around ability.

He enjoyed painting lessons in sixth grade and did quite a bit of this until his sophomore year in high school, when other activities took precedence; but he still had time for his drawing.

His "fall" began in sixth grade with loss of weight and sluggishness. He had many colds during that summer and when he went back to school in the seventh grade found that he hadn't grown an inch. The following winter he was in bed for two straight months. When he got well, his athletic career was "shot." He had lost his muscle and, what was more important to him, his courage. He feels that after this he was never much of an athlete. Today he plays only a fair game of ping-pong, tennis, baseball, and basketball. During his illness (seventh grade) he learned to play chess with such expertness that he beat all his relatives. He also learned to play bridge at this time.

Grope's account of his "fall" and subsequent lack of distinction at school is not wholly in accord with his list of high school accomplishments. In his freshman year he won the bantamweight boxing title and in his senior year the middleweight title. Despite illnesses he played varsity tennis and junior varsity football. He was skillful in managing the campaign of the seventh-grade class president and the junior-grade vice president, both of whom won. He was elected treasurer of his class sophomore year, and a member of the Student Council. Also, he was editor of the yearbook and an excellent comedian and master of ceremonies, talents which his classmates acknowledged by electing him "Biggest Joker" on graduation. In his studies he did well; he received the highest mark on a mathematics achievement test, was the only boy in his class to win a certificate on a nation-wide scholastic test, and passed the college board examinations with creditable grades. In his spare time he collected stamps, drew and painted, played chess and bridge.

He enjoyed building model airplanes.

His friendships were many but casual, never enduring. When he was a freshman in high school he was very close to a boy who lived on his street until a teacher happened to remark that familiarity breeds contempt. Both boys took this very seriously and their friendship deteriorated. At college he made no real friends until the end of his sophomore year. Currently he is extremely fond of one boy, a former member of his card-playing clique.

From eighth through tenth grade, Grope suffered from halitosis, which, he believes, made him much less popular and thus gave rise to a distressing inferiority complex. He thought he could make himself less offensive by speaking with a minimal expiration of breath, and now, six years later, his voice is habitually so low that his words are not always audible.

4. *Sexual experiences.* Grope's sexual potentialities were first aroused when he was about 8, the object of his "erotic tendencies" being the maid who was in charge of him. Seeing her breasts on one occasion started a sort of interior excitement which he did not think about or try to define but the nature of which was indicated in a dream in which he rode through the sky on the rump of this maid. He began to get inexplicable erections before urinating and when he was angry or frustrated. One of his more bizarre fantasies was that of flying over a city and urinating on the buildings, all of which were constructed out of women's bodies. A little later, his sex education began informally. Learning "dirty words and dirty jokes," etc., he began to get a general idea "of what females were for." One of his chief misconceptions was that intercourse was achieved when the male inserted his penis into the female anus. As time went on, however, things became clearer and his curiosity was appeased by reading the more pertinent parts of Clendening's *The Human Body.*

Outside of parties where Spin the Bottle and Post Office were played, he had nothing that approached an affair until he was 16, when he had a yearlong romance with an 18-year-old girl. This affair petered out because he had "never heard or imagined of going beyond the leg-wrestling stage without making it actual intercourse." When he was 17 he "went steady" with a girl his own age, but they never got beyond the mutual masturbation stage and they finally separated, his reason being "too much sex."

He had never seen any reason for masturbating and believed that his friends did it merely to prove to themselves that they were virile. But at a summer camp where he was employed after graduating from high school he had occasion to discuss masturbation with one of the dishwashers. When asked by Grope why he masturbated, the young man replied, "Well, for the *thrill.*" This was news! Grope determined to start that very night. He has been masturbating frequently ever since. He suffers no remorse as he keeps reminding himself that the more sexually active he is now according to Kinsey's findings), the longer he will retain his potency in later life.

At college, this form of sexual outlet has taken the place of dating. He had only a few blind dates in freshman year, none since. He is looking forward to marriage and right now would settle for any girl who is "attractive, intelligent, non-argumentative, has large lips, wide hips, and is willing and able to bear me about half-a-dozen boys."

5. *Family relationships.* Grope thinks that the relationship between his parents has been a "pretty good" one, despite occasional quarrels which are likely to terminate with his mother weeping. As for himself, Grope affirms that he has never loved either his mother or his father, his present attitude being one of confirmed indifference, mixed with a fair amount of "loyalty and respect." While working for the father's company last summer he gained some appreciation of this parent's business acumen; but his opinion of his mother is no higher than it was ten years ago. He thinks that her deficiencies of character outweigh her intellectual gifts. It is she who has disappointed him the most. Notwithstanding this, Grope insists that his parents have always been devoted and generous to him. They often tried to encourage him (with ill success) and were more thrilled than he whenever he was in any way outstanding. He is nonetheless disposed to believe that they must have made a lot of mistakes in rearing him, their first child.

When Grope's sister was born, a few years ago, his parents, "having read books on sibling rivalry," tried to heap an unusual amount of affection upon both him and his brother. This, he feels was ridiculous, since by that time he had long outgrown any dependence on their love.

During his teens Grope had many fierce quarrels with his parents, ending by his plotting various schemes for revenge, such as a six-weeks silent treatment. He often imagined his own death and his parents' subsequent grief, one particularly gratifying fantasy being that of resurrection from the grave as a ghost and then of gloating unseen over his mother's remorseful grief.

Grope's brother was born when he was 3, but, he assures us, there was no sibling rivalry in those early years. In fact, he hardly ever thought of him. His brother was a nonentity until the age of 8, at which time the two boys began playing together and getting into fights. They became good friends in high school, when Grope began to appreciate him a little more. He states that he doesn't fight with his brother now, the latter being an inch taller, ten pounds heavier, and solid muscle.

6. *Ambitions, goals, values.* As a child Grope wanted to be an orange grower. Later, after reading a book on China by Pearl Buck, he "became incensed with the desire" to go there, "an industrially backward land," and build bridges. He also thought of becoming a painter. As his estimation of his own powers increased, he became "more and more inspired and confident" about his role in life.

His major recurrent fantasy was one of landing on a desert island in the Pacific with a band of followers, discovering an inexhaustible spring of fresh water and an abundant food supply, and then founding a new civilization with himself as king and lawgiver. He often dreamed and daydreamed of self-propelled flights and of jumping off a high place and floating gracefully and gently to the ground. But he was almost equally hospitable to less extravagant fantasies: he considered becoming a prize fighter, an actor, an army general, a millionaire, an inventor, a psychiatrist, and a teacher. "It would be a lot of fun working with kids, teaching them with a sense of humor, and having them think you are a 'good guy.'" He has imagined himself a famous tap dancer, a singer, and a movie comedian. He is attracted by the stage and has a tentative plan of enrolling in some school of the drama. His more immediate intention, however, is to enlist in the Air Corps and become a pilot. Although in his opinion world wars are preventable evils, he expects another one within fifteen years, which will destroy much or most of civilization. The two worst things that might happen to him are (*a*) to be maimed in the war and (*b*) to lose his self-confidence. Finally, he writes: "If I could remodel the world to my heart's content, I would establish a sound World Government and would like to be the dictator, a good dictator." He would be "most proud" of having his name "go down in history as a leader, or as an artist, or as a discoverer or inventor."

He thinks that his insight increased most rapidly during his early teens when he was embattled with his parents. It was then also that he began working out his philosophy, the chief tenet of which is that every person's goal in life is happiness. Another tenet is that happiness is attainable in a number of different ways, depending on the individual. In his own case, the major sources of prospective happiness, and hence the most valued goals, are money, power, glory, and fame. "These are the alternatives of most normal men." He has never been to church and states that he is "sure there is no sort of God or vital force."

At the moment Grope feels that he is spiritually becalmed. In the past, his development has always occurred in "spurts or cycles." "If I did something well, I would be spiritually elevated, that is, my spirits would become gay. In the last few years my spirits have been in equilibrium and my development has more or less stagnated." Today he does not seem to be able to decide anything. He will either try to turn over a new leaf academically or get a job some place, such as opening a snack bar with a friend. Concluding this topic, he writes: "I am just biding my time and waiting for the day when my 'soul' will ignite and this inner fire will send me hurtling (two rungs at a time) up the ladder of success."

7. *Evaluations of self and others.* Grope highly esteems "all other people." Everyone seems to him interesting and exciting (more or less); but he especially admires the personalities and achievements of supremely great men. He has had many heroes—da Vinci and van Gogh in particular. At times, he tells us, he derives a lot of personal satisfaction from being gregarious, but he gets depressed if he is guilty of a *faux pas*: he "kicks himself mentally" for days.

Grope feels that the world's estimate of him is that he is a "pretty nice guy." As for his own estimate of himself, he used to think he was "pretty hot stuff," but now he "just agrees with the world."

COMPONENTS OF CURRENT MANIFEST PERSONALITY

In unfamiliar social situations Grope is keenly observant but shyly self-suppressed; he speaks little and with a very low voice. He waits for the alter to make the first move. Once his embarrassment has dissolved, however he becomes relaxed, tensionless, responsive, and quietly jocose. In this phase he strikes one as an easygoing, good-natured fellow—a "good guy"—with a keen, ever present, satirical, though somewhat juvenile, sense of humor.

Grope reports that a few months after his arrival at Harvard he came to the conclusion that he was a "small frog in a big puddle," surrounded by many far superior competitors for athletic, social, and academic honors. No hope for glory. Since then he has made the minimum amount of intellectual effort. He studies very little and cuts many of his lectures, especially if they come before noon. As a result, he is on probation, ranking well below the scholarship level predicted for him—an "under-achiever." He has joined no organizations, has accepted no roles or responsibilities, and dates no girls. This abstinence allows him to devote the maximum amount of time to sleep, relaxation, daydreaming, and playing bridge with a small clique of cronies. Of these the one he most liked has recently been flunked out of college. Except for this boy, he gives no evidence of affectional attachments.

Grope was rated (on a 1–6 point scale) by himself, by two of his acquaintances, and by six members of the clinic assessment staff on a large number of manifest behavioral variables. Only those variables on which he was almost unanimously rated among the lowest 25 percent of our subjects (1 or 2), or on which he was almost unanimously rated among the highest 25 percent (5 or 6), will be mentioned here.

Grope was judged to be unusually passive (inactive, indolent, apathetic) under current conditions, though not incapable of considerable, though spasmodic, activity under more favorable conditions (need Passivity 5). There were no *objectifications* of ambition (need Achievement 1). These two ratings (high passivity, low achievement) are confluent with our subject's inability to start on his own steam and to keep going without cooperation or without anticipation of a close reward (need Autonomy, Self-Sufficiency 1, and Endurance 1).

All of a piece with these estimates was the high mark Grope received on need Exhibition, Recognition (5), which was clearly a very strong disposition of his personality, though manifested during the current period only when he found himself in a familiar, congenial, and appreciative social group, at which times this need was likely to be fused with Play-mirth (6). He gained the attention he enjoyed by comical displays. It might be said that Expression, Exhibition was a part of Grope's overt *private* personality (behaviors manifested in intimate interactions with receptive, reciprocating alters), because in more public or less familiar situations this disposition was checked by his fear of committing a faux pas or "making a fool of himself" (need Avoidance 5, coupled with a persisting Inferiority Complex).

Grope was also rated high (5) on need Excitance (enjoyment of novelty, excitement, thrills, spectacles, etc.) and high (5) relative to other undergraduates on need Sentience (appreciation or composition of artistic forms), despite the fact that his drawings were not "serious art" but more in the nature of satirical cartoons (Play-mirth again predominating). Most questionable-in fact definitely wrong in retrospect-was the rating of 5 on need Affiliation, because, though habitually good-natured, smiling, and responsive, Grope had formed no firm and lasting friendships. He seemed to be existing without links, a free-floater in today's "lonely crowd," a passing acquaintance, with whom one is never seriously involved and on whom one can never seriously depend, a man of superficial contacts who does not attach himself for long to any one person and yet is dependent on everyone he meets. His self was open to friendliness—in no way distant, withdrawn, encased, aloof, resentful, or suspicious (need Rejection 2). He was rated below average on overt sexual behavior (need Sex 2) but rather high (5) on sexual and social curiosity (voyeurism).

Grope's room was always in a "mess"; he did not put his belongings in allotted places, and when he took off his clothes at night, he dropped them on the floor where they remained till morning. His appearance, handwriting, and written papers were all equally disorderly (need Order 1, and need Retention [conservation of possessions] 2). So much for the most striking of Grope's overt (manifest, or objectified) needs.

It was inferred on the basis of these and other evidences that Grope was very low (1) on degree of Ego Structuration and equally low (1) on degree of Superego Integration. He has very seldom, if ever, been concerned with moral questions and has no memory of ever feeling guilty or remorseful. No sociocentric interests or group identifications are apparent. His most valued goals-money, power, glory, fame—are perceived in a purely egocentric fashion. He has no religion. His dominant axis of evaluation is superiority-inferiority (of ability, wealth, social status, authority, and prestige); the ethical axis is absent or repressed, as it is in psychopathic personalities. This notwithstanding, Grope is guilty of nothing more hurtful or illegal than a few minor boyhood thefts. He seems to be free of vicious inclinations.

Grope rated himself high on Artistic Ability (6), Entertaining Ability (5), Social Ability (5), and Intuitive Ability (5), but very low on Self-Directive Ability (1) and Memory Ability (1).

Grope's responses on most of our questionnaires and inventories placed him in the middle range. He came out high (5), however, on Extraversion, and on the Studies of Values indicated more concern with Political issues than with the other five. On Level of Satisfaction he was low average and also low average in his estimates of the satisfaction level of other persons (supplementary self-projection).

INTERPRETATION OF CURRENT MANIFEST PERSONALITY

Since Grope showed considerable interest in athletics and scholarship at high school and was periodically quite energetic in organizing and promoting various social enterprises, we surmise that his current apathy, his lack of enthusiasm and will power, his submission to a sluggish id, is situational," rather than unchangeably constitutional. The current situation is one of being outclassed in all spheres by more talented and/ or more resolute associates. Evidently, he is not devoted to any form of athletics for its own sake, to learning for its own sake, or to any one of the numerous accessible extracurricular activities for its own sake; nor is he prompted by a need to learn some skill and to accomplish something for the sake of a resulting inner satisfaction or self-respect. It is glory he is after—praise, prestige, and fame—and since his present situation offers no prospects of these rewards, why should he exert himself?

Another significant attribute of Grope's current situation is the absence of parental support. During his school years in Illinois he had been constantly spurred on and, whenever in any way outstanding," applauded by his for-him-ambitious parents, and among his classmates, furthermore, during at least one glorious period of his life, he had been the "best" at everything. But at Harvard unhappily no such encouragements were at hand, and without encouragement he had no confidence, and without confidence he was nothing. He had to learn his worth from the lips of others. This conclusion was confirmed by the finding that a few sentences of "experimental" praise set him going at his books for a week or more on two occasions.

Another confirmation comes from the story Grope composed for Picture 7 of the Thematic Apperception Test (TAT):

[A gray-haired man is looking at a younger man who is sullenly staring into space.]

Here's a serious and intense young man, methodical, who the moment he entered Harvard knew he was going to be a pure physicist. He graduated Magna, Phi Beta Kappa, and went on to graduate school, where he was more or less a protégé of one of the great, good professors there, because he demonstrated unusual ability to learn, to grasp complicated theories as well as experiments in applied physics. Of course by this time, six years, he'd be in for a Ph.D. He is wondering if there is more to life than just studying. He's having his doubts about whether he can be happy being a physicist, working by himself instead of with others. This kind professor in the Graduate School sees the despondency of the last few weeks and decides to have a talk with him. He tries to encourage him at first, by saying,

"If you want, I have a very good job set up for you with one of the big companies." This guy shrugs and finally decides to tell the scientist about what's been bothering him. He does, and this scientist is very understanding, and says, "Well, when I was your age I felt the same way." He had a lot of insight. He told him exactly what he was thinking about. He said that he felt the same way when he was his age, and that he must look for a purpose in life. It was just a psychological talk, kind of bolstered him. Well, anyway, the young man goes along with this. He just needed that extra push.

Among the internal conditions contributing to Grope's present slump in his weak, unintegrated, and immature ego system (already mentioned)—the absence of work habits and the insufficiency of will power, the inability, when bored or tired, to force himself to finish something he has undertaken. Another determinant is his low tolerance of failure, his fear of "falling." This might stem from a childhood supposition that his ambitious parents would not respect him if it were proved that he was not among the best. By not competing, by not trying, he can avoid the demonstration of this humiliating probability. But in the sphere of scholarship it is a different matter: how can he both abstain from effort and avoid the stigma of being expelled from college? At this point another factor begins to operate, Grope's "spite complex": failure can be used as a weapon of condemnation. He confessed that by flunking out of college he could prove that his father had erred in urging him to go to Harvard rather than to Illinois or to some smaller college where he might have been a "big frog."

One final all-important determinant of Grope's collapse at Harvard is the height, diversity, and inconstancy of his ideal self-conception (a fitful sequence of heterogeneous ego-ideal figures, some of whom—a self-propelled sky flier, the founder of a new civilization, the dictator of a world government, a famous inventor-are far beyond his present reach). With these glorious visions running through his head, how can he bend down to day-by-day pedestrian exertions in order to make for himself a little name at Harvard? He says that, although he used to think he was "pretty hot stuff," he has finally come round to the world's view that he is merely a good guy.

This is what his intellect has decided; but the conflict is not thereby settled: to his soul a good guy is not nearly good enough. Hence, it is necessary for him to constantly refight the battle between his ideal self-conception and his real self-conception, as the following TAT story No. 8 makes evident:

> [An adolescent boy looks straight out of the picture. The barrel of a rifle is visible at one side, and in the background is the dim scene of a surgical operation, like a reverie-image.]

> *This picture seems to show the imaginations of a boy...The kid is a college student, leaning up against one of the pillars of Widener and thinking. He's a little frustrated by things at school—the competition, and the state of affairs, not only in school, but the fact that the world in his day is so much tougher. He feels that if he lived back in the days of, say, Aristotle he would certainly have thought up some of the fundamental concepts of physics or chemistry, or could have become a great doctor. If he wanted to be a premed student in this day, it would be very hard to achieve anything, any fame and glory. He takes time out to think back on the old days. Now he thinks he's a doctor on this warship, trying to perform an operation, using the light that comes through one of the portholes and a dim lantern. He thinks how people would look up to him the way he sterilizes everything, a practice not usually done then...The reason he's doing these daydreams is because he doesn't feel he can get much glory in this age, this civilization. He needs to go back to an older one in his thoughts. He finally realizes that perhaps there were geniuses in the old days too. He would not have had any more chance then to achieve glory than he does now. He feels he must be satisfied with his time and position, and must get happiness out of some of the fundamental personal things in life, rather than getting his name in a history book. Anyway, he finally realizes his mediocrity. Before he went to school he thought he was good and he comes to school and realizes there are many others better than him, who have intellectual intelligence over him. He thinks that due to all this competition he will never get anywhere in a society like this, where there seem to be so few inventions left. He daydreams about a past where he would certainly have made a name for himself, there was so much room for growth. After two more years of study he realizes he isn't such a hot shot and has to be content with an average existence.*

COMPONENTS OF COVERT PERSONALITY

1. *Urethral erotism.* Grope recalls experiencing (during boyhood) erections just previous to urination, as observed by Halverson[2] in babies; and he entertained the idea that babies were made by urinating into a woman's rectum. In short, sex was apperceived in urinary terms. Also he manifested, in high degree, every other concomitant of urethral erotism, as defined by Freud and his followers: cathection of fire, "burning" ambition, exhibitionism, and voyeurism. Remember Grope's bright saying: "Fire is a yellow-orange gas from outer space." Even today he "gets a thrill" by lighting wastepaper in his tin scrap basket and seeing it flare up. There is a high incidence of pertinent fire imagery in his projective protocols. Finally, there is the association of persistent enuresis and urethral erotism (dreams of urination accompanied by ejaculation) which we and others have found in a number of personalities. Thus, the evidence for the presence and continued operation of this rather enigmatic infantile complex is about as complete as one can reasonably demand without a full-length psychoanalysis.

2. *Ascensionism.* This is the name I have given to the wish to overcome gravity, to stand erect, to grow tall, to dance on tiptoe, to walk on water, to leap or swing in the air, to climb, to rise, to fly, or to float down gradually from on high and land without injury, not to speak of rising from the dead and ascending to heaven. There are also emotional and ideational forms of ascensionism—passionate enthusiasm, rapid elevations of confidence, flights of the imagination, exultation, inflation of spirits, ecstatic mystical upreachings, poetical and religious—which are likely to be expressed in the imagery of physical ascensionism. The upward thrust of desire may also manifest itself in the cathection of tall pillars and towers, of high peaks and mountains, of birds—high-flying hawks and eagles—and of the heavenly bodies, especially the sun. In its most mundane and secular form, ascensionism consists of a craving for upward social mobility, for a rapid and spectacular rise of prestige.

In Grope's case, ascensionism was fused—at the very start perhaps—with urethral erotism. Recall his dream of flying through the air on the

---

2. H. M. Halverson, "Genital and Sphincter Behavior of the Male Infant," *The Journal of Genetic Psychology* 56, no. 1 (1940): 95–136.

maid's rump (in conjunction with his urinary theory of intercourse) and his fantasies of urinating from the sky on the bodies of women. Then read the following story told to one of the (unpublished) TAT 2 pictures:

[Barn surrounded by snow. A winged horse is flying across the sky. The head of a bearded man is in right lower corner. In the snow, is the dim outline of a girl's face.]

An old hermit went out into the woods and built himself a farm. After thirty years of living all by himself on the crops he produced, he got pretty tired of this humdrum existence, so he decided that he wanted to re-enter the competitive world and try to sell, was planning on selling his crops, planning to build some sort of a fortune. So he worked for a few years, couldn't seem to get very large crops, really good crops. They wouldn't grow. What he needed was more fertilizer, but he couldn't afford fertilizer in any quantity, so he was practically at his wits' end, and one night he decided to turn to religion; and as miracles will happen, the very next day Pegasus flew over and fertilized all his plants. Not only that, but the cow in the barn bore him a daughter; something he had always wanted. In the picture here, he is squinting in his happiness; feeling that life has really been rewarding. So the picture is the spirit of happiness.

Grope reported many dreams and daydreams of rising in the air and flying, sometimes in a car or in a horse-drawn chariot, like Apollo's. Other fantasies were of shooting through space and landing on the planet Mars.

In his autobiography, he proudly tells us that he learned to walk at 12 months and to ride a bicycle at 7 years; and he devotes a long paragraph to a detailed account of each stage of his baby sister's progress in overcoming the pull of gravity. In addition to these items are Grope's passion for climbing trees, swinging out and down, his fantasy of becoming a tap dancer, the model airplanes he built, his admiration for Leonardo da Vinci's flying machine, and his intention of enlisting in the Air Corps, and the twelve or more flying creatures he saw in the Rorschach blots: two butterflies, two flying bats, a flying dog, a horse's head with hoofs emerging from a cloud bank, a pair of vultures being swooped on from above by a pair of eagles and these attacked by a flock of jumping woodpeckers. Asked by a hypothetical fairy godmother to make "seven wishes," he listed Height as his fourth wish.

3. *Cynosural narcissism.* This strikes me as a suitable term (more embracing than exhibitionism) to denote a craving for unsolicited attention and admiration, a desire to attract and enchant all eyes, like a star in the firmament. It is first supremely gratified at that *epiphanal* moment of babyhood when the grandparents and relatives arrive at the cradle, with gifts perhaps, to beam with wonder at this new emergence of pure potentiality, pure Being. No memory of this, of course, in Grope; but in line with it is the grandfather's astonishment (at a later date) when the child came out with his cynosural pronouncement about fire. The cynosural ego-ideal which Grope shaped for himself after he entered fifth grade and became the best at everything has remained to this day almost intact. In Draw-A-Family his self-portrait, twice the size of his father's and his mother's, was of a prodigiously strong athlete, corresponding in every way to his description of the image that came to mind when he was handed the blank card (No. 16) of the TAT:

> Well, I see a huge, powerful man. He is in the midst of throwing a shot-put. He weighs about 310 pounds and stands 6 feet, 6 inches high. He has no clothing except bathing trunks. There he stands with spectators all around him. He's about to win his third straight decathlon. Not only is he the most perfect physical specimen in all of Greece, but he is a nice guy, unspoiled. Everyone likes him. They practically worship him. He is a sensation; a wonderful box-office draw...

Already we begin to see a close, emotionally logical—indeed, an almost inevitable—connection, if not fusion, between ascensionism and cynosural narcissism: the way to attract all eyes is to be very tall, to stand erect above the multitude, and best of all to rise in the air like a god. Remembering that in Grope's personality ascensionism was fused with urethral erotism and that urethral erotism ordinarily reaches its peak in the phallic phase of psychosexual development, we may surmise that we are dealing with an imagination in which an ascending cynosural phallus was transmuted into an ascending cynosural body, both being "pretty hot stuff" and possibly on this account associated with fire, to constitute, in any event, the kind of burning ambition Grope portrays in his concluding sentence: "I am just biding my time and waiting for the day when my 'soul' will ignite and this inner fire will send me hurtling (two rungs at a time) up the ladder of success." Clearly this type of ambition depends on the carrying power of an unpredictable upsurge or excess of psychic energy (spontaneity, creative zest, self-confidence, enthusiasm), an excess which may someday be shown to consist of a quantum of sublimated erotic energy. In any event, little reliance is placed on will power, discipline, industry, conscientiousness.

Furthermore, since the youthful energy—passionate, romantic, fiery— that serves as motive power for this type of ambition is not likely to continue on a high level for very long without frequent reinforcements, its strategy entails a series of short, spirited, and spectacular achievements, never a long, slow, and methodical, solitary and inconspicuous, course of action.

The association of an ascending cynosural body and ascending fire is illustrated by Grope's story to Card 17 (TAT). *The fourth World War ended,* he said, *when a nation of supermen overran the globe, and now, in each conquered country, the victors are trying by means of strength tests to select other possible supermen with whom to start a new race.* He continues as follows:

> [A naked man is clinging to a rope. He is in the act of climbing up or down.]
>
> *...In this case this person elected to climb a rope; he was quite strong. The bottom of the rope was made of an inflammable-soaked in potassium chloride, I guess. They would set fire to the bottom of it and the flames would go at a certain slightly increasing rate. If the person failed to reach the rope before the flames did, of course he was killed. This person starts out like fury and by fifty yards the rope is burned only about five yards from the bottom...About seventy-five yards up his arms are like lead weight. He doesn't feel that he can go any further...He goes another five or ten yards and suddenly he slips back and barely manages to catch on five yards below. By now the flames are about half way up. Then he gets panicky, gets another tremendous burst, and goes about ten yards. He hangs on there and watches the flames increasing their momentum...He goes on taking about a foot at a time, the flames getting nearer. He can't rest—very hard to rest hanging on to a rope. He finally gets about ten yards from the top, that's the last thing he remembers.*

The end of this story suggests the next component.

4. *Falling, precipitation.* "Falling" denotes an undesired or accidental descension of something (usually a human body or the status [reputation] of a person, but it may be feces, urine, or any cathected object).

"Precipitation," on the other hand, means a consciously or unconsciously desired calamitous descension: the S allows himself to fall or leaps from a height (precipitative suicide), or he pushes another person over a cliff, throws something down, or purposely urinates or defecates on the floor. In one or the other of these two categories—it is often difficult to say which—fall a large number of items in Grope's case history: diurnal and nocturnal enuresis (eleven years of it), frequent micturition (checked on the Psychosomatic Inventory), several memories of fecal incontinence, fantasies of urinating and defecating from the air, the episode of throwing down a plate of string beans (his "martyr complex"), of dropping or throwing down his pocket watch, of shoving his little brother down a hill, of throwing stones down from a height on girls, of throwing down, one by one, every kid in his class, and recently, at college, his writing a comedy in which a rich man (father figure) is thrown by a huge gorilla down a water closet.

Finally, there is Grope's memory of falling off a bicycle and his statement that he often fell from trees, a resonance, perhaps, of earlier more traumatic falls during his learning-to-walk stage. The question of falling or not falling is central in the account he gives of his baby sister's efforts.

In all this we may dimly perceive an ascension-descension cycle on different levels; (*a*) fiery tumescense ascension) of penis followed by detumescense (descension) with urination (precipitation of water); (*b*) ascension of desire for cathected toy followed by descension of cathection and precipitation of toy; (*c*) ascension of body followed by fall or precipitation (as in the story of rope climber and several other stories); and (*d*) ascension of status (prestige) followed by descension (the "fall" after his phenomenal sixth-grade success and now his "fall" at college). This is an archetypal thematic sequence against which we are warned by the ancient aphorism: "Pride cometh before a fall." Very probably the Adlerian formula is applicable here: Grope's ardent desire to ascend is a counteractive disposition excited by one or more experiences of descent—let us say, some unremembered locomotive accidents coupled with recurrent enuresis, intensified by several falls of status, beginning at 2 years with his displacement from the cynosural center by the birth of that "nonentity," his younger brother.

This ascension-descension sequence is also reminiscent of the great cycles of nature, especially the solar cycle and the myth of the solar hero, his superior origin, humble foster parentage, rise to glory, decline, death, and resurrection. The precocious, importunate, and extravagant character of Grope's ascensionism suggests that he belongs with the adolescent, overreaching, would-be solar heroes, Icarus and Phaethon—father-superseding enthusiasts with unstructured ego systems.

Grope's early conflict on the physiological level between fire and water (heat and cold, erection and urination) was entertainingly projected into the weatherman on high in the story he told to Card 11 (TAT):

> This must be prehistoric times. A crowd of animals (live in this nice fertile valley). They are half baboon and half pig. And each year they have terrible weather. It would either be a drought, or a flood, extreme heat or extreme cold. So they all gather around and decide to send someone up to the weather maker's place...When he got up there he found that the place was a combination of all the weathers. It seems there was fire from one side and rain up above... "What do you want?"...This representative presented his case and asked why he had to send so many kinds of bad weather down on all this nice peace loving community. So this weather maker said, "Well, look at it this way, I have all weathers up here and I try to keep them all off you. I have hot weather cold weather, wet and dry weather up here all at once. How do you think I feel about it anyway? Most of the time I keep at least three of these different kinds of weather up here. I only get rid of one of them. If I wanted to be mean I could send them all out...

Limitations of space forbid the printing of more than these few items out of our large collection of to-me-convincing evidences of the dynamic interdependence, in the mind of this young man, of fire (heat, passion) and ascension of body (rising, flying), of ascension and descension (falling, precipitation), of fire and water, and of descension and water (falling water or falling of body into water). One illustration of this last, truly Icarian association (precipitation into water) must suffice. It is the sixth story on Grope's Multidisciplinary Association for Psychedelic Studies (MAPS) protocol:

> [A road skirting a deep chasm between high cliffs. On the road in the distance are obscure figures. Protruding from the rocky wall on one side is a long head and neck of a dragon.]

Well, the man in the striped tie, the Harvard tie, majored in physics (smiles). But he is not a good physicist. He doesn't work. He married a woman for the money she was capable of earning. (But the wife's rapid promotion aroused the envy and ire of the assistant buyer, her unsuccessful male rival at the department store. The buyer, armed with a gun, waylaid her one evening on the Cottage Farm Bridge.) He said to the woman: "Either you resign or I'll shoot you." "No, don't," she said and kept backing away, until she tripped and went over the railing into the river hundreds of feet below. (Two policemen arrive on the scene, followed shortly by the drowned woman's husband and son. The husband, realizing that he and his son have lost their one means of support, pushes the boy over the rail into the water, and then pushes one of the policemen after him.) The salesman sees his chance to make amends. So he shoots the husband, and turns to the other policeman and says, "Can't I go free? Have I paid my debt to society?"... The policeman shoots the man, but on the way bark he is so drunk with delight that he stumbles over the rail. To this day, no one really knows what happened out there. (Six deaths, four of falling into water.)

Evidences of matricidal and patricidal fantasies (of an anal aggressive type), as well as of castration anxiety, are fairly plentiful; but these are common occurrences in the minds of young men and to stress them here would divert attention from the less conventional integrate of themata that constitutes the thesis of this paper.

5. *Craving for immortality.* No doubt the narcissistic core in every man yearns for perpetual existence; but of all our subjects Grope is unexampled in giving Everlasting Life ("I might settle for 500 years") as one of his seven wishes for himself. If everlasting life on earth is impossible, then one can conceive of resurrection of the body or the soul. As illustration we have Grope's fantasy of breaking out of his tomb, digging his way up, and hovering in phantom form over his parents' house. In three of his stories the hero dies and comes to life again. If resurrection (re-ascension) is not to be vouchsafed a man, there is the possibility of replication, which may be defined as the process whereby one or more persons are transformed in the image of the subject. It is the complement of identification, or emulation: the implanting of a memorable and impelling image of the self in the minds of others. This is the evolu-

tionary significance of Grope's overreaching need for attention, worship, fame—glory in the highest. But if this is denied a man, there is still the possibility of immortalizing his likeness through reproduction. Grope was not invited by the idea of an enduring, stable marriage.

For himself, he prophesied divorce. What he did crave, however, was a number of tall sons with profiles somewhat better than his own. To Card 13 of the TAT he told the following story:

> [A young man is standing with downcast head buried in his arm. Behind him is the figure of a woman lying in bed.]

> *John, the man pictured here, liked children. When he went away to school, he used to think a lot about children...As he liked them, he wanted to have his own, but he could never find a girl that he really wanted. So after he graduated, he came home, at night, and first he went into the maid's room—that's the room pictured here. He woke the maid up, and she said, "Oh, how good to see you again, John." John, who was not one for mincing words, said, "Listen, maid, I want children. Children mean a lot to me. How about it?" So the maid said, "No, no, John, no, I am already bespoken." So John said, "Well, in that case there is nothing for me to do." Well, I imagine the thought came to him that now that she was dead he couldn't have his children anyway. It suddenly hit him and he was quite peeved.*

Other data reveal a profound concern with the possibility of impotence or sterility.

6. *Depreciation and enthrallment of women, bisexuality.* Grope spoke contemptuously of his mother and cynically of women generally. Love was a never felt experience. But, as his projective protocols made plain, women were nonetheless important, if not indispensable, to him as glorifying agents: a female was (*a*) someone to be "swept off her feet," to be driven sex-mad" by the mere sight of him; (*b*) someone to applaud his exploits; (*c*) someone with "wide hips" to bear him sons; and (*d*) someone to mourn his death. As one might expect in such a person, there were abundant evidences of a suffusing feminine component coupled with some degree of homosexuality. This is best illustrated by a story he told in the Tri-Dimensional Test:

> *A king announces that he will give half his kingdom to the person who creates the most beautiful thing in the world. The last contestant (hero of the story) comes forward and says, "I have created a replica of myself." Whereupon the king says, "That is the most beau-*

tiful thing in the world, therefore you are the most beautiful thing in the world. Will you be my queen?" The king takes the hero as his male queen and gives this androgynous beauty half his kingdom (cynosural ascension of status).

INTERPRETATION OF COVERT PERSONALITY

1. *Icarus complex.* This integrate might be defined as a compound of (*a*) cynosural narcissism and (*b*) ascensionism, combined with (*c*) the prospection of falling. It seems to be derived, in its extreme form, from a fixation at the urethral-phallic stage of development, before object love has been attained. Consequently, it is associated with (*d*) the cathection of fire, and, if enuresis or incontinence become an issue, with (*e*) an abundance of water imagery. Furthermore, an offspring of this complex is (*f*) a craving for immortality (some form of re-ascension) as well as (*g*) a conception of women as objects to be utilized for narcissistic gains.

I am inclined to the tentative opinion that the Icarus complex is the immature (perhaps perpetually adolescent) form of what might be termed the Solar complex, a complex that is characterized by the same genetical components but, in addition, by a relatively strong ego structure supported by tested abilities, which serves to constrain the reckless aspirations of youth within the bounds of realizable achievements, and thus to neutralize the dread of falling.

If tendencies for genital exhibitionism and arsonism are both suppressed, an Icarus or Solar complex might be objectified on the physical and technical levels by such cynosural and ascensionistic enterprises as high jumping, pole vaulting, discus throwing, high diving, fancy skating, circus acrobatics, ballet dancing, tree surgery, reckless mountain climbing, stunt aviating, or parachuting. On the verbal-social level one might think of singing or acting on the stage (becoming a Hollywood star), charismatic oratory and leadership, messianic enthusiasm and prophecy. But for the fullest expression of the complex one must turn to ardent romantic poetry (Byron, Shelley), to mythic philosophy (Socrates in *Phaedrus,* or Nietzsche in *Thus Spake Zarathustra*), or to some form of up-yearning (erotic) mysticism.

2. *Predisposing determinants.* To explain the urethral-phallic fixation in this case, to explain the absence of emotional maturation to the stage of object attachment (oedipal love), one must go back in Grope's history to still earlier experiences and their chief resultant—a revengeful

(almost implacable) rejection of the mother, because she (scrupulously following her day's dicta: (*a*) that children should be fed by the clock and (*b*) that maternal nurturance should be minimal) let the child cry, with his oral and affectional needs unsatisfied, much longer than is tolerable at his age. According to Sullivan[3] and others, such unrelieved intensity of need, combined with "desertion" by the mother, is likely to result in a kind of self-protecting apathy with rejection of both the giver and her gift when they do ultimately arrive—too late. This hypothesis would explain why Grope can give no reason, can remember no incident, which might account for his never having loved his mother, as well as for his food memories, his finickiness about food, his peculiar attitude toward gifts, and, most particularly, the incident of dumping the plate of string beans on the floor and his "spite complex." The hypothesis is further substantiated by Grope's mother's fairly full communication respecting her trustful adherence to the then-fashionable principles of John B. Watson.

Among Grope's story constructions there is one of a young man whose father shuts him up in total darkness. "No light ever entered the room. He could not perceive himself or anything around him." After thirty years of this, the hero "sort of lost his virility." In another story the boy hero dies in bed but regains life when his father brings him a cup of chicken soup. A somewhat similar story ends differently: The child hero goes to bed and calls for one and then a second glass of water. When he calls for a third, there is no response either from his father or his mother. "He was in bed a long time. He started yelling." But no one comes. Finally, the boy puts on his clothes, leaves the house, and lies down across the railroad track to be run over by an oncoming locomotive.

3. *Unity thema.* The unity thema in this personality, as we have interpreted it, is a compound of the just-mentioned but not elaborated Mother Rejection complex and the less well-known and hence more fully illustrated Icarus complex. Assuredly there were other constituents of Grope's covert personality—particularly those of an anal expulsive derivation—but here again, the prescribed space limits prohibit even the briefest exposition.

---

3. Harry Stack Sullivan, *The Interpersonal Theory of Psychiatry* (New York: W.W. Norton, 1953).

The surmise that Grope's overt personality during his college years—marked by apathy and withdrawal—was situationally determined is substantiated by his "conversion" into an enthusiastic, self-involved, hardworking, and cooperative fellow within a few weeks after leaving college when he found in a summer theater an admirable channel for his cynosural narcissism.

First published in 1979 in *Puer Papers* and re-printed in *Dromenon* 3 (1981). Revised in 2005 for inclusion in *UE* 3: *Senex & Puer*.

Puer Wounds and Odysseus's Scar

JAMES HILLMAN

He was nuts, he was a psychopath. He was crazy, nearsighted,
always having trouble with women. He was very talented, very
sensitive, very clinging. There were gaping wounds in him.
—Elia Kazan on James Dean

Mythological figures of young gods and heroes often show laming, crippling, bleeding, and sometimes castration. The motif of laming has been
examined in some detail from a Jungian perspective by Stephan Sas.[1]
I would concur with his findings that the crippled one is also the creative one (Hephaestus as paradigm). He interprets the laming as a one-
sided standpoint. But even if the lamed foot and wounded leg express
the one-sided unbalance supposedly necessary to creativity, and even if
this notion is symbolically reinforced by the sexual implications of the
foot and the devilish associations of limping, we have yet to uncover its
deeper ground.

There has got to be more to it than that. That word "creativity" dulls
and blunts the spirit of inquiry; it covers over more than it reveals, and
is, in fact, a most uncreative word. The usual misty-eyed reverence with
which it is spoken is an invocation to the fresh, spontaneous, unreflect-
ing and beautiful, though tortured, spirit; that is, it refers us back again
to the puer that it is supposed to explain. When we account for puer
woundedness with "creativity," we have become redundant and circular.

---

1. Stephan Sas, *Der Hinkende als Symbol* (Zurich: Rascher, 1964); on foot symbolism
(mainly as sexual) see Aigremont, *Fuß- und Schuh-Symbolik und Erotik* (Berlin, 1909).
Cf. Murray Stein, "Hephaistos: A Pattern of Introversion," *Spring: An Annual of Archetypal Psychology and Jungian Thought* (1973).

Why does the puer spirit require such massive wounds and crippling distortions? We must inquire into the specifics of laming, placing it within puer woundedness. Here again, it will be difficult to discern puer from hero, since the wound itself seems to identify the puer spirit with heroic destiny. Therefore, this chapter will have to go where puer consciousness is embodied in heroic configurations. We can't keep them apart until we have discerned the necessity of the spirit's entrapment in the wounds of heroism. Our aim is to recover mythical images that lose the hero but save the wound.

Modern psychology tells us that parents can be the wounders. Everyone carries a parental wound and has a wounded parent. Today we go to therapy for healing the parental wounds. Ancient myths tell of wounding parents in various stories. Pelops is chopped up by his father, Tantalus, who served his son boiled to the gods to eat.[2] Pelops, however, regenerated, except for a shoulder. Is Pelops that young man who must shoulder his father-complex, and yet cannot because this same complex deprives him of his capacity to shoulder? Or is his mode of shouldering aesthetic: the ivory prosthesis replacing the irrecoverably missing part?

Other tales tell of other parental woundings: when maddened by Dionysus, Pentheus's mother cuts off her son's head[3] and Lykourgos cuts off his son's extremities.[4] The boy Odysseus is wounded while he is with his grandfather, and by a "parental" boar.[5] The soft spot in Achilles (and in Baldur) comes from the Mother. Achilles is held by the heel and dipped into the bath to make him invincible—except for where she held him. His fatal wound is precisely where his mother touched him under the guise of protecting him.[6] One wound of Hercules occurs in a bat-

---

2. Pindar, *Olympic Ode* 1; Apollodorus, *Epitome* 2.3.

3. Euripides, *The Bacchae* 1170–1330.

4. *Ausführliches Lexikon der griechischen und römischen Mythologie*, edited by W.H. Roscher (Leipzig: B.G. Teubner, 1884), II: "Lykourgos."

5. On "parental" boar symbolism, see Erich Neumann, *The Origins and History of Consciousness* (New York: Pantheon, 1954), 77ff., 94f.; John Layard, "Boar Sacrifice and Schizophrenia," *Journal of Analytical Psychology* 1, no. 1 (1955); "Identification with the Sacrificial Animal," *Eranos Yearbook* 24 (1955). Other boar deaths include Osiris by Typhon and Hackelbrand in German mythology.

6. The stories concerning Achilles's bath of invulnerability vary. Apollonius of Rhodes (IV, 869) says he was bathed in ambrosia; or he was bathed in fire (*Schol. Ilias* XVI, 37), or dipped in the Styx (*Quint. Smyrn.*, 111, 62). Cf. C.M. Bowra, *Heroic Poetry*

tle with a Father and Sons (Hippocoon and his sons).[7] This father-son conflict wounds Hercules in the hollow of his hand; and in another tale Hercules kills his own children.

The wound-in-reverse, or the wounded parent, is shown by Aeneas who totes his lame father on his back, and by Perseus who, with a discus, accidentally wounds his grandfather Akrisos in the foot.[8]

The mythical image of the wounding or wounded parent becomes the psychological statement that *the parent is the wound.* Literally, we hold our parents responsible, but metaphorically the same statement can mean: that which wounds us can also parent us. Our wounds are the fathers and mothers of our destinies.

I

Laming. Puer wounds always occur in specific images within specific stories, and more: they are local wounds to specific bodyparts: Achilles's heel, Pelops's shoulder. In Adler's terms, puer psychology is marked by quite specific organ inferiority; first of all by wounds to the lower extremities. Achilles's heel, Oedipus (swellfoot), Hercules (the crab at Lerna),[9] Alexander the Great (wounded in the ankle),[10] Odysseus's leg, Jason's single sandal,[11] Philoctetes, Bellerophon who limps—all these are marked in the foot.[12] Does the fact that every human descended

---

(London: Macmillan, 1961), chap. 3; on Achilles's death, Karl Kerényi, *The Heroes of the Greeks* (London: Thames and Hudson, 1959), 353. The heel (ankle) as spot of vulnerability is given witness in a sixth-century BC vase painting: Margaret R. Scherrer, *The Legends of Troy* (London, 1964), 99.

7. Pausanias, *Description of Greece* 3.15.5.

8. *Ausführliches Lexikon der griechischen und römischen Mythologie*, III: "Perseus."

9. Kerényi, *The Heroes of the Greeks*, 144.

10. On Alexander's wound see, J.R. Hamilton, "Alexander and his 'So-Called' Father," in *Alexander the Great: The Main Problems*, edited by G.T. Griffith (Cambridge: Heffer, 1966), 236ff.

11. On Jason *monosandalos*, see Kerényi, *The Heroes of the Greeks*, 248.

12. Paris, who hit Achilles in the heel, is himself mortally wounded in the ankle by Philoctetes, whose insufferable wound was in the foot (Robert Graves, *The Greek Myths* (Harmondsworth: Penguin, 1960), 2:326). Philoctetes's father, Poeas, shoots Talos, the winged, heroic, bronze Guardian of Crete, in the ankle (*Ausführliches Lexikon der griechischen und römischen Mythologie*, V). In Talos, the bleeding and the foot motifs coincide: his single long blood canal from neck downwards came unstop-

from Eve shall be bruised in the heel by the serpent say that each human being is susceptible to the puer?

The wounded foot (and its reverse, the winged feet of Hermes and the seven-league flight boots) says something basic about the puer condition. His stance, his position is marked in such a way that his connection with *res extensa* is hindered, heroic, and magical. The spirit does not fully reach downward into this world, since at that place of contact with the world, the puer figure is deathly weak. This consciousness cannot walk and thereby extend itself step by step. It is unable to be in the world with both feet on the ground, as if the transcendent seems unable to posit itself fully as human. Even the incarnated Christ, whose mission was to bring Heaven down to earth, himself was wounded in the feet and crucified above our heads, in the air. When transcendent, Heaven's Son, the puer, is superb—like Bellerophon on Pegasus piercing through illusions; but when fallen onto earth, like Bellerophon the spirit limpingly drags itself around Aleion, the "plains of wandering."[13] How important shoes then become—Maine boots, Guru shoes, earth sandals, thick-soled, thinsoled, holes, cleated, or air-filled with luminous heels: ritualizations and magic of the feet.

If the deeper implication of laming is the verticality of the spirit, we may expect to find images of laming as an advantage or achievement. The one-legged dance of a Shaman[14] is just such an example of unnatural distortion representing supernatural power. Another example is the alchemical image of the hermaphroditic uniped.[15] The double standpoint of left and right is unified into a single pivot. Movement no longer shuffles along, back and forth, now this side, now that; instead, consciousness has to hop and skip about. The left-right rhythm that

---

pered through the wound in the ankle and all his blood poured out. On five versions of how Philoctetes was wounded, see Graves, *The Greek Myths*, 2:292–93. Ajax's vulnerable place was the armpit; Cycnus, son of Poseidon, the head. Hercules's son Telephos is wounded in the upper thigh.

13. Kerényi, *The Heroes of the Greeks*, 84. For more on puer wandering, see Chapter 6.

14. On the one-legged Shaman: see his dance on the stick or hobbyhorse in Mircea Eliade, *Shamanism* (New York: Pantheon, 1964), 467ff.; also Jack Lindsay, *The Clashing Rocks: Early Greek Religion and Culture and the Origins of Drama* (London: Chapman Hall, 1965), 197, 200, 332–33. The broomstick of the witch can also carry one off into the verticality of spiritual flight.

15. CW14:720.

steadies one with the mutual self-corrections of thesis and antithesis is off-balance, and with it, man's relation to the earth as walker who paces the dimensions of reality, taking its measure with his footsteps and his tempo.

Instead of steadiness, there is the gift of leaping about in discontinuity and then being wholly identified (at one with) wherever one lands. And wherever one has landed, at once becomes the center so that one's motion is no longer locomotion but a self-turning on one's own axis. In this condition consciousness is single, centroverted, and also in precarious balance, which does imply that the exceptional state of wholly centered consciousness is less stable than we like to believe. Perhaps the uniped shows a state of continuous discontinuity, in which the alchemical achievement is less a solid-state stone than the wonky wobble, always teetering, susceptible to falling. Consciousness leaps to the center of things, is identified with its standpoint, but cannot stand there. Nor can it even observe itself since there is no longer any one foot in and one foot out. We are now into the genius and pathology of fusional states, the single standpoint of identification.

Whereas alchemy represents one-footedness as an accomplishment, usually this virtue—if such it is—of being "singled" out through the foot does not feel like an achievement. He who has it experiences its onus and usually not its blessings. At best the marked foot represents a condition of being singled out by an abnormal standpoint. Jason's absent sandal meant that he was pledged with one foot (the left) to the Underworld. Mopsos, the prophet whose "special skill in divination was concerned with birds. He could understand their language," was snake-bitten in the left foot.[16] (The odd relation between the marked foot and prophecy is brought out further in Melampus = "Black Foot," the earliest legendary prophet of Greek myth.)[17] The cost of sight into the divine (divination), and thus foresight into time, is a marking in relation to this normal world of here and now. To soar one must hobble too. The marked

---

16. H.W. Parke, *The Oracles of Zeus: Dodona, Olympia, Ammon* (Cambridge, Mass.: Harvard University Press, 1967), 14f.; Cf. *Ausführliches Lexikon der griechischen und römischen Mythologie*, II: "Mopsos." This seer, one of the heroes of the Argonauts, was called by some a "son of Apollo." He was a wanderer, colonizer, and a conqueror of Amazons (perhaps a different "Mopsos"?).

17. Parke, *The Oracles of Zeus*, 165ff.

foot is also a laming, a limiting hindrance, a frustration and a wound. The complex through which we gain our profoundest insight is also our greatest hindrance. The native sensitivity through which we receive the gods also continually hurts and may kill us.

In a sense the heroic puer is uniped, as Emerson suggests in his definition of the hero as the one "who is immovably cened." He is tied to the Immovable Point or World Navel, "for the hero is himself the navel of the world, the umbilical point through which the energies of eternity break into time."[18] The wound represents the immobility, the limits of destiny nailing one to the spot so that through one's wound these energies of eternity can flow. Or, at least so it feels. The hurt leg or foot then keeps one eternally bound to the archetypal realm by one's very immobility. One never has to descend from the cross. So, heroic puer-consciousness that releases energies is itself paralyzed—almost senex-like, stuck forever to and by its own eternality.

Furthermore, the wounded leg or foot calls for a crutch. We need someone to lean on, special inclines, footstools, wheels. Winged and frail as the puer figure may be, he still can dominate through the power of his neediness.

Laming also expresses the weakness and helplessness at the beginning of any enterprise. The initial moment is also the most vulnerable; first steps are tentative and uncertain. The whole project stands or falls with the first stroke since everything after that is but a further development of the initial act. We may improve, rectify, or transform, but always the source is that first sketch or draft tossed off initially by puer inspiration. This is the motif of "difficulty at the beginning," of youthful foolishness or fantastic bravado; here we experience the fragility of the spirit. The wounded puer personifies the spirit's structural damage and, maybe, damaging structure.

II

Maimed Hands. Sometimes the damage shows in the hands that cannot take hold, grasp the tools, comprehend the problems, seize the issues. Then, puer consciousness complains that it cannot "manage." The hands may be clever and manipulative, but there is difficulty at hanging-in

---

18. Joseph Campbell, *The Hero with a Thousand Faces* (New York: Pantheon, 1949), 41.

or hanging-on to the "matter at hand" so that it can be resolved. Knots are sliced open with a brilliant stroke, rather than carefully sorted out strand by strand.

The inabilities of the hands are sometimes repaired in dreams by surgical operations. A slug-like worm is pulled out of the metacarpus of a woman who feels herself slow at grasping ideas. A surgeon operates painstakingly, seemingly for hours, at the base of a young man's right fingers, as if careful slowness is the operation itself, giving a base to the patient's deft but fluttery fingers that drop everything too soon. A young potter's hand is cut open down to the bone. He is horrified and fascinated by the sight. The dreamer can now see that his hand that forms is itself formed by deep, hard, ancient structures and that the shapes he makes have a preformed interior pattern. The dream has released an archetypal sense of what he is doing.

To the hands belong two distinct spiritual functions: creative and authoritative, the wand and the mace. The creative function appears in the conception of the fingers as independent forces, the little gnomic phallic *dactyls* who fashion new shapes in their spontaneous play. Inventions are fantasies of the fingers. The spirit plays with things, pries them open with curiosity, picks them apart analytically, puts the incongruous together into symbols. Jung[19] associates the fingers directly with the *puer aeternus,* so that a wounded or maimed finger strikes directly at the archetype itself. At the fingertips we are at the growing edge, reaching into the unknown. "The hand reacts quicker than the arm, the arm quicker than the shoulder."[20] As we move outward into the extremities, the expansive, experimental vitality of the individual comes into play. Here, too, the unconscious spirit presents itself by doodling, automatic writing, free-hand drawing—and writer's cramp. Scratching, picking, drumming with the fingers, fondling stones, worry beads—the fingers must be busy. Even masturbating may be as much for the sake of idle hands as for the claims of the genitals. To lose one's fingers is to lose one's creative fantasy and one's childlike

---

19. *CW* 5: 180–84.

20. Nicolas Vaschide, *Essai sur la psychologie de la main* (Paris: M. Rivière, 1909), 478. For a fuller phenomenology, see Jean Brun, *La main et l'esprit* (Paris: Presses Universitaires de France, 1963).

vitality. It is a loss that may signify the sacrifice of "newness."[21] These imaginative and playful activities of the hands can be distinguished from their other spiritual function: the fist of will and oath, handling, seizing, and comprehending the world.

The two spiritual meanings of the hands, imaginative and executive, pull against and may even damage each other. After all, the fingers disappear into the fist and must serve its punch, just as the fist is gone once the fingers come into play. The gifts of the puer-man may be in his hands yet these same hands may be the place where he lets go of his own gifts. Perhaps, the executive hands must be wounded; perhaps the imaginative function of the hands wounds their executive capacity. The gift both blesses and curses. The talent placed in my hands does not necessarily become mine. To seize the talent may realize it, but it also may make the talent vanish. The man whose lifestyle follows the puer and lives from the spirit shows wounded hands when he cannot handle his gifts or manage that spirit that comes and goes of its own accord. His handicap reminds him of his limits, keeping him to the fingers of fantasy rather than the fist of control.

Perhaps, the puer spirit may not be meant to manage but to imagine. In the hands of the puer are shapes and gestures, and the puer touch, but not the reins of will. The desultory execution, the indecision that cannot grasp the sword hilt and slash a way forward may be symptomatic not only of what is wrong. It may also hint at something right: that

---

21. The finger lost may have been given up for the social good, preventing anything new being formed that may disturb the archaic conservatism of tribal law. Among the Hottentots, but also in tribal societies in South Africa, America, the Pacific Islands, India, and in ancient Palestine, fingers are dedicated for sacrifice and mourning. Fingers have been found in graves with goddess figures, which recalls Attis whose little finger still lived even after his death (cf. M.J. Vermaseren, *The Legend of Attis* [Leiden: E.J. Brill, 1966] and *Cybele and Attis* [London: Thames and Hudson, 1977], 91). A relation between the Finger Tomb of Tantalos (who chopped up his son Pelops) and the phallic creative dactyl (=finger) is mentioned by Jane Harrison in *Themis* (London: Merlin Press, 1963), 402-3. Orestes (Eumenides) bites off his finger in his madness, which may point to the sacrifice of a puer impulse (unlike Attis) and a dedication to a new, limited way of being. Cf. Rachel Levy, *The Gate of Horn* (London: Faber and Faber, 1948), 17, 49, 93; J. Lindsay, *The Clashing Rocks,* 191-92; Richard Broxton Onians, *The Origins of European Thought* (Cambridge, Mass.: Cambridge University Press, 1953), 496-97, where the fingers are associated particularly with the child.

one way forward is not via action but fantasy, the way of imagination. If maiming puts everything active out of reach, only fantasy remains. And fantasy is not wildly inspirational only. It has its laws and will, its intrinsic intelligibility of forms that the hands follow in each of the crafts. The strict demands of craft—that fantasies be crafted with precision into shapes—provide discipline and an ethic for an imaginal ego. By staying true to the puer archetype and its transcendent function, we work at our crippling from within the imagination.

A primary method for the crafting of fantasy is what the French call *bricolage*, pottering about with bits and pieces that are given.[22] The wound reduces one to an "occupational therapy," that is, making something of one's complexes *as they are*. We recombine them into new fantasies by becoming a handy-man who can make-do with the limitations of his psychic complexity. Here, the wound is a teacher to which one apprentices one's puer ambition. It is forced into the concrete, for *bricolage* is the "science of the concrete." One can take hold of only small things, one at a time, try this with that. This *bricolage* gives one the feel of the complexes, their blunt places and sharp edges, and above all, how they fit into each other. The wounded hand is clumsy, and the healing of the puer's messy concrete life begins in the experience of one's clumsiness. (So long as we are soaring, we have no notion of the mess we leave behind.) Moving around in this way among the complexes, becom-

---

22. Cf. Edgar Wind, *Art and Anarchy* (London: Faber and Faber, 1963), 160; Claude Lévi-Strauss, *La Pensée sauvage* (Paris: Plon, 1962), 26–47; Nathan J. Schwartz and Sandra Ross, "On the Coupling of Psychic Entropy and Negentropy," *Spring: An Annual of Archetypal Psychology and Jungian Thought* (1970): 77–80. Perhaps the earliest image of the *bricoleur* was "Eros the Carpenter," an image found already in Etruscan times. (Raymond Klibansky, Erwin Panofsky, and Fritz Saxl, *Saturn and Melancholy* [London: Nelson, 1964], 308, with illustration). The figure of Eros is surrounded by joiner's tools, making quite practical and on the level of a craft the usual high-blown notions of Eros (as a cosmogonic force of unions, lord of fantasy and emotional upheavals). This sober aspect of Eros shows the joining function not within the cosmos of Aphrodite, but perhaps in connection with Athene. "Hesiod uses the periphrasis 'Athene-Servant' for a carpenter" (Norman O. Brown, *Hermes the Thief* [New York: Vintage Paperback, 1969], 66). Daedalos, too, can be taken as a primordial *bricoleur*. He made new things out of what was at hand. From within the "Daedalos complex" the attempt to gain a wider perspective (Talos) or to soar above what is at hand (Icarus) ends in ruin. *Bricolage* seems to limit ambition, glory, wings.

ing more crafty because one is so clumsy, holds up the impulse towards idealized abstractions. The straight line of puer ambition is tamed by the wounded hand. And, because fantasy itself is wounded, that is, kept limited by its own inability, the wound saves puer consciousness from higher flights and worse falls.

The autonomous hand extends to manipulate the world and make all things its tools. *Orexis,* the most embracing Greek term for appetite or desire, etymologically means the extension of the hand, its reach and greed. Puer nightmares show autonomy of the hands and the fear of their strangling or stabbing. Sometimes suicidal wrist-slashing seems to attempt a self-cure by the autonomous hand of its own independence: if I offend thee, cut me off. The self-wounding act may be read less in terms of bleeding and more in terms of the hands themselves. Although the fear of the Autonomous Hand may pervade a puer person, the same puer consciousness worships this autonomy as creativity, believing himself or herself an artist.

Let us remember that our fingers let us fly. Phylogenetically our hands compare with birds' wings. The ascensional possibility in the hands is expressed by Darwin in literalistic fantasies; Darwin considered humankind's verticality to be the result of its hands.[23] We have pulled ourselves up from the bestial floor by our hands. In them lies our freedom; they are our wings.

So far we have discussed the two spiritual functions of the hand, the fist and the fingers,[24] suggesting that for the same hands to perform both functions—talent and the control of this talent—may be more than human. In fact, it may be devilish, since only by shaking hands with the devil can one have the creative spirit in one's own hands to do with as one likes. As long as we are driven both by the hand of will and by the hand of imagination, there must be wounds. Left hand has need to ring

---

23. This subject is examined beautifully by Brun, *La main et l'esprit,* chap. 2.

24. The distinctions between fist and fingers (will-power and fantasy) have often been literalized into right-versus left-handedness to the detriment (in our culture) of left-handed persons and to the bafflement of ethnologists who try to establish the right/left distinction universally (e.g., Robert Hertz, *Death and the Right Hand* [Aberdeen: Cohen and West, 1960]). But see Vilma Fritsch, *Left and Right in Science and Life* (London: Barrie and Rockcliff, 1968), who brings evidence contrary to the idea that left must be imaginative, hence sinister and gauche.

its fantasy with wedding bands, seals and signets, and right to relax its fist. Until the power of ambition and the power of imagination rest their struggle, they mutually cripple each other.

The healing of the hand depends therefore on bringing into play a third function of the hands, their soul aspect. Now we are speaking of the hand as healer, the flat of the hand, its palm, which is the etymological root of our word *feel*. All kinds of powers pass through the palms: soothing, blessing, warming, caressing, weighing, slapping, begging.[25] Here, in the palms, are the lines of our fate, and here we are nailed. Also here, we are naive, open-handed, bare.

So, another way of envisioning the three functions of the hand—fingers, fist, and palm—is in terms of puer, senex, and anima. This suggests that wounds in the palm go to the soul, both its peaceful simplicity and its crisscrossed complexity. Here the wound affects our grip on things and our handle on the world by means of tools. With the awakening of the anima through suffering the flat of our hands, we have to let go of the utilitarian connection. There is nothing more we can *do* about things (fist) or to things (fingers). Instead we learn about maintaining and holding—just keeping in touch. This the puer has least of all. His wounded hand betrays a structural inability of the spirit—or a charismatic superability—to handle what is today called "human feeling." He may show a sign, point a way, but can he give us a hand? He may brilliantly grasp, but can he hold on? Nonetheless, that same wounded palm opens the soul of the hand, making it excruciatingly aware of giving and receiving. Swift-footed boy, mimetic to Hermes, hitherto all cap and phallus, god of exchanges, commerce and *Handel,* may now experience by means of his hurt that what actually passes through his hands are values.

We begin to see that the wounded hand is a saving grace, because it keeps the puer spirit human. Were it not for this inadequacy, every puer-person would long ago have built his way to heaven and would never have let slip the reins of his sun-frenzied horses. The maimed hands are the necessary correlate of puer giftedness. The wound is a consequent of the gift; the gift wounds; the gift is a wound.

---

25. Cf. Brun, *La main et l'esprit,* chap. 10, "La main et la caresse." Contrary to the palm's feeling is the "back of the hand'—an expression for insulting dismissal.

The wound may also be a gift. To construe maiming in only symptomatic terms is to miss its necessity within an archetypal pattern. The feet that walked the waters had to be nailed but the legs left unbroken at Christ's final descent into humanity. The same foot that made Achilles the "swiftest" also carried that flaw that made him mortal.[26] Wounds contain a blessing as well as the evident curse. To assume that the curse can be cured—by exercising will power, by taking a grip to overcome a weak ego—without at the same time affecting the blessing is naive. It is also irreligious, i.e., neglecting the archetypal structure. The religious or spiritual must be kept foremost in mind when dealing with puer consciousness, since that is the archetypal substrate of every puer problem. What happens in ego-consciousness is only derivative of something transcendent. Thus organ inferiority cannot be adequately met with ego compensations in the Adlerian sense. Organ inferiority is indeed a ground of the weak ego, but the "weak ego" is merely pathology's way of stating that the ego is only human. Organ inferiority is the human condition, our liability to be bruised at the heel, our mortality. The ego is weak because it is mortal, with its specific lacuna or privations, deprived of ideal and abstract good by its complexes. These complexes keep us continually wounded, that is continually limited to our inferiority, our mortal condition. Every wound is a mortal wound, the realization of mortality. The crippling is indispensable for the puer, who, had he the gift without the wound, would be altogether inhuman. His handicap compensates his omnipotence, making his archetypal structure viable for human existence. His viability lies just in his vulnerability. The wound brings the senex virtue of limitation to an unlimited reach.

Ordinary psychologists, whose weight is upon analyzing the unconscious and strengthening the ego, berate the puerman for his fragile adaptation. He is so vulnerable to break-downs. In reply to them we shall remember that through the lacuna of the wound not only "the eternally pubescent individual"[27] shows, but also mortal man who is

---

26. In Greek thought, the main difference between humans and gods is that all men are mortal; whereas gods are *athnetos* (immortal).

27. Jolande Jacobi, *The Psychology of C. G. Jung* (London: Routledge and K. Paul, 1951), 40.

Wounded Man enters life. This "infantile, childlike individual" whom Jacobi berates is none other than the archetypal Child, chrysalis of the puer. The wound that makes adaptation so special or impossible also makes possible a new fate. A new spirit emerges in weakness, and through our holes the unexpected comes out. Hans Castorp's lung with its *petite tache humide* makes him unable for life. He has to go and live it on the *Magic Mountain,* where, through the little hole of his wound, the immense realm of spirit enters. A wound has this spiritual logos quality. It is a learner and a teacher both, and has been compared with a mouth (*Julius Caesar,* 3.1; *Henry IV,* 2.1.3). It has a message.

One meaning that speaks particularly through the wounded hand has to do with gestures. Imaginal reality, which informs puer consciousness, gives to acts and deeds a fantasy quality of gestures. Puer consciousness can transform the acting-out of the complexes into gestures, giving another style to a complex, a style that has been called fantastic and irresponsible, even hysterically theatrical. Yet, for puer consciousness, whatever role is played, however the hands are used, life itself is a gesture of the spirit; life as *mudra,* a significative gesture.

Damage to the hand discloses the fate of one who is purely and only puer: life as broken gesture, unachieved, a fragment that points beyond itself. At the same time, this damage offers the very possibility for moving from this fate into a human world where handicaps give soul.

Our hands are exposed to all the risks of daily life. They are our first touch with the concrete, how we defend ourselves, how we express ourselves, what we give each other. In them lies our sensitivity. Little wonder that the puer's hands break at this direct contact. Because hands are particular to the human species, playing a special part in shaping each destiny that we can never really read, we turn to hands to read fate. Their lines, like the prints at each finger-tip, are unique, as personal and changing as those on our faces. Yet, they are also indelible and inherited. So the wound to the hand is a wound in fate and the fate of woundedness, the fuller meaning of which we are trying to place within the phenomenology of the puer archetype.

III

Bleeding. Another aspect of woundedness is bleeding. Here we may recollect Baldur, and the Near Eastern figures of Attis, Tammuz, and Adonis,[28] also the dismembered Osiris and the dismembered Dionysus, and Jesus, too. Why must the young god bleed? Why does he bleed to death? What does bleeding to death signify for this kind of consciousness?

On the face of it bleeding would seem to signify castration. The sons of the Magna Mater are emasculated, die of their hemorrhaging, and from their blood comes the flowering of nature. Their male substance fertilizes mother earth. By losing their external sex and bleeding from the genitals as women, they are transformed back into the female body from which they came. They are re-absorbed into nature, becoming "gardens," *kēpos,*[29] another name for the vulva in Greek. Castration and subsequent bleeding states a primary identity of the son with the mother: one makes oneself one with her by making oneself into her. As such, castration bleeding is more appropriate to the son of the Great Goddess.

Another aspect of bleeding, however, is more authentically puer. With Jesus, Baldur, certain saints, knights, and heroes, bleeding is primary, as if before the wound, as if the wound releases and reveals essence. Let us focus upon the continuous bleeding that cannot be stopped. Of course, this image has been given overwhelming religious significance through Jesus. The bleeding stigmata and the bleeding heart and the relics associated with the blood stir the most profound emotions of Christianity. It is said that the bleeding of Christ tells of love, of compassion, of suffer-

---

28. Every year in Lebanon, it was said, the river Adonis turns red, flowing to the sea stained with the blood of the beautiful slain lover (*Ausführliches Lexikon der griechischen und römischen Mythologie,* V: "Tamuz").

29. Liddell and Scott, *A Greek-English Lexicon;* compare Latin *hortus* (garden) as a term for female pudenda; further, *Myth, Religion, and Mother Right: Selected Writings of J.J. Bachofen,* translated by Ralph Manheim (Princeton, N.J.: Princeton University Press, 1967), 131. The most complete study is by Marcel Detienne, *The Gardens of Adonis: Spices in Greek Mythology,* translated by Janet Lloyd (London: Harvester Press, 1977). Detienne works from J.G. Frazer's Adonis section of *The Golden Bough,* but radically revisions the cult so that, in Detienne's words (122): "Adonis is not a husband or even a man: he is simply a lover, and an effeminate one…an image of seduction."

ing and of the endless flow of the divine essence into the human world, and of the bond through blood kinship and blood mystery of the human world with the divine. The bleeding of Jesus is a transfiguration of a basic puer motif onto a theological plane.

What does this specific form of woundedness say about the psychology of the puer? His bleeding reveals his archetypal structure in several ways. *First,* it is an image for vulnerability in general, the skin too thin for real life, the sensitivity to every pointed instrument of attack, the defenselessness of youngly naive and open truth. The bleeding tells of the puer propensity for victimization, for the constellation around him of the psychopathic attackers: Loki, Hagen, the Roman soldiers, the crowd of arrows into Sebastian.[30] He draws the assassins to himself, a hero-in-reverse, noble for his martyrdom, remembered finally less for what he does than for what is done to him. The bloodthirsty aggression that comes to him from the outside belongs to his fate, but he is unaware that it belongs to his character too. He points up the ancient idea that "character for man is destiny,"[31] so that the insights arising from the complexes composing our character also tell us about our fate. (*Amor fati* thus also means loving one's complexes.) To draw blood or to have it drawn is part of the same constellation of bloodletting. As the hero, i.e. puer, cannot stop his manic seizure of slaughter (Achilles abused Hector's corpse for twelve days), so the hero-in-reverse cannot staunch his own bleeding. He has no tourniquet partly because his bleeding is so beauteous.[32] Why stay such blood, a blood that is latent

---

30. An example closer to our times of one who draws the psychopathic attacker is Johann Joachim Winckelmann, the great classicist, who "invented," in the eighteenth century, the modern fields of archeology, the scholarly art museum, and an aesthetics based on classic models. His life is rife with puer phenomena: logos obsession in childhood, out of obscurity to fame by following his childhood fantasy, idealized homosexuality, falling in love with an idealized idol (Apollo Belvedere), dedication to aesthetics, and finally bleeding to death in 1768 from brutal knife wounds suffered at the hands of a thief-homosexual psychopathic liar named Arcangeli.

31. Heraclitus, DK 119.

32. The beauty of the bleeding wound evokes a love that is more than compassion for the sufferer. The bleeding calls to the lover, not only to the nurse. Greek paintings of young men of the Trojan war binding the wounds of comrades and the love expressed in the act continues as a theme in war films today. The bleeding heart of

with flowers? Myths tell us again and again that from slain pueri spring wondrous blooms.[33] The puer is transfigured by his wounds into glory. It is as if he does not sense his broken vessels, cannot smell blood, only flowers. Aestheticism can defend one even against pain. Parsifal has only to ask Amfortas "What ails him?" but the question of the wound never occurs to this beautiful young man, single-minded on his quest for the grail. So Amfortas's wound continues to suppurate—ailing is all in the King, the senex; there is none in the pure young knight.

There are other wounds, suppurating and bitter, leading neither to death nor cure, serving instead as focus of psychic complexity. Prometheus's liver is always being torn at; Hercules burns in his poisoned shirt; Philoctetes's foot is continually infected. No flowers here, but rather the stuff for reflection for thousands of years in myths, dramas, and poems. These bitter wounds hurt; they stink and give rise to continual complaint, and, in Philoctetes's case, the complaint gives the dignity of an individualized destiny.

It might be well to relate complaining to woundedness, rather than to a search for mothering and a childish inability to take the hardships of life and "be a man." Complaint then may be regarded as part of woundedness, a first realization of imperfection. The shield is pierced, life is seeping away in a process of decay. A touch of Saturn. Sometimes with the puerman the wound is evident only in the complaint betrayed in the voice or posture. The breakdown begins in a cry. "I broke down and cried." The invulnerable spirit becomes human just by feeling miserable. To wail is *the* human sign, as the first emotion of the infant is crying, as the last statement of Jesus was his complaint on the cross.

Human existence is wounded from beginning to end, and the puer complaint reminds that physical nature, life of the body, the only-natural perspective is not enough. The puer body is broken through; his is an opened *physis*. The complaint, like the so-called accident that suddenly ends a promising sports career, states that consciousness is no longer contained by only the physical mode of experience. The "accident" dis-

---

Christ stands as a central icon of the beauty inciting the most passionate love.

33. Cf. Paul Kugler, *The Alchemy of Discourse: An Archetypal Approach to Language* (Lewisburg, Penn.: Bucknell University Press, 1982), for phonetic relations between "blood" and "bloom."

engages puer from the heroic carrier who has anyway been accidental to the essential puer fate that is beyond the heroic. Puer comes into his own, but complainingly. The complaint tells of separation from nature and announces the call of spiritual destiny. Mistakenly, we who hear a puer complaining consider him calling out to mother, whereas his cry is over a fate that now announces Mother Nature gives us no support and the body's life is not enough.

Bleeding also expresses the outpouring dynamus of the puer. We see it in inflation and enthusiasm. The vitality of the puer spreads and stains like the red tincture of the alchemist's *lapis*. His bleeding is a *multiplicatio*, the infectious giving out of essence for the sake of transforming the world around. The archetypal structure of the puer insists on gushing forth, hyperactive, charismatic, sacrificial. So Hotspur, for the honor of Mortimer would "empty all these veins,/And shed my dear blood drop by drop..." The magic touch of the puerman is not spurious; it is his life-blood that he puts into his projects and his friends. He pours out his heart despite himself.[34] His bleeding seems mere display, but it is an enactment of those god figures whose bleeding is the emanation of their essence, the exteriorization of creative vitality. Through this enactment of them he participates in them and so has superabundant energy; his bleeding seems never to exhaust him. Through their wounds these god figures are recognized as divine, so that entry into the god's love is through the divine wound, a mimesis of the archetypal infirmity, which paradoxically gives power, as the Christian mystics so triumphantly declared. A superhuman power emanates through the open wound and through being wounded. Thus puer consciousness by continually giving out and spilling forth keeps in touch with his style of power.[35] Thus, too, the puer man, mimetic to "suffering Jesus" may be playing a power game, dominating by means of his disregard for himself. His egoless generosity and self-sacrifice keep him high on his cross.

---

34. Ann Belford Ulanov (*The Feminine in Jungian Psychology and in Christian Theology* [Evanston, Ill.: Northwestern University Press, 1971], 236) misses this point when assuming that a young man's pouring out and spilling over derive from an anima not yet separated from the "maternal instinct." Readings in terms of the Mother always miss the spiritual authenticity of puer phenomena, in this case a phenomenon as important as love.

35. See my *Kinds of Power* (New York: Doubleday, 1995), "Charisma."

But, *third,* he has no clotting instinct. Giving becomes spilling, a psychic hemophilia. The inhibiting senex factor does not function or overreacts; both sudden borders and no limits. Here we touch upon the puer difficulty with eros. Because the heart's blood can flow so freely, the puer structure makes a man tend to draw back, to protect himself, closing off and trying to control the seepage with ego strictures of the senex. He never feels able to contain his life energy or eros: it pours through him and out of him, or he stops it up, unlovingly cold. It is an all-or-nothing phenomenon, beyond human intervention. He does not know how to feed on himself, to partake in his own essence, as the pelican could nourish its own children from its wounds. Through his wounds the puer may feed others, but may himself be drained thereby. There is a curious fault in his love for himself. Modern attempts to deal with this condition, such as Kohut's psychology of narcissism, tend to miss a main point. An archetypal force has no true care for its human incarnation. A power beyond the ego demands such immense service that we must bleed for it. Were we able to supply ourselves with enough narcissistic counsel, we would not be wounded, of course, nor would we be dominated by the puer archetype, that demonic angel.

To find that caring love of self, puer often constellates—not senex and the instinct of survival—but the nurse. Myths show divine-child figures each with special nursing attendants. In the individual puer person, nursing plays a subtle role, now one's sustenance, now one's doom. Indeed the spirit needs nursing, from the milk that philosophers drink from Sophia to the glass at night for a burning stomach. But with milk may come the Great Mother and the decline of the puer spirit into whimpering for physical aid and pampering with concrete solutions. Milk has many sources, and one can be nursed in various manners. Dionysus, too, brings milk.[36] The Dionysian nurses are *daughters* of the spirit, followers, a troupe of participants, enjoying and serving spirit as their mode of mothering it. They drink, dance, and bring humor. Puer spirit, when nursed through the maiden-maenad-daughter, is no longer forced into the role of child of the mother, but instead becomes the troupe's "father." The daughter-nurse reconnects senex and puer.

---

36. Walter F. Otto, *Dionysus: Myth and Cult,* translated by Robert B. Palmer (Bloomington: Indiana University Press, 1981), 96.

IV

Leaking and Containing. Fourth—which sums it all—is the problem of the vessel. Socrates in Plato's *Gorgias* refers to an Orphic tale that says the soul of "foolish uninitiated being" is like a leaky vessel (493b). The uninitiated are the most unhappy in the Hades depths of the psyche because there they are undergoing a process of senseless repetitive compulsion: they carry water in a sieve and pour it into a perforated jar.[37] The uninitiated have no proper vessel; they are unsealed and unretentive, says Plato. They are filled with eagerness for more because they do not hold what they have. When everything passes through, the person himself is only passing through, without substance. The open wound may here refer to the *unbuilt psychic body,* which originally, in Plato, is the guard and keeper (not imprisoner) of the soul. Then the rush of life energy bursts the thin bag of psychic skin and the reddening comes too fast, which, as the alchemists said, shows that the work was spoiled.

Thus, what is fundamentally missing in the puer structure is the *psychic container* for holding in, keeping back, stopping short, the moment of reflection that keeps events within so that they can be realized as psychic facts.[38]

Let us regard this vessel as a womb that—for two thousand years from Hippocrates until Charcot—was considered to be the special cause of hysteria. When this feminine vessel, the uterus (*hystéra*) was out of place (wandered) it caused that leaking, dripping, outpouring of substance, or hysteria. Without a proper feminine vessel, we can gestate nothing, nourish nothing, bring nothing to complete birth. Through the same unstopped vessel out of which one pours oneself, one is subjected to the invasion of influences. Or, as Plato puts it, the leaky soul "can be swayed and easily persuaded." These souls are sieves that cannot close on themselves and so worship at springs (continually bubbling forth) and riversides, trusting in flow. The worship of flow, however, means also to be continually flowed through, provisional, suggestible,

---

37. A full discussion of the leaky vessel can be found in Eva Keuls, *The Water Carriers in Hades: A Study of Catharsis Through Toil in Classical Antiquity* (Amsterdam: A.M. Hakkert, 1974).

38. Compare Socrates's self-reflection and his use of the image of the vessel in regard to his own soul, *Phaedrus* 235c.

receptive to sinking into any surrounding. Now we meet another danger to puer consciousness: dissolution into water, oblivion. Nothing ever really happens. The virginal Yes that is both continual renewal and indiscrimination, all wet. Wide eyes, open mouths, ready laps.

The proposition that the wound is an opening further proposes that the wounded one is *afflicted by openness*. Puer openness appears as innocence, which means literally "without hurt," free of noxiousness, out of harm's way. The wound that is so necessary to initiation ceremonies ends the state of innocence as it opens one in a new way at another place, making one suffer from openness, bringing to a close the world as wonder. Now it hurts, and I must protect myself. I am no longer unharmed and harmless. So, the puer impulse will force a car crash or a ski spill, not merely for risk or the penchant for destruction, but as well because these adolescent accidents may move the soul into a harmed and initiated body. It is as if the soul can find no path out of innocence other than physical hurt.

This lets us look again at castration, so usually imagined to be the root problem of puer states. The usual view considers puer woundedness reducible to castration: he has been weakened by the mother or become her hystericized ineffectual son because of the father. Let us start from the usual view, although revisioning it anew. Let us imagine that puer castration is indeed a return to the mother—but less as her son than as a disembodied wandering spirit searching for one's *hystéra*, one's internal "mother" as the womb has been called.[39] The return to the womb is to find shelter and enclosure for one's leaky, hysterical suggestibility. In other words, like cures like: my very sickness shows the mode of its healing. Hysterical regressions to the mother reveal my profound vulnerability, how utterly exposed I am, like an exaggerated wound, and I enter into my woundedness so that it may mother me. Instead of hysterically fleeing castration I am initiated by it. Here, the fantasy is wound = womb. Now, the womb is in the right place, inside the deep belly, no longer wandering in hystericized woundedness, seeking a little help from friends, love in a restaurant, straws in the wind.

When wound = womb, then castration is the very ground and carrier of fecundity. One's weakness bears one's future; one's inability is the

---

39. On the implications of hysteria for the psyche, see my *The Myth of Analysis* (Evanston, Ill.: Northwestern University Press, 1972), Part 3.

place of one's potential. So often we read this truth in the lives of sickly, hystericized young persons whose "castration complex" is precisely the locus of their genius. So, we may consider the puer's castration (how he is cut off from his phallic force and seminal thoughts) as a mutilated and desperate recognition of the need for a womb-like soul that can gestate his embryonic values. My self-castrations may be my mother teaching me how to mother; they are attempts at holding myself in. Rather than wounded bleeding into the world, there is internal, rhythmical bleeding like a womb, moving more easily between openness and secrecy.

Openness and secrecy—so puer! The bleeding puer reveals his naked life and his soul is a sieve. It is all there for anyone to come and look; he will tell you all about himself. The puer influence in any complex lays out its wares in public, and passers-by are amazed that anyone can be so open, so unpsychological. This public display is enacted by writers, painters, performers, whose complexes compulsively insist on being widely published, hung upon the wall, or shown to applauding audiences.

Together with this openness, a countermovement of paranoid anxieties begins to cloud over. A peculiar secretiveness darkens the innocence. One feels that emotions can be shared with only a few; whom can one really trust, on watch for betrayals. To be open only leads to hurt. These anxieties initiate a sense of isolation, enmity and separation—cunning, exile and silence—in contradistinction to the charmingly naive defenselessness. Paranoid worries come as answer to overexposure; they are self-protective and indicate closure. This happens, however, only when openness begins to hurt—hence betrayals are so important for moving consciousness from the only-puer condition.

As wounds heal, they close in on themselves. Paranoid anxieties, therefore, may be therapeutic for the innocent puerman. By sealing up in secretiveness, he moves toward initiation; he has a secret without which there is no separate individuality. The secret that seals one off has often to do with the paranoid anima: a secret fantasy, a secret love, a secret goal. Curled inside the paranoid suspicion is the chrysalis of one's special individualized soul. My soul wants something unique from me. Anima is one meaning and one cure of puer-woundedness.

The paranoia of the enclosed anima in its reaction to puer openness can go to extremes. Interior life is sealed up tight, like those images of Mary, the Closed Gate, Enclosed Garden, *Semper Virgo*. The virginal anima that has not been pierced to the emotions by the experience of *physis* (which we literalize as sexual and physical experience) keeps puer persons youngly innocent while offering another way of denying woundedness.

Moreover, the eternal virginity of Mary in soul constellates a Christ identification in action. There is let loose a fresh round of bleeding into the world that never really stains one's interior life. This version of the Christian mother-son drama plays itself like a routine repertoire, season after season, in the psyche of those mimetic to this particular pattern of the puer. Yet from all that repetition little awareness comes since the anima remains *virgo intacta* and the man remains crucified by spiritual questions—the relations of spirit and flesh, God and world, ego and self, east and west, one and many—never moving past the psychological age of thirty-three. (Fortunately there are other images of Mary and other modes of the Mary-Jesus tandem, and even other less literal modes of being in the *semper virgo* pattern.)

Building the psychic vessel of containment, which is another way of speaking of soul-making, seems to require bleeding and leaking as its precondition. Why else go through that work unless we are driven by the despair of our unstoppered condition? The shift from anima-mess to anima-vessel shows in various ways: as a shift from weakness and suffering to humility and sensitivity; from bitterness and complaint to a taste for salt and blood; from focus upon the emotional pain of a wound—its causes, perimeters, cures—to its imaginal depths; from displacements of the womb onto women and "femininity" to its locus in one's own bodily rhythm.[40]

Whatever is necessary and missing gains in importance, so anima assumes grotesque, compulsive and mystical proportions in puer-consciousness, receding only as this consciousness takes on its own wound that is its container. But the opus of woundedness is counterculture. It must move Western history itself. For we stem from adventurers, missionaries, and especially crusaders. The crusading impulse that laid cities to sack and stormed through centuries of our heroic history—and still sets sails in our heroic hearts—was in grotesque search of a mystical Grail, the Crusader's noble Quest for a Vessel to contain the endlessly

---

40. For a discussion of anima and bleeding, see Penelope Shuttle and Peter Redgrove, *The Wise Wound: Menstruation and Everywoman* (London: V. Gollancz, 1978), "Animus, Animal, Anima."

flowing blood of an uncontained Christ-modelled puer consciousness. To recognize that the soul is this grail returns puer consciousness to itself. In the chalice of the wound is soul. This means that psyche is the aim of our bleeding love and that the wound is a grail. The opus is not in Jerusalem; it is right here in our own wounds.

V

Wound Consciousness and Dionysus. Although the wound may be experienced through a symptom, they are not the same. A symptom belongs to diagnosis, pointing to something else underlying. But the wound, as we have been imagining it, takes one into the archetypal condition of woundedness and gives even the smallest symptoms their transcending importance. Every symptom would turn us into its fantasy, so that skin spots make us lepers, diarrhea makes us little babies, and a sprain turns us into old has-beens on the bench. The *magnificatio* that wounding brings is a way of entering archetypal consciousness: an awareness that more is going on than my reason can hold. One becomes an open wound, hurting all over, as consciousness is transfigured into the wounded condition. We experience affliction in general, afflictedness as a way of being-in-the-world. The wound announces impossibility and impotence. It says: "I am unable." It brutally brings awareness to the fact of limitation. The limitation is not imposed from without by external powers, but this anatomical gap is an inherent part of me, concomitant with every step I take, every reach I make.

Because limitation is so difficult and painful for the puer structure, its statement, "I am unable" is exhibited by the painfulness of the wound. He stands before you, still radiant and cheery, as innocent as ever, all the while grossly demonstrating his incapacity by the thick plaster cast on his leg. Puerman hides his wound, since it reveals the secret that weakens this mode of consciousness. It fears feeling its own inability. For, when the wound is revealed at the end of the story, it kills one as a puer. Each complex has its symptom, its Achilles's heel, its opening into humanity through a vulnerable and excruciatingly painful spot, be it Samson's hair or Siegfried's heart.[41]

---

41. Ajax's wound is said by Graves to be in the armpit. Does this not tell us something about the vulnerable place of the man of mighty arms, that he is wounded in the underside of his very strength? Maybe it also tells us about our heroic obsessions

Therapy must touch this spot; it must move from the beautiful wounded condition into the actual present hurt. The archetype generalizes, because archetypes are universals. So drive the nail home! Go into the crippling, maiming, bleeding; probe the specific organ—liver, shoulder, foot, or heart. Each organ has a potential spark of consciousness, and afflictions release this consciousness, bringing to awareness the organ's archetypal background, which, until wounded, had simply functioned physiologically as part of unconscious nature. But now nature is wounded. The organ is now inferior. Deprivation of natural functioning gives awareness of the function. We realize for the first time its feeling, its value, its realm of operations. Limitation through the wound brings the organ to consciousness, as if we know something only as we lose it; as if the knowledge death gives is the knowledge of what a psychic thing is in itself, its true meaning and importance for the soul. A "dying" consciousness is released by the wound.

This dying awareness or awareness of dying may heal the wound, for the wound is no longer so necessary. In this sense, a wound is the healing of puer consciousness and, as healing takes place, the wounded healer may begin to constellate. We must admit, after all, to a curious connection in fact between puer persons and the vocation to therapy.

The "wounded healer" does not mean merely that a person has been hurt and can empathize, which is too obvious and never enough to heal. Nor does it mean that a person can heal because he or she has been through an identical process, for this would not help unless the process had utterly altered consciousness. Let us remember that the "wounded healer" is not a human person, but a *personification* presenting a kind of consciousness. This kind of consciousness refers to mutilations and afflictions of the body organs that release the sparks of consciousness in these organs, resulting in an *organ or body-consciousness.* Healing comes then not because one is whole, integrated, and all together, but from a consciousness breaking through dismemberment.[42]

---

with deodorized armpits, especially in view of the relation between sense of smell as the preferred sense in the underworld of soul (as discussed in my *The Dream and the Underworld* [New York: Harper & Row, 1979]).

42. I have elaborated on the theme of " wounded" and "disintegrated" consciousness in several other places: "Dionysus in Jung's Writings," *Spring: An Annual of Archetypal Psychology and Jungian Thought* (1972): 199–205; "On the Necessity of Abnormal

The moments of localized consciousness are the healers in the wounds. This is a dismembered, dissociated consciousness, one that speaks now from the heart, now from the hand, now from the feet that are hurt and can't walk. It is a wounded consciousness that is always sensitively inferior. And, this dismemberment and dissociation allows conversation between two persons to go on through the wounds. My wounds speak to yours, yours to mine. Wounded consciousness is less threatened by decomposition fantasies of decaying parts (aging, cancer, circulatory disorders, psychosis) because it is itself built upon specifically localized wounds and has emerged from the decay into parts. When disintegration anxiety is no longer paramount, the compensatory emphasis upon ideals of wholeness, order, and union can fade into the thin spiritualized air that is its jinn.

The archetypal root of this dying consciousness that is brought on by wounds may be found in the Dionysian aspect of dismemberment. The tendency of the puer to hysterical dissociation may refer to the vital life-force breaking into bits of consciousness as occasional, multiple insights. Dismemberment is thus not only a matter of passion and of being pulled apart by opposites. For such would be to place Dionysus upon the Cross and to formulate with ego conceptions movements on the vital level. Rather, dismemberment refers to the decomposition or decentralization (and thus decerebralization) of consciousness into primordial regions of organs, complexes, and erogenous zones. Through dismemberment we may also contact the sensuousness of the complexes and not only their suffering. Sometimes, and especially for the puer, the sensuousness comes through suffering, i.e., the first discovery of the body complexes is through a craving skin, straining rigid back, thin breathing, cramped anus, and neglected arches in cold feet. The puer structure often shows this peculiar mixture of suffering and sensuousness. There is both narcissistic body-love and masochistic body-pain, both hypochondria and heroic disdain for the fleshly aspect of the complex. Yet, just this is constellated by the wound that joins in one the psyche and the libidinal body. A wound may be a mouth that speaks spirit, but the spirit is in the flesh.

Psychology" *Eranos Yearbook* 43 (1974): 91–135; *Healing Fiction* (Putnam, Conn.: Spring Publications, 1994), Part III; *Re-Visioning Psychology* (New York: Harper & Row, 1975), chap. 2, "Pathologizing."

Dionysus was *zoé*, the divided/undivided life force, what we might today call the libido (a cognate of Dionysus's Roman counterpart, Liber) at that psychoid or genetic level where information and living matter are difficult to distinguish. Dionysus is a consciousness that occurs in "loosened," "democratic," uncontrolled and disintegrative states. As systematic integration decays and the organs are liberated into differentiated experiences, we feel wounded. And we are wounded by the profound body-consciousness that Dionysus brings, for "Dionysus and Hades are one."[43] The experience of the Dionysian body is also a death of our own habitual physical frame. Woundedness is initiatory to meeting Dionysus. It starts us into the subtle body.

VI

Odysseus's Scar. Still another Greek figure bears on our theme—Odysseus (Ulysses). One derivation of Odysseus's name (Latin, *Ulixes*) is *oulos* = wound and *ischea* = thigh.[44] Evidently his wounded thigh is essential to his nature if it has given him his name.

A singular difference between Odysseus and the other wounded heroic figures we have mentioned is that Odysseus does not die from the goring. His wound becomes a scar. "It was a common form of royal death to have one's thigh gored by a boar, yet Odysseus had somehow survived the wound."[45] *Somehow?* Evidently there is a specific quality in his character allowing him to survive. On the one hand, like the others, he is a puer—always leaving for another place, nostalgic and longing, loved by women whom he refuses, opportunist and tricky, forever in danger of drowning. On the other hand, he is father, husband, captain, with the senex qualities of counsel and survival.

The story of Odysseus's wounding is revealed toward the close of the *Odyssey.* As his old nurse washes his feet, she espies the scar and almost gives him away.[46] We are even told in this scene that Odysseus's name

---

43. Heraclitus, DK 15.

44. Cf. Graves, *The Greek Myths*, 2:170.

45. Ibid.

46. *Odyssey* 19.276ff. There is an ambiguity concerning exactly where the wound is. Is it in the foot or ankle that the nurse washes, or is it higher in the thigh that she sees while crouching below Odysseus, washing his feet? The ambiguity discussed by scholars need not be univocally settled, inasmuch as his foot wound (puer hero) is also a thigh scar (*puer-et-senex*).

derives from the incident of his wounding. As Auerbach[47] points out, this tale is suddenly introduced, and thereby the whole fate of Odysseus is revealed. This is not only a stunning literary denouement, but the revelation of his psychic essence: he is the one of the wounded-thigh.

The sexual symbolics of the wound, and by a boar, especially to the groin or thigh, has already been discussed above. In the case of Odysseus, the wound suggests that he had been violated and opened while still a youth. His wounded thigh is a symbolic vulva, like the thigh of Zeus that brings forth Dionysus. Moreover, this wound is there before the story begins; he comes on the scene wounded, not in the history of the tale but in his nature or essence. The others, like Achilles, begin invulnerable and thus must be wounded. In other words, Odysseus is never innocent and this shows in the *Odyssey* as his being continually in harm's way.[48] He is not innocent (*innocere*) because of his inherent wound that is also the symbolic incorporation of female fecundity.

Odysseus is the one hero—if we must call him that—who had differentiated relations with many female figures and goddesses, relations that furthered his journey making survival possible. It is hard to point at any one of these figures—Wife, Mother, Queen, Nurse, Mistress, Enchantress, or Goddess Athene—as most telling. ("He recognized all these women," concludes Book 22.) There is, however, a subtle seachange in Odysseus after the encounter with Nausicaa, who bears traditional traits of what Jung calls "anima." After bathing in her stream, Odysseus is renewed.[49]

I would suggest that his multiple relations with anima, implied by the scar and the suffering that lie in his name, is the secret of his epithet, *polytropos*, "of many turns," or "turned in many ways" by which he is described in the very first line of the epic.[50] Odysseus is not locked into

---

47. Erich Auerbach, *Mimesis* (Princeton, N.J.: Princeton University Press, 1968), chap. 1: "Odysseus's Scar."

48. Cf. G.E. Dimock, Jr., "The Name of Odysseus," in Charles H. Taylor, Jr., *Essays on the Odyssey* (Bloomington: Indiana University Press, 1963). Dimock derives the name from *odyne*, "to cause pain, and to be willing to do so." Odysseus thus becomes the sufferer, the pained one, and the one who brings suffering and pain. Dimock also suggests the name "Trouble" for Odysseus; others have suggested the "Odd-Man-Out" or "Oddball," "Man of Odium" (hated or angry one), etc.

49. *Odyssey* 6.216f.

50. Cf. W.B. Stanford, *The Odysseus Theme: A Study in the Adaptability of a Traditional*

opposites. He does not suffer from one-sidedness. In him there need be no conflict between senex and puer. His is an "anima" consciousness, which also helps account for his successful descent to the Underworld.

We see an easy commerce between young and old in his special relationship with Nestor (called *senex* in Latin versions) and also with the son of Achilles (called *puer*); as well, there is remarkable love between him and his father and him and his son, Telemachos. Odysseus is emotionally bound in both directions. Only Aeneas, at the beginning of Vergil's *Aenead*,[51] who leads his little son by the hand and carries his lamed father on his back, can be compared to the senex-puer integrity in Odysseus. The very last page of the book has the new day dawn with Odysseus rising and, together with his son, going to join his father.

Of course, it is Athene who helps maintain this integrity. But so does Penelope. For instance, Telemachos says: "My mother says I am his son, I myself do not know: no one of himself knows his own father." Penelope could have told another tale to turn son against father. Instead, she acted as did the mother of Horus, encouraging the son's search for the father's redemption. "One general feature emerges from the study of Odysseus's more intimate personal relationships. He seems to have met none of the suspicion and distrust of his male associates among the women who knew him well."[52] Little wonder that a theory has been put forth that the Odyssey was written by a woman.

It has been said that Odysseus is the most human of the heroes. He certainly does not fit within the divine pattern of the puer or into that of the senex—yet both are present in an array of traits. What "humanizes" the archetypal configuration is the scar. He cannot be only unblemished or bleeding puer. Nor can he be deformed and crippled senex, for the wound has healed. He has been spared by his thigh from the perfections of archetypal identification. Thus, he says flatly that he resembles no god, but is like only to mortal men.[53] He refuses divinization. When Calypso offers to make him immortal and ageless, he chooses the usual

Hero (Thompson, Conn.: Spring Publications, 2022 [1954]), 112.

51. For more on the puer-senex in the *Aenead*, see Stephen Bertman, "The Generation Gap in the Fifth Book of Vergil's *Aenead*," in *The Conflict of Generations in Ancient Greece and Rome* (Amsterdam: Grüner, 1976).

52. Stanford, *The Odysseus Theme*, 74.

53. *Odyssey* 7.208f.

path.[54] "No, I am not a god. Why liken me to the immortals? But I am your father," he says to Telemachos.[55]

A scar is a blemish, a weakness, and from the outset we meet Odysseus as weak. He is no usual hero. The senex qualities of judgment, sobriety, prudence, patience, deviousness, isolation, and suffering are reinforced by yet one more character trait that separates him from the heroes. He is a man of little power. He has no massive army like Achilles, Agamemnon and Menelaus; he contributes but one ship. Nor has he the strength of Ajax and Diomedes. Often, it seems, he'd rather eat than fight. He is not past feigning madness to avoid going to war. It is as if Odysseus proceeds by means of depression. When we first meet him, disconsolate on the shores of Calypso's isle, he broods in melancholy like Saturn and yet with the *pothos* of the sailing wanderer. His most usual disguise is outcast of the islands, ragged beggar, connected with dogs. (Yet as direct descendent of Autolykos and Hermes, he has a slippery kind of puer blood in his veins.) Even his pale alter-ego or double, Telephos, who is also wounded in the thigh, is a man of counsel and does not fight owing to his relation to his wife.[56]

With all this in mind we may turn again to the scene of the nurse washing Odysseus's legs and feet, understanding now this moment of recognition-through-disguise as revelation of essence. The scar by which he is known is the mark of soul in the flesh. It is the seal of anima, the somaticized psyche. His flesh has become wound, just as our flesh "hurts all over" when we enter wounded consciousness. Now, we can see that this generalization of a symptom into the pathologized condition of complaining pain is an attempt at giving full body to the wound by letting the body be fully sensitized by the wound. Odysseus, the pained one, is the personification of pathologized consciousness—like Christ in his way and Dionysus in his. The wounded body has become the embodied wound; and, as embodied, as built into his existence in the leg that carries him and walks with him, his woundedness is also his hidden understanding and grounding support.

---

54. *Odyssey* 5.81, 135, 203–24; 23.335.
55. *Odyssey* 16.187.
56. Graves, *The Greek Myths*, 2:160.

A clue to the nature of this understanding is to be found in Montaigne, who wrote: "So I do not want to forget this further scar, very much unfit to produce in public: irresolution, a most harmful failing in negotiating worldly affairs. I do not know which side to take in doubtful enterprises. 'Nor yes nor no my inmost heart will say' (Petrarch)."[57] The scar reminds consciousness of its wobbling uncertainty, the dark vulnerability in the heart of its light.

VII

Conclusion: The Union of Sames. As we have been elaborating, the open wound belongs with the puer structure; the scarred wound, however, suggests the person whose soul can care for him, the person whose life-blood circulates through his complexes, feeding and washing them, a self-contained eros. Healing is not expected to come from somewhere else. It emerges from the wound's depth and leaves a scar, a scar that is always visible to one's own nurse.

In Odysseus, the senex urge to persist and endure takes care of the puer spirit that is always ready to risk and die. Healing and wounding alternate, or, as healed wound, tender scar, they present the complex image of weak-strength, of soft-hardness. The scar remaining is the remainder, the soft spot recalling the body to its tenderness. The scar acts as a *memento mori,* recollecting the Grandfather and oneself as a Hunting Boy. That scar gets Odysseus through twenty years of unparalleled dangers, like a talisman of dying consciousness, keeping remembrance of death. "Few in the *Iliad* are as conscious as Odysseus of why they are at Troy, and death [to the others] is a recurrent surprise."[58]

This scar could have become a deformity. It could have meant lameness, which characterizes the only-puer or only-senex onesidedness of the archetype. Then the scar would have been the deformity that, as Jung writes,[59] separates father and son, man and boy, large and small. Odysseus, however, is not deformed by onesidedness in as much as he

57. Translated from Montaigne's Essay "Of Presumption," in Philip P. Hallie, *The Scar of Montaigne* (Middletown, Conn.: Wesleyan University Press, 1966). Cf. 130–33, "The Scar."

58. John H. Finley, *Four Stages of Greek Thought* (Stanford: Stanford University Press, 1966), 15.

59. *CW* 5: 184.

signifies the twice-born man: father-with-son, male-with-female, body-with-soul. This initiated consciousness has been discussed elsewhere in regard to *pothos* and the mysteries of Samothrace where Odysseus was said to have been initiated.

Initiation refers to the transition from only-puer consciousness, wounded and bleeding, to *puer-et-senex* consciousness, opened and scarred. It is experienced as well in the transition from the sense of oneself in a story to the sense of oneself as an image, all parts inherent and present at once. Heroic puer consciousness enacts its story, racing forward with its narrative into its denouement. This kind of consciousness can remain invulnerable because the mode of story can put off wounding until the end. Moreover, puer consciousness remains "at the beginnings" because the end is only the puer's sudden undoing and his conversion into the opposite—failed, crippled, ashen. Story tells puer and senex into beginnings and endings, first half and second, keeping green and gray apart. Odysseus's scar, however, builds the wound in all along the way. It belongs to the image of Odysseus, necessary to his very name, and therefore it is not a fatal flaw that brings his fall.

The heroes—Ajax, Theseus, Philoctetes—nursing their hurts have fallen for their stories. Even in the underworld where they are sheer images, they are still stuck in their stories, as if it is essential to the heroic mode never to realize oneself as imaginal even when undergoing the most prodigious exercises of imagination. A separation of puer from hero takes place when one's account of oneself moves from history and epic destiny to imaginative fantasy. Our fiction changes from epic and tragic to comic or picaresque. Simply by moving out of its story, consciousness may move out of the heroic mode.

We might extend this thought further by saying, along with Patricia Berry and David L. Miller,[60] that story consciousness will set us up as heroic *pueri,* fatefully leading us into the woundedness that is inherent to the story but comes at its end. "Ourselves as epic stories" might well be a good way of defining the puer neurosis. Then we must go to therapy

---

60. Cf. Patricia Berry, "An Approach to the Dream," *Spring: An Annual of Archetypal Psychology and Jungian Thought* (1974): 68–71; David L. Miller, "Fairy Tale or Myth," *Spring: An Annual of Archetypal Psychology and Jungian Thought* (1976): 157–64.

to "reversion"[61] the story, that is, to integrate the symptoms by discovering their inherent necessity. This discovery takes us out of story and into image, for we realize that the wound, like that of Odysseus, has been inherent to us all along, a realization that turns wound into scar. In other words, image consciousness heals. The sense of ourselves as images in which all parts belong and are co-relatively necessary keeps ends and beginnings together,[62] like the wound remembered by the scar.

"Much in the *Odyssey* suggests that it is an old man's poem. Its analogue is Shakespeare's *Tempest*...a world shared, so to speak, between the old Prospero on one side and the young lovers and the beauty of nature on the other...The battered Odysseus has sympathy for old people who have endured as much as he...but the young Telemachus and Nausicaa give freshest renewal, and the green islands of his travels confirm nature's persisting youth...It is the old and the young who jointly effect the marvel of life made new, as if Homer were conscious of the transformation and in some part saw himself now in Odysseus."[63] The sea, ever-renewing and freshening, yet the oldest father, Okeanos, is background to both the *Tempest* and the *Odyssey,* and finally from this sea will come Odysseus's death.[64] The sea, the great long poem, Homer, Odysseus, are each "ever young yet full of eld" (Spenser). Is this why that figure, Odysseus, "thigh-wound," continues to shape himself again and again in our Western imagination?[65]

There are many reasons for the imaginal power of Odysseus, but surely a major part of his greatness is that Odysseus resolved a morbid division fundamental to the Western psyche. The major genealogical

---

61. "Reversioning" is a term I have borrowed from Edward S. Casey's phenomenological investigation of memory. Cf. "The Fiction of Case History," in my *Healing Fiction*.

62. According to the ancient Pythagorean physician, Alcmaion of Croton: "Men die because they cannot join the beginning to the end."

63. Finley, *Four Stages*, 11-12.

64. Odysseus does not die in the *Odyssey,* but the post-Homeric tradition, especially in the Latin Middle Ages, told the Trojan legends mainly according to the version of Dictys of Crete (in *The Trojan War,* translated by R.M. Frazer (Bloomington, Indiana: Indiana University Press, 1966). In these tales, Odysseus has a dream of death coming from the sea that is fulfilled by the arrival on the shores of Ithaca of his son (by Circe) Telegonos, who then in an unwitting battle between father and son kills Odysseus with a special spear.

65. W.B. Stanford and J.V. Luce, *Quest for Odysseus* (London: Phaidon, 1977).

myth of Uranos, Kronos, and Zeus the youngest son—leaving aside the Biblical patriarchs and their sons—is present in all the wrenching horror of the father-son, puer-senex struggle.[66] Our torturing battles with our fathers and with our sons was raised by Freud to the central explanation of our culture and our soul. That this struggle between senex and puer is at the heart of our culture has also been attested to by Christian doctrine, which insists that recognition of the unity of Father and Son is the way of redemption. But that very union of sames is threatened by the Son's last words on the cross, perhaps a residue of puer consciousness not joined with the Father.[67]

Odysseus is not in this dilemma, and the entire *Odyssey* holds senex and puer together, as at the end in the most obvious and heroic climax Odysseus and Telemachos battle side by side against the common enemy who would take Penelope from them. But the union of sames is also more subtly woven through the whole text. It gives us Homer's answer—or is it Odysseus's answer—to this unbearable psychic affliction.

The last scene of rejoining Odysseus with his home takes place with old Laertes, his father, wearing a tattered tunic and goatskin hat, hoeing alone in a briar patch: Saturn, the gardener, squalid and in mourning. Until now, Odysseus had always been father, and Telemachos, the son, in search of the father. But now at the end,[68] facing Laertes so perfectly sketched in his outcast senex condition, Odysseus is son, remembering the wound, the hunt, and the garden of his youth. And by these signs he is known.[69] As *senex-et-puer,* Odysseus comes home, and his odyssey tells the tale of the diversified, polytropic process of homecoming.

---

66. For listings and discussions of these struggles, see Bertman, *Conflict of Generations,* 22–23 et passim. On the relation of the classic myths to Freud, there are interesting comments by Mark D. Altschule, *Roots of Modern Psychiatry* (New York/London: Grune and Stratton, 1957), 162.

67. Matthew (27: 46) and Mark (15: 34) attest that the last words were the cry of being forsaken by the Father; Luke (23: 46) does not mention this cry, but instead re-unites Father and Son: "Father, into thy hands I commend my spirit." It is noteworthy that the ambiguity about the Father-Son relation is itself reinforced by the variant accounts of the last words.

68. Cf. Dorothea Wender, *The Last Scenes of the Odyssey* (Leiden: E.J. Brill, 1978).

69. *Odyssey* 24.327ff.

First published in 1979 in *Puer Papers* and
emended for this edition.

Puer's Wounded Wing:
Reflections on the Psychology of Skin Disease

RANDOLPH SEVERSON

Active ambition is a skin disease of the soul.
—Nietzsche

Carl Jung said that the gods have become diseases.[1] From the practice
of therapy he had learned that in the curtained coolness of the consulting room the gods appear just as they once did in the healing temples of the ancient Greeks. Paled by the presences, Jung realized that if
he could know to which deity a disease must be offered, then he might
become a medium through which a god spoke and thereby healed a
reluctant votary who had until that moment seen himself only as a
manic, a depressive or even a schizophrenic. Jung phrased his insight
in this way: "To serve a mania is detestable and undignified, but to serve
a god is full of meaning.[2]

Not all share Jung's wisdom, his knowledge of things divine. Our consciousness is much more Biblical than Greek. How foreign to our souls,
how unconscious, for example, is the acute ability of Achilles to discern precisely who among the Immortals had caught him by his golden
hair when be reached for his sword. Homer says: "Achilles in amazement turned about, and straightway knew Pallas Athene and the terrible eyes shining."[3] The modern psyche is much more akin to the Hebrew
prophet Samuel who when he heard the voice of Jahweh murmuring in
the rustling leaves of a midnight wind thought it was his father snoring,

---

1. *CW*13: 54.
2. *CW*13: 55.
3. Homer, *Iliad* 1.199–200 (trans. Richmond Lattimore).

not once but three times! If a true *therapeia* depends so much on the discernment of what Sophocles called the divine destiny of & disease, then what are we who come from Samuel's line to do?

Of course the problem is overstated. The Greeks did not always know straightway who the god in the disease was; instead, they asked the oracles "to which god must I sacrifice in order to be healed?" And St. Paul taught that the discrimination of spirits was one of the gifts of the Christian Holy Ghost. Even so, as Dodds points out, had any cultivated pagan of the Hellenistic Age been asked about the difference between his own view of life and the Christian one. he might well have replied that it was the difference between *logismos* and *pistis*.[4] (Dodds is emphatic that the main issue between paganism and Christianity "was not a debate between monotheism and polytheism."[5]) To the Greeks, *pistis*, which the Christians defiantly made the rock upon which they built their church, was the very lowest grade of cognition, the state of mind of the uneducated. "There is nothing in your philosophy beyond the one word 'Believe,'" exclaimed the Emperor Julian, who probably knew the Christians better than anyone. To the pagan eye, the Christians enjoyed courage, will, belief, and desire but they lacked *phronesis*, discrimination, the knowledge of the soul. The pagans, however, despite their glorious tradition, had lost their nerve. Even the priestess of Delphi did not have much to say or so she told the emissary of Julian. Jung knew that if healing is to occur in the knee-to-knee encounter of patient and therapist, then not only psychological knowledge, an eye that sees that all things are full of gods, is necessary, but also psychological faith, the faith in the reality of the psyche given to Jung by the dream of the descending dove.

"What has Athens got to do with Jerusalem?" Tertullian thundered centuries ago. The answer is Alexandria and alchemy. Alexandria, with her famous library of 700,000 manuscripts, was the fourth great city of the ancient world. During her zenith she had more than one million inhabitants, but by the last years of the rationalist nineteenth century Alexandria had become little more than a village where a few shopkeepers watched their children play among the crumbling ruins of the

---

4. E.R. Dodds, *Pagan and Christian in an Age of Anxiety* (New York: Norton Library, 1965), 120.
5. Ibid., 116.

library. Still, the mysterious city remains buried deep in the imagination. Yeats dug deep enough to uncover Holy Byzantium but below even Byzantium lies Alexandria. Once upon a time through the winding and crowded streets of Alexandria walked neo-Platonist and Christian believers, intently listening to the rambling ravings of one of the practitioners of the *opus divinum.* Alexandria was the home of Ammonius Saccas, a veiled figure who has vanished into the air of scholarly fantasy. At the feet of Ammonius sat both Plotinus and the great Christian theologian Origen. Not much else is known about this strange man. Scholars have seen in Ammonius a Buddhist monk, and a somewhat unorthodox Christian writer.[6] I believe that Ammonius Saccas was an alchemist because it is in an alchemical image that all these strands of fantasy can be woven together, Many times neo-Platonist philosophers and members of the sect who ate their god must have met behind a locked door. inscribed with the signs of the zodiac, in a room filled with bubbling retorts and strange colored fires. It was surely in rooms such as these that the soul had its singing school, and studied monuments of its own magnificence.

---

6. *The Cambridge History of Later Greek and Early Medieval Philosophy,* edited by A.H. Armstrong (Cambridge: Cambridge University Press, 1970), 197. Enormous controversy still surrounds Ammonius. Porphyry, whose testimony is suspect since he certainly had an ax to grind, says that Ammonius was born of Christian parents but later converted to the Greek religion. Of his education nothing is known. William Ralph Inge believes that he was self-educated. We do know that Ammonius had an extraordinary impact on Plotinus. In describing his youthful search for a true teacher, one well versed in the mysteries of existence, Plotinus says of Ammonius. "This is the man I was looking for." There is even some question about whether the Origen taught by Ammonius was the Christian Origen, although both Armstrong and Dodds are content to believe that he was. Cf. Armstrong's discussion cited above, and Dodds, *Pagan and Christian in an Age of Anxiety,* 106. It is probably best to say with Rist that "Exactly what these pupils learned from Ammonius we do not know"; J.M. Rist, *Plotinus: The Road to Reality* (Cambridge: Cambridge University Press, 1967), 5. For two of the discussions of the Ammonius question, see K.H.C. DeJong, *Plotinus of Ammonius Saccas* (Leiden: Brill, 1941), and E.R. Dodds, "Numenius and Ammonius," in *Les Sources de Plotin,* Fondation Hardt, *Entretiens* 5 (Vandoeuvres and Geneva, 1960). For our purposes these arguments are soul barometers, measuring the fantasy pressure of the image. Ammonius taught in Alexandria, a city which is not on any map, for as Melville said, true places never are.

Another in the Alexandrian line was Paracelsus. Paracelsus, the alchemist, who once confessed "that I write like a pagan and yet am a Christian."[7] Paracelsus never bothered with the apparent contradiction between paganism and Christianity; the White Woman[8] and the Red Slave lived together in a true domestic bliss within the bridal chamber of Paracelsus's psyche. The conflict between these two visions of reality was to give many of Paracelsus's followers a multitude of sleepless nights, especially Gerhard Dorn. It did not worry Paracelsus though. He no doubt felt all the spit and fire was the sign of a lovers' spat, fully aware himself that each vision added a necessary something to what was simmering in the retort.

Jung, too, was advised of how the Greek and Biblical psyches melted and flowed into one another when put in the vessel and placed on the fire. Jung on most occasions spoke of alchemy as if it were primarily a Christian heresy, to be understood principally as a compensation to official Church dogma. Tucked away, however, in a footnote in *Mysterium Coniunctionis* is a story told by Jung about Asclepius. At the end of the tale Jung commented briefly on the relationship between Greek mythology and alchemy and said that "alchemy, although the alchemists did not know it, was a child of this mythology."[9]

In alchemical fantasy, the union of the Red Slave with the White Woman, the marriage of Christian Spiritus and Greek Psyche, gives birth to psychological consciousness. Through his numerous studies and case histories, Jung demonstrated that the inner alchemist is still alive and dreaming in all of us, even if we be for the most part unconscious of his presence. Scratch the surface of the skin and you will find an alchemist. For moderns, a sorcerer's apprenticeship in an alchemical laboratory could provide a way through Samuel's dilemma. The alchemist can instruct us on how to recognize the archetypal personages who announce themselves, as Jahweh once did to the Prophet, in an unexpected way. The analyst trained in alchemical fantasy can discern the

---

7. *CW*13:148.

8. Armstrong, *Cambridge History*, 443. The appearance of the White Woman in the dreams of many early Christians may be a compensation for the repression of Greek imagery. What we deny in our waking life returns in our dreams.

9. *CW*14:122n.157.

coming and going of the gods in the changing colors, smells, and sounds of the base elements of the psyche, which are now called complexes. By sniffing the sulphurous air that surrounds a complex the analyst will know which gods are there. In a jar in the alchemist's laboratory is preserved the Greek gift of recognizing the god in the disease. The gift of the Christian spirit to the laboratory is a blazing fire that keeps the temperature so incredibly hot—"He who is near me is near the fire" says Christ in one of the uncanonical sayings-that images can never solidity into idols; that is, their hermetic qualities are kept alive. If an image is to be a guide of souls, a psychopompos, as Hermes was said to be, then it must stay moist and fluid. It must be kept on the fire.[10]

In what follows alchemy is the method. A pathology is to be cooked in the imagination until the fluttering fantasies congealed in it bubble and boil and appear on the surface of the retort. The *prima materia* in this case is an unpleasant and unsightful skin disorder: neurodermatitis. To the material the hot explosive sulphur of individual fantasy shall be added first. Next comes the dry, briny salt of literature that will prevent the brew from bubbling over by drawing the vapors back down to earth, the bottom of the vessel. The quicksilver of myth will set the vapors rising again to create a *circulatio* as the wildly spinning fantasies begin to move into an orbit around a central theme. More than this cannot be promised since the vessel is no crystal ball. Alchemy is not magic.

WHAT IS THE MATTER

In 1935, Joseph Klauder remarked: "The psyche exerts a greater influence on the skin than any other organ."[11] D.W. Winnicott has said that

---

10. The importance of the fiery spirit to authentic psychological work has been pointed out time and time again by James Hillman. One of the direct statements appears in his article "The Great Mother, Her Son, Her Hero, and the Puer" in *Fathers and Mothers: Five Papers on the Archetypal Background of Family Psychology*, edited by Patricia Berry (Dallas: Spring Publications, 1973), 84. [Reprinted in *UE3: Senex & Puer.*] There Hillman says: "Psychology is not dissolution into psychic magic; psychology is a *logos* of the psyche; it requires spirit." Also see his "Anima (II)," *Spring: An Annual of Archetypal Psychology and Jungian Thought* (1974): 145: "...psychology cannot omit spirit from its purview. The syzygy says that where soul goes there goes spirit too."

11. Joseph V. Klauder, "Psychogenic Aspects of Diseases of the Skin," *Archives of Neurology and Psychiatry* 33 (1935): 221.

"the smallest skin lesion...concerns the whole personality."[12] Since Freud, it has become generally accepted that the skin can function as an object of intense libidinal attachment. The skin can bear a multiplicity of psychic meanings. Experienced by almost everyone, the intimate link between soul and skin is obvious. Psyche unveils herself in pale, cold, damp foreheads, hot flushed checks, sweaty palms, tingling, prickling goose-pimples. The skin is a peacock's tail, blackening, reddening, whitening, purpling with emotion. Thass-Thienemann notes that "the skin is for these reasons like a screen upon which repressed fantasies become projected."[13] Because the connection between the fantasy soul and the surface of the skin is so immediately given, it occurred to experimentalists to devise a technological method for flushing out the secrets of Psyche when she herself would prefer to remain hidden behind a white veil. The result of the experimental fantasy on skin and soul is the Galvanic Skin Response test (G.S.R.).

Since the laboratory is the place of this opus, let us consider this laboratory phenomenon before actually initiating the alchemical work. The G.S.R. is a method used to detect the existence of hidden or repressed psychic meanings by measuring the intensity of electrical current which shoots across the surface of the skin. The experimenter attaches two electrodes to his subject and then introduces prepared stimuli into the situation, noting the subject's response by means of the deflection of a needle on a galvanometer. When a complex is touched, the needle records its existence as an increase in electrical current. In fact the experiment is now called the electrodermal test. Charles Féré, who invented the G.S.R. in 1888, thought the phenomenon was due to static electricity generated by dry skin, but it is now known that the current intensifies because when a complex is touched, small drops of sweat appear on the skin's surface thus making the skin a better conductor. What is important in

12. Eric Wittkower and Brian Russell, *Emotional Factors in Skin Disease: A Psychosomatic Medicine Monograph* (New York: Paul B. Hoeber, 1953), 23. In addition to this text, two other books that are important for understanding the psychology of skin disease are: W.J. O'Donovan, *Dermatological Neuroses* (London: Kegan Paul, 1927), and Maximilian E. Obermayer, *Psychocutaneous Medicine* (Springfield, Ill.: Charles C. Thomas, 1955).

13. Theodore Thass-Thienemann, *The Interpretation of Language*, vol. 1: *Understanding the Symbolic Meaning of Language* (New York: Jason Aronson, 1968), 214.

this context is that the experimental fantasy binds together electricity and skin, suggesting that it is the crackling current in the complexes that appears on the skin.[14] In fact, one observer has described the manifestation of psychic conditions in the skin as a " sparking over" from mind to body surface.[15]

Although the G.S.R. was utilized by other psychologists, it was really Jung who, along with Peterson in 1907, first demonstrated that the G.S.R. could be used as a "complex indicator."[16] Jung said that "the galvanic phenomenon, like reaction-time and alteration of reproductions, may give evidence of an unconscious complex."[17] In the paper he co-authored with Peterson (which is still deemed a major contribution by experimental psychologists), Jung reported on how he came to this discovery. While working with the G.S.R., he was surprised by a sudden deflection of the needle when the stimulus, phrase "sun/burns" was offered to the subject. Further research indicated that the phrase was but the tip of a network of feeling-toned ideas—a complex. Is there not an archetypal image here that tells us something about what it is in the soul that touches the skin? Jung's discovery came as a consequence of an electrical spark plunging through the beads of sweat, the salt water sea, on the skin after the "sun burns." Is not this the story of Icarus, who fell into the ocean because the sun burned his wings? If so, then perhaps it is the Icarus-winged spirit, the *puer aeternus,* who lives a special relationship to the organ of the skin. Emma Jung believed that the spirit could leave its mark on any organ.[18] The crackling current in a complex is the puer spirit.

---

14. For a discussion of the many fantasies that constellate around the theme of electricity, see Ernst Benz, *The Theology of Electricity: On the Encounter and Explanation of Theology and Science in the 17th and 18th Centuries,* translated by Wolfgang Taraba (Eugene, Or.: Pickwick Publications, 2009).

15. H. Musaph, *Itching and Scratching: Psychodynamics in Dermatology* (Basel and New York: S. Karger, 1964).

16. Jung's study of the G.S.R., which includes a brief history of the test, is found in *CW* 2:1015-35. For another view of the phenomenon, see Robert S. Woodworth and Harold Schlosberg, *Experimental Psychology* (London: Methuen & Co.; New York: Holt, Rinehart and Winston, 1961), 133-60.

17. *CW* 2:1136.

18. Emma Jung, *Animus and Anima: Two Essays* (Thompson: Spring Publications, 2022), 14.

The stars are right: it is time to commence cooking. As already stated, the specific skin problem to be touched on here is neurodermatitis, a painful and embarrassing psychosomatic illness. The skin breaks out into a scaly crusty rash, which comes and goes, appearing now in one place and then in another. Sometimes the rash will vanish for long periods of time, only to be resurrected whenever victims finds themselves in a stressful situation. The rash burns; neurodermatitis is a skin inflammation, a fire in the skin, a flickering flame licking the delicate surface of the flesh until a pus-pouring sore begins to form. The rash can flare up anywhere on the body: scalp, groin, arms, knees, or face. Frequently the sufferer will scratch until the wound bleeds and becomes infected. Kolb notes in his introductory text that this unbearable itching "often represents a voluptuous or tantalizing sensation so that the rash seems to be experienced as if it had a sexual component."[19] Dry, red, scaly, burning, itching sensations in the flesh and scratching, scratching, scratching until the fingernails are worn away.

After a generalized description of the affliction, it is customary in psychiatric literature to include a case study. This ritual must be adhered to, but there is a great danger in moving too fast at this stage of the *opus*. The temperature of the *materia* must not rise too quickly lest the container shatter. The pathology should be allowed to soak in. While watching the stove and the soaking, simmering stew, let each recall the chapped lips, prickly heat, chigger bites, boils, chafed windburned cheeks, summer rashes, acne, infected knee sores, dandruff, sunburn, peeling tans, and pus-filled sores which are the doors into the house of neurodermatitis.

SULPHUR: THE RASH, THE WING, AND THE LITTLE PRINCE

Case histories always ignite a few fantasies. The case history to be studied here is thieved from Franz Alexander's classic text *Psychosomatic Medicine*.[20] Our story begins with a young, white girl, aged twenty-two, who was referred to psychotherapy for treatment of severe recurrent

---

19. Lawrence Coleman Kolb, *Modern Clinical Psychiatry* (Philadelphia: W.B. Saunders, 1977), 585.

20. Franz Alexander, *Psychosomatic Medicine: Its Principles and Applications* (New York: W.W. Norton, 1950), 166–68; the case is J.P. Spiegel's.

bouts of neuro-dermatitis. The lesions flared on the face as well as upon the upper and lower extremities. They consisted of discrete, red, raw, itching areas. Because of the frightful itching, the young girl frequently scratched until the wounds wept and bled, and this was particularly likely to happen during sleep. Due to the incessant scratching, the girl had become quite disfigured. Having been told by a number of physicians that the lesions were a consequence of emotional disturbances, she decided to see a psychoanalyst.

The skin problems had come and gone all through the patient's life, originally appearing as eczema only a week after her birth. Her mother had been very upset during the pregnancy by the accidental death of her seven-year-old son, and by the subsequent desertion of the father. As the girl grew up, she and her mother moved from place to place. Shy and socially backward at school, the patient was nevertheless exceptionally bright in her studies. At college she blossomed out and became popular. Following graduation, the girl found a satisfactory job and began to form intense sexual attachments to men which were always broken off with the resurrection of the rash.

After some time in therapy this cycle was brought to a close by "the appearance of a masculine protest, much attention to her job, a turning away from close ties to men and women, and a lightening of affect and clearing of the skin."[21] With insight into the "repetitive pattern" of her life the patient was able to form a relationship with the man she ultimately married; the skin lesions disappeared and did not recur.

Jung sometimes spoke of archetypes as "repetitive patterns." Archetypes are styles of consciousness, patterns of behavior, forms of fantasy. To which archetype should this case be referred? Perhaps it is the puer. The rash itself resembles the puer. Like the rash, the puer comes and goes and is always on the move; one might imagine a handsome youth disappearing into the dark body of the forest, only to be glimpsed on rare occasions by city folk. The rash is a superficial disorder, that is, it stays on the surface of the body, never setting down any roots that would endanger the more important organs. The puer also refuses to set down any roots. He is cityless and homeless, an exiled vagabond eter-

---

21. Ibid., 167.

nally wandering across the dry open spaces of the earth. Lastly, the rash is a skin inflammation with a sexual reference, an erotic flame, young Eros bearing a torch

Other puer charms in the patient's story should be noted. The case begins with a striking image of a young boy meeting an early death, and, perhaps, soaring back to his home through the spheres of the seven planetary governors. I suspect that the spirit of this Little Prince presides over the inner galaxy of this young woman. Doomed to wander, following the father's desertion, the story repeats a familiar mytheme in puer lives: spirit wandering. Shy and socially backward, yet bright in her studies, the patient resembles the archetypal puer, Hippolytus, who surely would have been out of place at a school dance, but, as Theseus says, took Orpheus as his King and worshipped the "vaporings of many a scroll." Probably both the patient and Hippolytus often burned the midnight oil as they poured over romantic poetry and esoteric philosophy. At college, however, the young lady "blossomed" out-which should not be unexpected since universities have habitually furnished a place for the pothos of flower children to bloom. The numerous affairs, direct and unmediated, signal like a red light the feeling lacuna of the puer complex.

The psychoanalyst reports that the bleeding rashes dematerialized in the course of therapy. If the "puer diagnosis" is accurate, then it might be possible to learn something about the proper destiny of the spirit from the study of the case. The rash vanishes when there is " a lightening of affect," that is, when the soul regains its puer wings. Once the winged spirit is liberated, then he is free and able to go about his father's business, which in this instance is called the development of "masculine protest" and "much attention to her job." Despite the clearing of the skin, the puer remains the puer. The healing is synchronous with "a turning away from close ties to men and women": the puer seems fated to go it alone. Even so, this does not necessarily indicate a faulty feeling function. After all, one can certainly feel his fate. In addition to being with the father, there is another possible destiny for the puer once his wounded wing is healed, or so the case intimates. The wing may be healed by a coniunctio—a marriage.

From the seething material in the retort an image has now come forth. One image of skin disease is that of a Broken Wing. Expressed conceptually, this means that neurodermatitis is the mark of a wounded puer consciousness, a windhover spirit who cannot fly and therefore cannot fulfill his fate. Using traditional language, skin disease might be simply called the stigmata of the Spirit. To name a raw, red rash the stigmata of the Spirit is by no means to romanticize psychosomatic pathology. Skin disorders and stigmata have always been imagined as belonging on the same continuum. Under the heading "Stigmata," *The New Schaff-Herzog Religious Encyclopedia*, for example, says: "The phenomenon is one that is known outside of religious circles. The exudation of blood through the skin is recognized by the medical profession and is described in many books on dermatology."[22] In order for neurodermatitis to reveal its archetypal value, we must reverse the natural perspective and view neurodermatitis as a sign of spirit rather than reducing all tales of stigmatization to dermatological cases.

Long ago, at a time when a sufferer from bleeding rashes on the hands and feet might claim that the marks were stigmata, there was a necessity for noting the visions which accompanied the materialization of the wounds. On the testimony of these visions the truth of the claim was ruled upon. What were some of the fantasies? The most famous of the cases of stigmatization recorded by the Church is that of St. Francis. According to Thomas de Celano, who published his biography of the Saint only a few years after the death of St. Francis, the stigmatization happened on 14 September 1224, during the Festival of the Elevation of the Holy Cross,[23] With a few friends and disciples St. Francis had gone to a mountain retreat and there he dreamed a vision of a seraphim, with six wings, being crucified. Two wings were raised above the head, two were outstretched for flying and two covered the body. After St. Francis felt a brief rapture, the angel departed, leaving behind a "fleshy excrescence" that covered the hands, feet, and side. St. Francis is said to have "revealed this secret to few or none." Like most who suffer from eczem-

---

22. *The New Schaff-Herzog Encyclopedia of Religious Knowledge*, edited by Samuel Macauley Jackson, with the assistance of Charles Colebrook Sherman and George William Gilmore, 12 vols. (New York and London: Funk and Wagnalls Company, 1911), 11:96.

23. For a detailed report on St. Francis's stigmatization, see the *Encyclopedia of Religion and Ethics*, edited by James Hastings, 13 vols. (New York: Charles Scribner's Sons, 1908–21),

atous rashes that exude blood and pus, he must have kept his hands in his pockets.

In the image of the Crucified Angel with trapped wings, the two concepts of skin disorders as the mark of the wounded puer consciousness and as the stigmata of the spirit unite. In his "Visions Seminars," Jung recounted several dreams and images similar to that of St. Francis.[24] The woman whose individuation process provided the gross matter of the study dreamed once of pulling thongs and arrows out of the body of a young man. In the next vision the figure becomes the winged Icarus who chooses not to fly off to the sun, although he is apparently free to do so, but to serve the feminine soul instead. Linking this *angelos* to the skin is the next vision. The text reads: "I was descending many steps into the black earth until I came at last to a catacomb...I came to a dead man whose *flesh was red*" (my italics). Angel and red rash go together. Jung titled the section which includes these dreams and visions "The Imprisoned Animus" and remarked that the liberation of this spirit marked an important stage of the woman's psychic development.

At this stage it is timely to ask why the puer chooses the skin and not the bowels or the liver or the heart as the living canvas on which it paints its pathology. The astrological and homeopathic traditions have always insisted that there is a specific psychic connection between each of the body parts and organs, and particular stars, planets, and deities. This is the microcosm-macrocosm fantasy. The puer chooses the skin because the skin is in many ways the most visible of the organs and the puer demands that his wounds be visible, out there in the open. Each morning the puer is drawn to the mirror to gaze not upon his beauty, as did Narcissus, but upon his skin sores. Touching the rash, popping the pimples, stroking the sores; the puer wants to see what is wrong with him. The puer does not, however, necessarily desire others to see the rash, that is, he is not always an exhibitionist. When he gets to school, the rash will more than likely be covered with a cream or clothing. Neither Narcissus nor exhibitionist, the puer says with Shelley: "I fall upon the thorns of life, I bleed," and he knows he is hurt, wounded and bleeding because he can see the blood on the surface of the skin.

---

24. C.G. Jung, *The Visions Seminars: From the Complete Notes of Mary Foote,* 2 vols. (Zurich: Spring Publications, 1976), 1: 239–47.

Can we agree that neurodermatitis is visibility of the Broken Wing of the spirit? Has the opus touched the soul of the reader and made it, too, an element in the vessel? There is still the question of prognosis. Will the spirit rise again on wings lighter than the air? The planet whose signature is neurodermatitis—is it a burning or a dying star? The question is important, for there are some puer spirits who, upon falling from the inner firmament, are content to give up and dissolve into the primal sludge, all the while mumbling platitudes about decay being inherent in all living things. One way to sidle up to this prognosis question is by investigating the clichés that are concerned with itching. It is through cliches that pathology enters the psyches of those who do not literally suffer from the disease. Jung said that archetypes are first and foremost figures of speech,[25] which may be taken to mean that cliches are archetypes and archetypes are clichés. Many clichés about itching dot our language: itching to get started, itching to move, itching to go, itching with ambition are just a few examples. No wonder the latin verb *prurio* means both to itch and to long for a thing.[26] Our clichés can persuade us of the truth of etymologies and vice-versa. An image comes of a fair skinned youth with blonde curling locks, nursing its wounded wing but at the same time bursting with uncathected energy, glowing and reddening (reddening too soon an alchemist would say) with libido. This puer is like the American Icarus Grope, who says: "I am just biding my time and waiting for the day when my 'soul' will ignite, and this inner fire will send me hurtling (two rungs at a time) up the ladder."[27] Who does the angel with the itching, burning wing long for? The case study of the young girl indicated that the puer desires both a Father and a Bride. Without them the wound continues to fester with fever, growing worse and worse. The prognosis is uncertain: to be cured the puer must seek out those who have caused the affliction. He has the energy to do it, as well as the desire. The puer seeks the Father and the Bride; he must hope that they are the ones who have caused his suffering. Are they?

---

25. *CW* 9.1:157. In Hull's translation, the quote actually reads: "An archetypal content expresses itself first and foremost, in metaphors."

26. Thass-Thienemann, *The Interpretation of Language*, 217.

27. Henry A. Murray, "American Icarus," in this volume.

SALTING THE WOUND: ORESTES, JOB, AND SONS
WITH WHOM THE FATHER IS NOT SO WELL PLEASED

The active Sulphur has sparked not a few fantasies which have rapidly risen to the skies of the retort, there to thunder and lightning or to dance through the wispy vapors like an Arabian dancing girl. A healthy dose of salt is required to bring the clouds back down to the earth sitting at the bottom of the vessel. The fantasy of neurodermatitis as the wounded wing of a puer's unfulfilled obligation to the senex father must be cooled and condensed. The fantasy must be given the body that literature can provide.

Aeschylus can supply the requisite materials. Let us reminisce for a moment about the *Oresteia*. It will be recalled that Orestes is charged by Apollo to avenge Agamemnon's murder. This means that Clytemnestra must be slain. To serve the father Orestes must drive a bloody sword deep into the maternal body. Should Orestes leave the shade of his father unappeased, should Agamemnon howl in Hades for a blood libation that is never offered, then Apollo makes quite clear what will follow. Orestes repeats what the god has told him:

> Apollo will not break his faith, by whose
> Almighty oracles I am commanded
> To take on me this hazard. Loud and long
> His prophetess predicted chilly blasts
> Of pestilence to turn the heart's blood cold,
> If I should fail to seek those murderers out
> And put them to the death my father died,
> Their lives for his...
> Or else the penalty, he said, would fall
> On my own soul—a host of horrors, some
> Sent up from earth by the resentful dead,
> Which he named thus, ulcers to mount the flesh
> With ravenous jaws and eat the substance up,
> And out of them a crop of hoary hairs;
> And worse, he told me of the fierce assault
> Of Furies, sprung out of a father's blood.[28]

---

28. Aeschylus, *Choëphoroe*, translated by George Thomson, in *An Anthology of Greek Drama: Second Series*, edited by Charles Alexander Robinson, Jr. (New York: Holt, Rinehart and Winston, 1954), 44.

The message is clear: the most gruesome ulcers creeping like worms through the flesh are the deserts of refusing to go about the father's bloody business.

Orestes is important to our project in another respect. It would be uncomfortably easy to mistake Orestes for a hero instead of a puer. Skin disease would then seem to be the mark of the Hero instead of the Angel.[29] Yet Orestes is *not* a hero and the *Oresteia* is not a night sea journey! Heroic consciousness is primarily concerned with the world of matter. Heracles must continually labor to save and clean up the material world. It is the fate of Ganymede, on the other hand, to serve the gods; Zeus absolves him of all terrestrial duties. The puer belongs to the spirit world, the *archai* of the imaginal cosmos. Orestes is much more like Ganymede than like Heracles, for he is first and foremost a libation bearer, serving the spirits who roam the netherworld. The hero believes only in what he can see and touch, despising the phantasms of the underworld. The *puer aeternus* responds to the hero with Orestes's words: "To me they are no fancies—only too clear."[30]

Clytemnestra dreams of Orestes as a young snake who bites her nipple, drawing blood and water; thus she connects her son to the *eidola* of Hades, since they, too, in antiquity were imagined as snakes.[31] A serpent among serpents, Orestes moves freely. Here begins the analyst's fantasy of the puer as a snake in the grass. Cold, slippery, furtive, the puer sheds his skin and wriggles out of the analytical grasp. But where does he go? Into those holes, perhaps, which were thought by the Greeks to be entrances to the under-world. It is precisely his slipperiness which lets him slide out of reality, through the holes that open into the imaginal world. And underneath the skin he leaves behind, empty in our hands, is a new skin. Mottled and scabby at first, this tender new skin

---

29. For a careful discrimination between the hero and the puer angel, see Hillman's "The Great Mother, Her Son, Her Hero, and the Puer."

30. George Devereux in his *Dreams in Greek Tragedy: An Ethno-Psycho-Analytical Study* (Berkeley and Los Angeles: University of California Press, 1976), devotes two chapters to Clytemnestra's dream; see 171–218. Devereux ties together the serpent, the son, the father, and the dead in this quote: "Since both Orestes (in dream) and the dead (chthonian) Agamemnon are 'snakes,' they are equivalent in every significant respect"; 191.

31. Aeschylus, *Choëphoroe*, 67.

must heal not in the light of analysis, but in the dark and shadowy world of *phantasia.*

Someone else from the past had problems with the father complex. He, however, was not so lucky as Orestes and ended up bedeviled with boils. "My skin is broken and become loathsome,"[32] says Job. Since Job failed to comprehend the mysterious ways of the Father Who is in Heaven, he found himself sitting in the ashes, scraping and scratching the blood from his blisters. Although Job was a just man (he had a strong ego), his spirit was not with God. Because of this, he itched terribly. Alluding to the misery of Job, St. Augustine recollects a time when his inner angel did not know God. He says: the spirit "did not grow healthy, but it was ulcered over, and cast outside itself and in its misery was avid to be scratched."[33] When Job let his spirit fly to God and meditate on the mysteries of the Lord's majestic creation, his flesh ulcers melted away.

RISING MERCURY: A SON, A LOVER AND THE WING AGAIN

The fantasies have indeed congealed into the images of Orestes and Job. One Greek and one Biblical: a nice combination for an alchemist to make. Through these images it has been shown that the affliction of skin lesions does belong to the father, and so—since the puer does desire the father—healing becomes a promising possibility. The puer naturally longs to love and know more fully that which has made him ill; the prognosis is therefore favorable. However, we wish to keep the fantasies of neurodermatitis fluid and alive. Other seasonings should be added to the brewing pot or we will have nothing more than a dry, tasteless interpretation of skin disease, which would locate neurodermatitis in a faulty puer-senex relationship. While this is true, there are still a few more truths to come, all of which revolve around the image of the Wounded Wing. Let's add a little quicksilver.

One of the most famous puer in mythology is Icarus, whom we have discovered in the Galvanic Skin Response test. Icarus was the son of Daedalus. Daedalus, or so the story goes, was jealous of one of his helpers in the workshop and so he killed him. Forced to flee from Athens to Crete, Daedalus eventually managed to offend the King in the land

---

32. Job 7:5.

33. St. Augustine, *The Confessions,* translated by John K. Ryan (New York: Image Books, 1960), 77.

of his exile and was imprisoned along with his son Icarus. In his soli-
tude Daedalus designed a pair of wings for both Icarus and himself so
that they could fly across the wide waters which surrounded the prison
tower. Daedalus severely cautioned his young son not to fly too close to
the chariot of Helios or the wax which held his wings together would
certainly melt. Once in flight, however, the boy flagrantly disobeyed his
father and soared off to the sun. As Daedalus watched in horror, the
wings melted and poor Icarus plunged into the salt water.

What was Icarus's experience like? One poet has described the day
of Icarus in a poem entitled "Flight":

> Oh Father, I am in flight again,
> That last incarnation on the horizon
> (I see it in my dim side-vision
> Like a ruffle of swans);
> And though I planted my wandering feet,
> My leaping feet, in the deep mud,
> And refused to look upward or outward for weeks on end
> For fear of the beckoning;
> And though I thought only of vultures as birds,
> With their plucked necks, where plumage
> Should hide the natural deformity;
> And though I focused my heart on night
> And the walls of the hut,
> I arose in my sleep, saved candle-ends,
> And feathers from dead things the cat brought in—
> And awoke, melting gaily
> In the face of the sun.[34]

I doubt if the melting was quite so gay. Imagine Icarus as he nears the
sun. The wax starts to burn, melt and drip as the youth finds his motion
impeded. Feathers flutter through the air and Icarus' face flushes and
pales with dawning recognition of what is happening. The oozing wax
sticks to his skin and scorches it. Finally, the flight is over and the spirit
ceases to hover over the waters and falls into them.

The analogue for the melting wax, the wounded wing, in mortal existence is, as has been seen, the experience of skin problems. (The author

---

34. Cecile Gray, "Flight," *The Otterbein Miscellany* (December 1980): 34.

of this poem, incidentally, had eczema.) The analogy between wax and skin is a vivid one as anyone knows who has visited a wax museum where the statues are so lifelike that one's skin begins to creep. In plants, vegetables and fruits there is often a wax covering which functions as a skin. Like the wax skin of a vegetable, the skin of a mammal protects it from the sun and regulates temperature. Wax is to vegetable as skin is to vegetative nervous system. In the melting, burning, and itching wing of Icarus is a rich image of skin disorder. The image of the skin disease and of a split between son and father, Icarus and Daedalus, is the Wounded Wing.

Mythology offers another image in which wax, wound, wing, and a burning, itching sensation all have a place. The image, of course, is that of Eros. In the myth Eros slept with his bride, Psyche, many nights while forbidding her to look upon his form. His comings and goings were always in the dark. Soon tiring of this charade, Psyche decided to have a look at her lover, so during the night, as Eros slept, she suddenly lit a wax candle. Startled, Eros jumped and a drop of the melting wax seared the delicate thin membrane of his wing. Quite angry and frightened, Eros flew off in a huff. He returned to the emerald house of Aphrodite, there to nurse his itching wound.

The experience of Eros in his mother's house, seething with anger and scratching the scabs off the slowly healing wing, is again very much like the experience of skin problems. Schoenberg and Carr found in their investigation of neurodermatitis that there is in most cases a high degree of anger and hostility. Significant in their study is a fantasy of one of their patients, the only fantasy to be included in the article. Of this woman the investigators say:

> Miss W. was judged to be one of the most successfully treated patients. Nevertheless, on both initial interview and on the basis of psychological testing, she was recognized as an overtly psychotic 20-year-old girl...The content of her responses to the Rorschach test was highly personalized, expressive of blatant hostility. The essence of a thinking disorder is reflected in such responses as, "Well that looks like a butterfly, I see it going toward a flame...mostly I thought of the operetta *Firefly*."[35]

---

35. Bernard Schoenberg and Arthur C. Carr, "An Investigation of Criteria for Brief

No wonder this patient was cured of her neurodermatitis after only twelve sessions with the therapist. She had already fantasied her healing as a union of flame and butterfly, Eros and Psyche. By implication, then, the disease was the split between them. The patient had accurately diagnosed her pathology as the divorce of Eros and Psyche and imagined her cure as their *coniunctio*. The wedding march was appropriately not the Song of the Moth but the *Firefly* operetta.

In a similar vein, the eczematous Icarus poet diagnosed her pathology. She writes:

> I fear to watch the ragged moth
> Curve knowingly to flames,
> And see the blackbirds, close behind,
> Fat from crushing butterflies,
> Bumble through my mind.[36]

Moths in flames and butterflies in the belly of a bird also signify a rift between erotic-spiritual and psychic reality. What these images of a patient and a poet say is that eczematous rashes may appear not only when the puer fails the father but also when the spirit flees from connection to the psychic principle. Neurodermatitis is a psychosomatic disease, an outcome of being burned by the light that Psyche carries, and is healed when the lights go out and Eros and Psyche lay down together. As in the case of the father, the imaginal person who causes an affliction can also cure it. The puer apparently has a double destiny: both to wait on the old senile King and to win the golden-haired young girl kept locked in a tower by the King.

There is an additional character, covered with old and greasy rags, who has trailed our company all along, but at a healthy distance. He must now be spoken of. The cloaked figure is the Leper. Mackenna, in 1944, described a psychic condition displayed by many patients with extensive dermatitis which he termed the "leper complex."[37] In most societies, skin diseases are usually thought of as infectious and dirty.

Psychotherapy of Neurodermatitis," in *Psychosomatic Medicine* 25, no. 3 (May 1963): 261.

36. Cecile Gray, "The Moth," *Bachet* (Spring 1970).

37. R.M.B. Mackenna, "Psychosomatic Factors in Cutaneous Disease," *The Lancet* 244, no. 6326 (25 November 1944): 679–81.

Wittkower and Russell say that "many patients and their relatives regard skin diseases as being due to dirt and those who suffer from them are best avoided…mostly unjustly in view of the genetic basis of many dermatological types of reaction."[38] The person with a bleeding rash is like a leper, ridiculed and set apart. Many people feel uneasy around skin problems, which may lead to friction at school and work. Develop a weeping sore on your face and in a week or two you'll be looking for a new job. To these sufferers marriage is an unimagined possibility. Like the lepers who hid among the tombs and empty streets of ancient cities, those who have been touched by the "heartbreak of psoriasis" see themselves as pariahs.

To imagine the Leper is also to imagine the Spirit: Christ healing the lepers, St. Francis kissing their sores, Godfrey the leprous crusader king of Jerusalem, and Father Damien setting sail for an island colony. Foucault reminds the forgetful that "if the leper was removed from the community of the Church visible, his existence was yet a constant manifestation of God, since it was a sign of both His anger and His grace."[39] Bruegel's famous painting shows the lepers eternally accompanying Christ on the long road to Calvary.[40] The very word leprosy derives from the Greek *lepos,* which means scales—perhaps the scaly skin of the fish, the secret sign of the Spirit who rules our Christian Aion.

---

38. Wittkower and Russell, *Emotional Factors in Skin Disease,* 23.

39. Michel Foucault, *Madness & Civilization: A History of Insanity in the Age of Reason,* translated by Richard Howard (New York: Random House, 1965), 6.

Leprosy is a field from which the soul can harvest much food. For our fantasy of skin disease as the wounded wing of a puer who has refused to go about his father's business, it is of note that in the Middle Ages leprosy belonged to Saturn. Also, leprosy was often announced as the visit of an angel. Constantine the Great, for example, contracted leprosy after he dreamt of an angel pouring water on him. For this and other information, see Saul Nathaniel Brody, *The Disease of the Soul: Leprosy in Medieaval Literature* (Ithaca and London: Cornell University Press, 1974). Two other books of importance are *Leprosy in Theory and Practice,* edited by R. G. Cochrane and T. F. Davey (Bristol: John Wright & Sons, 1965), and Paolo Zappa, *Unclean! Unclean!,* translated by Edward Storer (London: Lovat Dickson Limited). The Hebrew ritual cure for healing helps ballast our fantasy. The leper was purified by the priest transferring the pollution to a bird that was carried outside of camp and then released. When the spirit bird in the soul is set free and allowed to soar, skin disease can be healed.

40. Pieter Bruegel the Elder, *Procession to Calvary* (1564; Kunsthistorisches Museum Wien).

Lastly, leprosy plays a role in alchemy. The *Rosarium* says:

> Our gold is not the common gold. But thou hast inquired concerning the greenness, deeming the bronze to be a leprous body on account of the greenness it hath upon it. Therefore, I say unto thee that whatever is perfect in the bronze is the greenness only, because the greenness is changed by our magistery into our most true gold.[41]

In the leprosy of skin, disease is the true spirit waiting to be transformed by the *opus alchymicum,* an idea to which we will soon return.

In the history of leprosy, an enigma is encountered. Leprosy disappeared from Western Europe at the end of the Middle Ages. The leprosariums were emptied until new residents could be found. Foucault says this: "In the margins of the community, at the gates of the cities, there stretched wastelands which sickness had ceased to haunt but had left sterile and long uninhabitable...they would wait, soliciting with strange incantations a new incarnation of disease."[42] The new disease was madness. Like Eros with his wounded wing and Psyche, the Leper and the Madwoman just missed meeting each other as they marched across the stage of history. Two crazy ladies ran to the tomb only to find the spirit had gone on before them. Had the Leper and the Madwoman bedded down together in some cold damp tomb, then our age might not find itself with a wounded spirit and an unhappy soul. The churches might be full and the butterfly of fantasy free.

The first distillation is at last complete. To review what has been said, let us look once more at the images who have manifested themselves in the retort. The purpose of imaginal psychopathology is to free these images from their total embrace in the material of sickness. Once free, they have room to maneuver and set up new fields of force, other galaxies of psychic significance. Then the experience of disease may be transformed by being fantasied in a different way. Before actually beginning this opus, we puttered around in the laboratory with the G.S.R. test and discovered that it is the Icarus spark in the complexes which shoots

---

41. Quoted by Jung in *CW*12: 207.
42. Foucault, *Madness & Civilization,* 3.

through the skin like a falling star on a clear summer night. The first operation was to work through a case history of a young woman. These skin diseases were imagined as the sign of a puer whose wings are hurt, the stigmata of a wounded spiritual consciousness. Although this angel be crucified (St. Francis), other operations indicated that he itches to get going, to continue ascending and descending on the three-runged ladder of *nous, psyche* and *materia*. Images of Orestes, Job, Icarus, Eros, and the Leper flared in the vessel and in these burning bushes a voice spoke and said that in the affliction of neuro-dermatitis both the claims of the senex and of the soul announce themselves to the spirit. If the wing is to stop itching, then the puer must somehow find a way to work for his father all day and spark the girls all night.

FINDING THE PHILOSOPHER'S STONE IN THE GALL BLADDER: JUNG, ADLER, AND THE PSYCHE OF THE BODY

One of the main ingredients in the treatment of neurodermatitis and related skin sicknesses is diet. When a patient first goes to the dermatologist's office, he is almost without exception instructed to change his diet. He must eat only bland and spiceless food and get in touch with his digestive processes. Diet is also important to puer consciousness. Of the American Icarus, Grope, Murray says that he "has always been somewhat finicky about food."[43] Grope's early memories, his archetypal reminiscences, were almost all about food. Much of the spirit's life is a fasting and feasting on the way to the last supper. In this instance—analysts take note—one had better feed the complex all it wants because spirits hungry for immortality can do a lot of damage. How is the significance of the link between puer and diet to be fantasied? Paracelsus gives a hint: He says that the stomach is the alchemist.[44]

It is through alchemy, as the Rosarium suggested, that the spirit-skin complex can be kept moving. If the essence of the soul is motion, as the ancients taught, then all that can be expected from psychological therapy is to keep the complexes from getting stuck. Since the rash is a skin inflammation, a fire in the flesh, the alchemist might see in this psychosomatic phenomenon a sacred alchemical flame without which

---

43. Murray, "American Icarus."

44. *Paracelsus: Selected Writings*, edited by Jolande Jacobi; translated by Norbert Guterman (Princeton: Princeton University Press, 1951), 143–44.

the work could not proceed. The *opus alchymicum* is initiated when the adept hears the cries of a decrepit old man, the dying senex. By turning a skin inflammation into an alchemical flame, the puer starts paying his debt to the father; he heeds the voice of the senex. Alchemy is work. Thus the puer needs a mentor, an older man, who will teach him about work, time, order, and limits. Otherwise, the *opus* is impossible. If the work is alchemy, then the puer can, as Jung and von Franz believe, be cured by work.

When the rash is a fire, the body becomes the prime matter. Put on the fire where it bubbles and boils and eventually melts, the unity of the body dissolves into a variety of parts. Sparks from the flame fall into each individual organ igniting the body part into soul significance, the sleeping psyche of an organ is awakened with a burning kiss. This would reverse the direction of libido development postulated by Freud. The genital organization would fall apart and each libidinal zone would regain its consciousness, and come alive. We would all walk, work, love and play differently, adepts in the Western analogue of Kundalini yoga. If the body were truly experienced as alive, as a jungle where a thousand exotic species prowl and howl and growl instead of just crowing, purring and braying below the belt, then the polytheistic psyche could find a mirror in the multiple organ zones. With this image it might fall in love. Body no longer bruised to pleasure soul. In the delicate touch of skin and spirit, gross matter and fire, the psyche of the body is born. The res cogitans and the res extensa embrace in the bridal chamber.

If the alchemical fire can create "organ consciousness," then Jung, in his fascination with alchemy, and Adler, as well as many of the mavericks in the tradition of depth psychology such as Ferenczi, Róheim, and especially Reich, may share a common fantasy. In point of fact, there are many similarities between Jung's understanding of the archetypes and Adler's vision of the organs. The archetypes are the foundation of psychic life, as are the organs for Adler. Both the archetypes and the organs are imagined as multiple: a polytheistic soul and body mirroring each other. For Jung; every archetype posits its own world; for Adler, each organ is a functional structure that sets up its own landscape. Like the archetypes, the organs are alive and pulsating with psychic meaning; both have a particular impression on the psyche, leaving their signature as it were. Jung and Adler seem to agree that every archetypal organ has its own style of pathology. Adler put the insight in this manner: "I wonder whether there are any criteria for distinguishing 'healthy' organs from inferior ones...According to our conception an organ may be found quite healthy, but inferior."[45] An organ can be "healthy" while displaying the most hideous and inferior traits.

Jung and Adler steer the ship of fools in the direction of re-imagining the psyche of the body. Active imagination in the body, Lopez-Pedraza calls it.[46] Concretely, this means that the body is transformed from being a piece of raw matter into an imaginal cosmos with manifold topoi. Where in the body, in what sacred precinct, is my anger, my desire, sexuality, grief, depression, mania, and even schizophrenia? These are just a few of the questions that should be asked. The method here is that of Freud and Adler, who identified psychic conditions with body parts, but the vision is that of Jung, who fantasied the body as a microcosm, a mirror sparkling with reflections of the star-studded Milky Way of the imagination. In the Western tradition the soul has been placed at different times in different organs. Not always was the soul identical with the brain. When the body becomes a cave of fantasy pocked with the glowing eyes of myriad animal images, biography might then repeat collective history and my angry soul would be today in my stomach and tomorrow in my skin. The soul could stay in motion.

Reading Jung and Adler, however, is simply not enough if our own complexes do not speak psychosomatically. Yet all complexes do, if only we would hear them. Normally, they are heard when they shout as symptoms, but perhaps by listening carefully we could both hear and discriminate among the quiet whisperings. Aristotle's idea was that the body could speak best nocturnally, that is, in dreams, because only during the night was the soul not too busy to be bothered. Even to listen requires courage though, because when the Tower of bodily unity crumbles, as in disease, an awful babbling arises. But the babbling soon becomes distinct languages. "Organ speech" is what psy-

---

45. Alfred Adler, *Study of Organ Inferiority and its Psychical Compensation: A Contribution to Clinical Medicine,* translated by Smith Ely Jelliffe (New York: The Nervous and Mental Disease Publishing Company, 1917), 21.

46. Rafael López-Pedraza, *Hermes and His Children* (Zurich and New York: Spring Publications, 1977).

SEVERSON *Puer's Wounded Wing* / 161

chologists have pejoratively named the phenomenon. Through listening to these speeches, the moods, feelings, emotions, sounds and smells to which we are a captive audience, it is possible to learn the rhetoric of the organs. An analyst could then tell from a dream image in what part of the body the soul is singing. Were this in fact to occur, it could be said that analytical psychology had advanced so far that it had caught up with Hippocrates. The old physician devoted a treatise to the subject of the body's rhetoric in dreams.[47]

This work on skin disease began with Jung's epigrammatic remark about the gods relation to pathology. That quote reads in full: "The gods have become diseases; Zeus no longer rules Olympus but rather the solar plexus." When Eros rescued the swooning Psyche from the Underworld, he took her to Olympus, where they celebrated their wedding ceremony. Unto them a child was born who was called Pleasure. In the modern soul, or so Jung implied, the body has become Olympus, so that the place where Eros and Psyche marry, the contemporary vessel of the *coniunctio,* is the body. For this archetypal necessity has the body become such a *fascinosum* in contemporary culture. Both alchemy and modern psychology offer persuasive proof of the immense personal and cultural significance of this conjunction. Yet few alchemists claimed to have produced the philosopher's stone, and when Jung was asked during a seminar whether or not anyone had actually ever seen the diamond body—a metallic image of the conjunction—he answered that it was absolutely certain that no one had.[48] Jung insisted always that the conjunction is within the individual. If, as Jung believed, cultural change follows on individual transformation, could it be that by working out his own fate the person plagued with skin disease will accomplish a collective metamorphosis of extraordinary importance? In the miserable rash, or in any organ inflammation, is the felt fire, the efficient causality for the *coniunctio* of the spirit and soul in the vessel of the body, precisely in the place Jung suggested it must be. Without this fire the divine *opus* could not begin. The unbearable itching of neurodermatitis propels the puer to search for soul, and because of this

---

47. "Regimen IV or Dreams," translated by W. H. S. Jones, in *Hippocrates,* vol. 4 (London: William Heinemann; New York, G. P. Putnam, 1931).

48. Jung, *The Visions Seminars,* 1:240.

pathos he cannot rest until he finds her. In his pursuit the puer takes the cross of our culture upon his back, thus drinking from the cup his father has prepared for him.

Before the planets change their houses, allow the alchemist to touch your soul with one more image. This fantasy, however, he thieves from his neo-Platonist friends. During the Renaissance there was a mystery cult that involved an image of skin pathology. The gloomy image was known as "the flaying of Marsyas" and was painted by beautiful Raphael, who played the puer to Michelangelo's senex. Because Marsyas had dared to challenge Apollo (ego confusing itself with spirit?) and lost, he was flayed alive. To the music of his screams, his skin was scraped and scratched and peeled away. Edgar Wind believes that this mystery enjoyed a special connection to the tale of Eros and Psyche.[49] He points out that the neo-Platonist meditating on the fate of Marsyas would recollect that in the Symposium Socrates was called a Marsyas and that this appellation immediately follows Alcibiades's drunken description of Socrates as a Figurine with many secret doors which, upon being opened, revealed the presences of the gods. The Renaissance fantasy that binds the flaying of Marsyas with an image of the body as a divine cosmos with numerous topoi suggests that the experience of skin pathology in scaly, peeling rashes can open into an archetypal imagining of the psyche of the body. Were it not for the promptings of the spirit in skin disease, the doors of the somatic soul might remain locked and bolted.

As the banners of anima consciousness are unfurled, the alchemist slips away into the crowd. Hidden in the pommel of his sword is the miraculous philosopher's stone which the medieval mind believed to be the cure for the most virulent forms of skin disease.[50] (Dante parodied this folk wisdom by condemning all alchemists to the Inferno, their flesh ravaged by running sores and rashes as punishment for their occult dabblings.) Although gone, the alchemist has left behind the memory of a strange afternoon which began with a knock on the door. When opened, the oak door revealed a funny dwarfish little man dressed in rags. Upon being conducted into a back room with pots and foul smell-

---

49. Edgar Wind, *Pagan Mysteries in the Renaissance* (New York: Norton Library, 1958), 175.

50. Brody, *The Disease of the Soul*, 72.

ing substances, the little man pulled a potion from his pocket and projected it onto a bit of pathology and transformed it into gold, the fool's gold of the imagination. Unwilling to remain for even one night, the visitor vanished with the twilight. Despite his promise to return, do not look for him. He will not be back. The shooting stars of this long and belabored alchemical fantasy have fallen, but they have left the air all awash with angels. Puer and Psyche are asleep, the burning wing is cooled by the caress of the soul. This is my son, says the father.

First published in 1979 in *Puer Papers*
and revised in 2005 for inclusion in
UE 3: *Senex & Puer*.

Notes on Opportunism

JAMES HILLMAN

I

Chance and system are other words for puer and senex. Senex consciousness lives from the plotted curve of expectations. Establishment requires predictabilities: we must plan for eventualities, provide for the future, run no risks. Within a senex cosmos chance will be either reduced to meaninglessness by calling it "random events" or fit into order as "statistical probabilities." Otherwise, chance becomes chancey and those who follow it chancers; opportunity becomes opportunism and those who follow it opportunists—major charges against the puer. Puer existence, however, is based on opportunities and therefore an archetypal aspect of existence is reflected through this style. What we may learn about opportunism may tell us as well something about the puer aspect of existence itself.

Let us begin with the word "opportunity." The word derives, according to Onians, most probably from *porta, portus* (*angiportus*) "entrance," "passage through." Portunus was associated with doors. "*Opportunus* would thus describe what offers an opening, or what is in front of an opening and ready to go through."[1] Onians associates this meaning of opportunity with the Roman *porta fenestella*, a special opening through which Fortune passed, and the word window (*fenestra*) "was used symbolically in the sense of 'opening,' 'opportunity.'"[2] Cognate with *porta*

---

1. Richard Broxton Onians, *The Origins of European Thought* (Cambridge, Mass.: Cambridge University Press, 1953), 348.

2. Ibid. The window in dreams (coming in through a window, seen through a window, the "woman in the window") can be elucidated in terms of this opening that

and *portus* (meaning "passage," "way," "means") is the Greek *poros*,[3] who, according to Plato's *Symposium* (203b–d), is the father of Eros. Curiously, *poroi* are passages and connections in the body for its flowings (veins, ducts, etc.).[4] "Pores" are openings in our skins.

A similar set of meanings appears in English in connection with the word "nick,"[5] another of those words, like chancer and opportunist, that can be applied to the shadowy traits of puer consciousness. "To nick" means "To win at dice, to hit the mark just in the nick of time, or at the critical moment."[6] A nick in time is a hole in it, that slot in the system of law and order through which an opportunity may be seized. The "nick" is slang for prison; to be "nicked" is to be cheated; and a "nickel" is false-copper. "Old Nick," of course, is the Devil, and St. Nicklaus (Santa Claus) who can never be caught, always disguised, slipping down chimneys in the night, was originally a goblin, a kind of *Augenblicksgott* (epiphanic daimon). The close association, even identification, between Old Nick and the Christchild, bringer of miraculous gifts, gives a wholly hermetic, mercurial aspect to the Christmas moment of the Christian year.[7]

The main Greek term for opportunity is *kairos*, which referred in Homeric Greek to a "penetrable opening." Let us listen to this sentence from Onians in terms of the puer-senex opposition: "To get past fortifications, armor, bones, the early Greek archer practised by aiming at an opening or a series of openings...*kairos*, as appears from Pindar, Aeschylus, etc., described that at which he aimed."[8]

---

allows a glimpse "beyond" or permits passage of "wind" into one's "room." For a marvelous constellation of puer imagery interconnecting wind, wings, Eros, windows and doors, see Robert Duncan's "Chords: Passages 14," in *Bending the Bow* (New York: New Directions, 1968), 46–47.

3. Ibid.

4. Ibid., 29; Liddell and Scott, *A Greek-English Lexicon* (Oxford: Clarendon Press, 1968), under "poros."

5. Onians, *The Origins of European Thought*, 29.

6. Captain Grose, *A Dictionary of Buckish Slang, University Wit, and Pickpocket Eloquence* (London: C. Chappel, 1811).

7. Clement A. Miles, *Christmas in Ritual and Tradition* (London: Fisher Unwin, 1913), 229–38.

8. *The Origins of European Thought*, 345. See Theodore Thass-Thienemann, *The Interpretation of Language* (New York: Aronson, 1973), 1: 371.

The same idea of "opening" can be evolved not only from *kairós* but also from *kaīros*, a term from the art of weaving. Weaving, time, and fate are often connected ideas. An opening in the web of fate can mean an opening in time, an eternal moment when the pattern is drawn tighter or broken through. The weaver shot the spool or shuttle through the opening in the warp-threads at a critical time, the right moment (*kairos*), for "the opening in the warp lasts only a limited time, and the 'shot' must be made while it is open."[9]

The image of Kairos presents another of those astoundingly vivid personifications exemplifying an experience as a puer figure, like Pothos who presents the nostalgias of longing, and Eros who images the burning and moody complexities of love.[10] These puer figures bespeak archetypal experiences. They therefore tell of a consciousness that affects young and old, male and female, and are not limited only to young and special men.

The earliest large-scale visual image of Kairos that has been recorded was fashioned by Lysippos (of Sikyon), the principal sculptor in the Peloponnese during the fourth century BC. Reconstructions of this statue show Kairos as a wingfooted runner, a naked young man on tiptoes with head shorn except for forelocks. He carries a razor (in his right hand) and a balance scale, and often stands upon a wheel or sphere.[11] Later he added other attributes, becoming more emblematic, e.g., winged time (wings on his back), hurrying time (carrying a whip).[12] Another trait could not easily be shown: deafness.

The poetic personification of Kairos appears in a fifth-century hymn where he is called the youngest son of Zeus, and he had his cult in associ-

---

9. Ibid., 346.

10. These figures are discussed, with references, in Pothos: The Nostalgia of the Puer Eternus," and in my *The Myth of Analysis* (New York: Harper & Row, 1978), Part 1.

11. Pauly-Wissowa, *Real-Encyclopädie*, under "kairos"; also Arthur Bernard Cook, *Zeus: A Study in Ancient Religion*, 5 vols. (Cambridge: At the University Press, 1914–40), 2: 859ff., and Roger Hinks, *Myth and Allegory in Ancient Art* (London: The Warburg Institute, 1939), 117ff.

12. Ibid. See Erwin Panofsky, "Father Time," *Studies in Iconology* (New York: Harper Torchbooks, 1962), plate XXI. These later versions bring *kairos* into visible relation with time, that is, they attempt allegorical connections between puer and senex. This same connection is made by the etymological fantasy that derives Kronos and Kairos "from the same root" (*Zeus: A Study in Ancient Religion*, loc. cit.).

ation with Zeus of Olympia.[13] (A somewhat comparable figure is Tages of the Etruscans who was a little boy spirit, yet had grey hair. He, too, was an *Augenblicksgott,* an epiphanic appearance at a certain moment, who had something to do with insight into time through magic and foretelling).[14]

II

By considering opportunity as a nick in time (senex) through which Kairos (puer) may pass into the established order, we may better understand puer openness and suggestibility. This is a consciousness that must leave its door ajar; nothing closed down; "toujours ouverte, toujours disponible," as maxim for the young man in André Gide's *The Counterfeiters.* We may also better understand the necessity of puer wounds and the supposed weak ego with its omissions and holes. These, too, are doors, ways for the spirit to come in. The gaps in learning, the absences in remembering, the spottiness in systematic work especially in regard to time (appointments, schedules, deadlines) may be necessary for keeping open and available and superior to the senex style of order. Puer integrity would mean never covering these holes, and so personality integration, when imagined by puer consciousness, always retains gaps and absences, unshielded.

Kairos is vulnerable to the senex who says: "Prove it. How do you know?" Or, more simply, "Say that again." This puer consciousness can never do. It cannot repeat because it is deaf and has never heard what slipped out of its own mouth. And it has no hair on the back of its head. Nothing of the brainstorm can be pulled back after it has skated by. Puer truth may be public but it is not repeatable.

As puer is vulnerable to senex charges, so in turn it threatens senex systems by espying their holes. Often a penetrating shaft simply mobilizes massive defenses and the puer is surprised at what he set off by just a "chance remark." When puer spear is countered with senex shield, a paranoid reaction is the consequent of an opportune insight.

The holes in puer consciousness allow for a two-way traffic. A new idea is never only a wind-fall, an apple to be eaten. It takes hold of us as much as we take hold of it. The hunch that breaks in pulls one into an

---

13. Pausanias, *Description of Greece* 5.4.9.

14. "Tages," in *Ausführliches Lexikon der griechischen und römischen Mythologie,* edited by W. H. Roscher (Leipzig: B. G. Teubner, 1884).

identification with it. We feel gifted, inspired, upset, because the message is also a messenger that makes demands, calling us to quit a present position and fly out. The puer person is susceptible to the archetypal call of the message, becoming the very angel that has come to him.

What comes through the hole has its source beyond the wall and cannot easily be detached from the gap (chaos) of its entry. Opportunities are not plain, clean gifts; they trail dark and chaotic attachments to their unknown backgrounds, luring us further. One insight leads to another; one invention suggests another variation—more and more seems to press through the hole, and more and more we find ourselves drawn out into a chaos of possibilities.

This chaos that an opportunity initiates also constellates a Zeusian fantasy of cosmic generativity. We feel called to create new schemes, new forms, new visions. At first the puer comes only as a little hole, a brush of wings, as a naked runner on tiptoes; quick now, here, now. And, before we have taken thought, we have been seduced into enterprises beyond our resources. The Zeusian vision of mastery from Olympus takes Ganymede[15] right straight up on eagle's wings way beyond his light-weight body, and a fantasy of lucky power can be the effect of a visitation by Hermes, son of Zeus, messenger of Zeus.

III

Although it has been said that *kairos* "has nothing in the least to do with luck and the fall of the dice, but has much more to do with the propitious moment that must be seized through one's own power and insight,"[16] we do find later associations between Kairos and Hermes, Tyche (Fortune) and Nemesis,[17] just as there are similarities between opportunity and luck. "It was good luck to meet him (Hermes), and a piece of good luck was called a gift from Hermes."[18] The older idea of *kairos* as something

---

15. Besides the homoerotic, religious, and aesthetic interpretations of the Ganymede image, there is also a Christian reading that carries a useful insight: a gloss on the image refers to Christ's "Suffer little children to come unto me." The uprush on eagle's wings catches us when we are most childlike, or childish. (See Jean Seznec, *The Survival of the Pagan Gods: The Mythological Tradition and Its Place in Renaissance Humanism and Art* [Princeton, N.J.: Princeton University Press, 1972], 103).

16. Pauly-Wissowa, op. cit., 1510. (*Der kleine Pauly*, III, Stuttgart, 1969).

17. Ibid.

18. W.K.C. Guthrie, *The Greeks and their Gods* (London: Methuen, 1968), 91.

to be seized, as a target to hit with one's arrow, emphasizes the heroic puer. Kairos as luck, on the other hand and to make the distinction sharp, stresses the role of the gods, the hand of Tyche or Fortune in the fall of the dice. Emphasis upon what one does with an opportunity (by means of power and insight) helps to bring it into the existing order; emphasis upon the *fall of chance* brings the element of uncontrollable disorder (and thus bad luck too) to the foreground. Walter F. Otto notes these two divergent aspects of opportunity in connection with Hermes: From him comes (both styles of) gain, cleverly calculated, or wholly unexpected, but mostly the latter. That is his true characterization. If a man finds valuables on the road, if a man has a sudden stroke of luck, he thanks Hermes. The regular word for any windfall is *hermaion*...It is Hermes in whom the merchant trusts; from him comes the art of sly calculation, but also the lucky chance without which his shrewdness is futile.[19]

When Kerényi differentiates Hermes-Mercurius from the Trickster figure of the American Indians[20] and when Otto differentiates Hermes-Mercurius from Pushan (of the Vedic Hindus),[21] their point is relevant for the order-disorder problems raised by Hermes. For all the similarities of Trickster, Loki, and Pushan with Hermes, the God of classical antiquity did not govern a special section of the world, nor did he represent a separate principle of disorder, or of evil.[22] Hermes's realm and Hermes's order are not distinct from and opposed to our world.

Hermes is the world itself. "Hermes" refers to a way of living in the world, a *Daseinsform* or specific kind of consciousness that creates a

---

19. *The Homeric Gods* (New York: Pantheon, 1954), 108.

20. Karl Kerényi (with C.G. Jung and Paul Radin), *The Trickster* (New York: Greenwood Press, 1956).

21. Otto, *The Homeric Gods*, 121.

22. See Karl Kerényi, "The Problem of Evil in Mythology," in *Evil* (Evanston: Northwestern University Press, 1967), 8ff., with reference to Wilhelm Grönbech, *Kultur und Religionen der Germanen* (Hamburg: Hanseatische Verlagsanstalt, 1942), on Loki. A correction of Grönbech and Kerényi in regard to Loki has been presented by Margrit Burri, "Repression, Falsification, and Bedeviling of Germanic Mythology," *Spring: An Annual of Archetypal Psychology and Jungian Thought* (1978): 91–92. See also, Norman O. Brown, *Hermes the Thief* (New York: Vintage, 1967), 24–25, on similarities and differences between Hermes and Prometheus, Loki, and Trickster.

"cosmos" (lawful order, intelligible arrangement, beautification) in like-ness to itself.[23] Each style of consciousness, such as Hermes, regards the world in a self-consistent way, thereby creating world and man-kind according to its image. There are not a multiplicity of worlds and mankinds, yet there are many gods. Thus for the gods to create after their likenesses, they must be able to use the same world in many man-ners, creating styles of being and perception so that our one and only world may participate in a shifting realm of many perspectives, at one moment mimetic to Zeus, and the next to Aphrodite or Ares. Or, they all may be present at the same moment, and we see but one. As the same world can be a likeness of different gods, consciousness can be quali-fied by many forms. This very variety of divine forms is the first mes-sage of Hermes-Mercurius, who, Jung said, "consists of all conceivable opposites."[24] Hermetic awareness guides souls by bringing conscious-ness to experience the ego-strictures of opposites as messages of divine multiplicity. Then all things provide divine opportunities for the gods.

IV

The mercurial opportunist, having no fixed position, no sense of being at the center, keeps his eye on the door, the thresholds where transien-cies pass over from statement to implication, from fact to supposition, from report to fantasy. Mercurius is messenger of the gods, so he must be able to hear their messages in whatever is said. This is the hermeneu-tic ear that listens-through, a consciousness of the borders, as Hermes was worshipped at borders.[25] And borders spring up anywhere as soon as we enter that duplicity of mind that hears two modes at once.

For the opportunistic eye, every wall and every weave presents its opening. Everything is porous. As the surrealists say: "There exists

23. Karl Kerényi, *Hermes: Guide of Souls*, translated by Murray Stein (Thompson, Conn.: Spring Publications, 2020 [1976]), 42–43.

24. C.G. Jung, "The Spirit Mercurius," *CW* 13: 269, 284; on the Hermes-Mercurius relation, see par. 278–83. For a complete catalogue of the epithets of Hermes—all his traits, powers, and associations—see William G. Doty, "Hermes Heteronymous Appel-lations," *Arche* 2 (1978): 17–35.

25. The border-consciousness of Hermes is brilliantly presented by Rafael López-Pedraza, *Hermes and His Children* (Zurich and New York: Spring Publications, 1977). His work extends beyond Hermes manifestations in the puer.

another world. But it is assuredly in this one."[26] The bricks and mortar are firmly real, and surreal at the same moment. These sudden openings that shift perspective with a shaft of insight are hermetic opportunities.

The cosmos of one God, via Hermes, suddenly swings open into that of another. We see one viewpoint from that of another. This is Hermes operating in our vision—the God of betweens, keeping us to the world and guiding us out of it at the same instant. "A swing-door is in us leading to the memoryless spaces of a metahuman condition."[27]

Opportunities are also *voiced*. They are seized not only by heroic action or the gambler's hand, but also by hermeneutic formulation. Hermes's gift to Pandora was "voice," and we may hear opportunities as hallucinatory hunches, as dreams speaking direct meanings. A puer waits for these voices, or when he is one, carried by it, he tells you how and what and where, himself an electronic bit of information, a fiery *logos spermatikos,* fervent fugleman of a goldrush.

Because the usual senex ego that we each embody cannot easily grasp these opportunities, they seem slippery and shadowy. We do not trust our hunches and are suspicious of what comes through luck. Puer messages are not familiar; they are so new and young. An opportunity after all is mere *status nascendi.* Sometimes it originates as a schizoid neologism, a fused poetic nugget; or it sounds no better than a pop-slogan or commercial. Yet this almost surrealist absurdity contains a revelation for which puer consciousness will chase to the ends of the earth. The puer word is not composed into solid verbal forms by the elephant of *visuddha,*[28] not established into a commanding voice of authority based on knowledge. Puer consciousness has no footnotes and you can't get a handle on its idea. Its word breezes through the window, freshening but ungraspable. Then to make it concrete, puer consciousness becomes

---

26. Attributed to Paul Eluard by J.H. Matthews in a chapter entitled "A Swing Door," *An Introduction to Surrealism* (University Park, Penn.: Pennsylvania State University Press, 1967), 67.

27. Attributed to Simon Hantai and Jean Schuster in Matthews, *An Introduction to Surrealism,* 62.

28. See C.G. Jung, "Commentary on Kundalini Yoga," *Spring: An Annual of Archetypal Psychology and Jungian Thought* (1976): 14–17, and James Hillman, "The Elephant in the Garden of Eden," *UE9: Animal Presences.*

schizoid or surrealist, as André Breton makes a huge literal Manifesto of a little phrase that seems to "tap at the window pane"[29] without warning or premeditation. The Word becomes Flesh in a flash without ever passing through the soul. In the window, out the door: opportunity literalized into a venture.

Puer consciousness neither possesses what it knows nor knows what it intuits. Knowledge, anyway, belongs to the senex, and puer knowing is at the threshold, dawning, where pure meaning is fullness before knowing. It shrugs off knowing its own ideas so that they may remain messages: "I had a thought," "This idea came to me," "Let me tell you this." Mind unsullied by the bowels of digestion.

Opportune ideas come like Hermes, stealthily, or even as actual thefts from others, cryptomnesias, blocked recollections. Kairos is deaf—perhaps in order to hear only his own autochthonous processes. The puer idea flowers in the air of the moment without roots in senex authority. Its hallmark is newness, so that new truths come with puer accoutrements. It is announced as a "discovery" and wholly self-authored (authorized by the Self). Hence those vicious disputes in science about priority in connection with new ideas and inventions, leading into the paranoid senex machines of patent lawyers and copyright offices. When truth is newness and newness truth, then priority is a sign of truth. Opportunism and duplicity are inherent in originality.

Even duplicity does not adequately characterize this consciousness, since doubleness implies a fixed position—one foot in and one foot out, fence-sitting, talking out of both sides of your mouth. This is not really a puer place because it literalizes the border into a Janus-Saturn stance of the wise-guy who can argue either side. A more precise conception of hermetic opportunism is *eccentricity,* being at the edge, on the windowsill. Then our senses must be acute in order to survive; then we need even a sixth sense. We *have to* listen through, else we lose our luck, and fall. So we find in puer dominated lives an affectation of the crazy, that odd-ball quality in clothes and gait, that signal disconcern for normalcy—a funny hat, a torn sleeve, a car unlike all others, talismans to keep the wall and weave of regular life off center, surrealistically open for chance.

---

29. Matthews, *An Introduction to Surrealism,* 63.

The puer perceives the *discontinuity* of spirit.[30] It comes and goes as do his inspirations and his moods. We are best in touch with it by being discontinuous ourselves, living by chance and loving synchronicities that prove a secret order is guiding our destiny, beyond senex categories such as time, space, and causality. So puer consciousness worships Kairos at the altar of chance: *I Ching*, a dream, even someone else's dream, spot words on a page will send one off to California. The Dadaist movement elevated chance to a law. Hans Arp was led "to conclude that the laws of chance are 'the highest and deepest of laws, the law that rises from the fundament' "[31]—how much like the new Puer Religion (formulated in senex *Weisheiten*) of Synchronicity. These two Zurich schools, Dadaism and Synchronicity, use similar methods: "When Surrealism interrogates chance, it is to obtain oracular replies."[32] Analysts as usual blame a mother complex for this magical indecisive provisionality. The force at work, however, is not Mama but Dada.

V

In puer consciousness, the tendency to lie, to do the devious, to cut out and around the system, would seem a moral problem. Analysts consider the opportunism to belong to the shadow and to result from a weak ego that cannot take a stand and face consequences (as a hero should). But if opportunism has archetypal substrate, having *archetypal necessity* within the puer structure, then we must re-assess the psychological function of puer deviousness and opportunistic duplicity independently of our preconceptions of right and wrong.

Our usual notion of ego is Emersonian, Faustian, and Apollonic. The German old man of Weimar, whom Faust spent so many years creating,

---

30. "Discontinuity" is a characteristic concept of our times, discussed by physicists, and by thinkers as divergent as Erich Neumann and Gaston Bachelard. It informs our contemporary consciousness also in literary forms (poetry) and in Orient-derived disciplines of "suddenness." (See Karl Heinz Bohrer, *Suddenness: On the Moment of Aesthetic Appearance* [New York: Columbia University Press, 1994].) Discontinuity is today invoked as an explanatory principle even in classical scholarship much like "fertility" once was: cf. R.F. Willetts, *Cretan Cults and Festivals* (London: Routledge, 1962), 199, on the Minoan Mother Goddess as "continuity" and the "youthful god" as "the element of discontinuity."

31. Matthews, *An Introduction to Surrealism*, 24.

32. Ibid., 99; see also 110.

died supposedly calling for "more light." If we elevate this archetypal aspect of our natures by knighting it Sir Ego, we promote solar consciousness to rulership. But what then of Brother Mephistopheles who lives in the twilight?

The thief, the lie, the deception of magic, the surreptitious borderline areas fall into shadow and can but return (opportunistically) to attention through tricks and theft.

In the sunlight world, the artful dodger is an opportunist. Psychology calls him shadow. But Hermes is not shadow cast off by light, not Lucifer. He is dark to begin with. He belongs to the night.[33] From the hermetic perspective and the serpentine eye, it is rather the hero, sun-fixed and immovably centered who is the benighted one. His is the consciousness that sees in terms of black and white, and points to evil to justify the enormous destruction we always find in his myths. From the viewpoint of a genuine shadow psychology, a hermetic psychology, the sun-ego is a *sol niger*, in darkness because of its light, like the untrustworthy blackbirds that appear so often with the sun.[34]

Where there is hero, there is shadow. Depth psychology has too long insisted that the hero integrate the shadow, whereas maybe the heroic is actually a product of the shadow. When Hercules was born, a weasel attendant at his birth was the first to recognize and proclaim Hercules to the world.[35] The sneaky moment calls up the heroic from the beginning; something tricky is going on whenever a heroic impulse comes into being. Does the weasel want the hero? And if so, are our heroisms and egoisms emboldened weaselings? At this point the terms "ego" and "shadow" begin to dissolve into each other. We have begun to be guided by Hermes towards the serpentine roots of consciousness, the

---

33. Otto, *The Homeric Gods*, 115ff.

34. On the blackbird-sun motif, see *Picatrix*, translated into German from the Arabic by Hellmut Ritter and Martin Plessner (London: Warburg Institute, 1962), 115 and 119; it appears in Mithraism, and in late paintings of Van Gogh. Apollo was "represented" by a black bird, supposedly meaning his prophetic gift. Why does prophecy that sees so clearly, see doom, and what is the secret desire of Apollo for Cassandra? The inherent relation between the spirit of clarifications and the spirit of destruction remains an enigma, and a tension of the psyche.

35. Karl Kerényi, *The Heroes of the Greeks* (London: Thames and Hudson, 1959), 132–33.

imagistic impulses that cannot be contained by concepts such as ego and shadow.

When we stand in the image and view hermetically, the problem of black and white becomes irrelevant: one could as well be the other, and Hermes's son Autolycus[36] (who is also Odysseus's ancestor) changes them back and forth, opportunistically in accordance with the situation. Besides, there are so many colors in the spectrum of messages that Hermes carries that black and white need no longer be paired.

Yet, for all the independence of the hermetic viewpoint, Hermes the thief is indeed Apollo's smaller brother.[37] He comes into the world in relation with Apollo, as his shadow, and carries his deception, his cleverness, his weakness. This myth reminds us that the mercurial aspect of the puer is in some shadow league with the Apollonian. When we are Apollonic in ideals, Hermes in his darkest (i.e., most literal) aspect is not far. Together they make a fine pair: the golden gleam of noble ends achieved by sly means. The brothers go together as well in the mercurial ego personality who has a perfectionist computerized shadow.

Rather than following the psychologist's maxim of integrating the shadow, an integration that tends to mean by the hero into the light, we might take the Hermes-Apollo filiation as a model, not of substance, but for its structure. Hermes appears in a "shadow" relation with various gods, especially these: Hades, Zeus, Athene, Aphrodite, Dionysus. It is within these tandems that shadow can be integrated, not by us, but into them. This is a hermetic mode of shadow perception: noticing how Hermes moves *together with* various structures of consciousness, and this hermetic awareness of archetypal shadow is itself a message of each god through Hermes.

But there is something about Apollo that cannot bear his little brother. Zeus, Dionysus, Aphrodite, even Athene can work well with his wiles. So, what makes it so difficult for Apollonic consciousness to keep this hermetic awareness? Or should we turn the matter on its head? That is, perhaps Apollo is Hermes's shadow, simply cast-off older light, a

---

36. The tale of Autolykos is told succinctly by both Robert Graves (*Myths, Dreams and Religion* [New York: Dutton, 1970], 1: 67) and Kerényi in *The Heroes of the Greeks*, 77.

37. See Rafael Lopéz-Pedraza's *Hermes and His Children* for insights into the Apollo-Hermes relation.

rationalized and distant awareness that may illumine but no longer has a cutting edge or door into crazyland.

Although the Apollonic temperament loses its Hermes, it is the task of hermetic consciousness to learn to travel with Apollo and with all that light. Hermes can carry messages from any god, Apollo too. Puer consciousness in the Hermetic pattern may follow Auden who says of the Apollo/Hermes strife: "if thou must choose Between the chances, choose the odd."[38] But we must go beyond Auden and the notion of brother strife and opposites, by finding opportunities also for the even, the clear, and the calm, rather than merely literalizing opportunity into chance and oddity. Hermes literalized is not Hermes but a Hermes caught by his Apollonic side, a puer secretly senexed.

VI

Now we can return to opportunism from another vantage point. It manifests not merely the chancy provisionality of puer existence. Opportunism is a way of living the world, creating a Mercurial cosmos.

We might borrow from the language of existentialism for another entry into this puer mercurial cosmos. A *kairos* appears as a situation, where *situs* refers to the invisible structure or lay of things. The puer spirit is the voice of the moment and the puer spirit seizes the situation in an instant. The ethics are situationalist.

A situationalist ethic permits one to move in accordance with a constellation as it is (not as it should be), so that for puer consciousness no situation ever becomes "wrong" or "impossible." There is always a way, or way out. Every human complexity and every psychological complex, perceived from the puer perspective, is a situation serving its own purposes. There is intentionality in all psychic life, when perceived in terms of the puer. Every situation is always headed somewhere.

Here, mythology shows Hermes knowing the ruse and deception that opens the way until the constellation shifts. Hermes here is like Eros, whose father was Poros, "resourcefulness," "way-finder;" love, too, finds a way, and Hermes had a special function in finding the way at night for lovers. His ethic was situational, but it favored eros. Here,

---

38. W.H. Auden, "Under Which Lyre," a long humorous poem on the Apollo/Hermes contrast in academia.

Hermes is like his descendent Odysseus who, too, finds his way through tight spots. Opportunities excite puer consciousness because they evoke these archetypal spirits of resourcefulness.

Since situations require this opportunistic knowing about where the openings are and when the time needs voice, *the master of a situation is the master of the complex.* In an encounter (let us imagine a Mafia negotiation, a master's chess class), the lacuna, the weak place of the other's psyche gives the opportunity. Perception of opportunities requires a sensitivity given through one's own wounds. Here, puer weakness provides the kind of hermetic, secret perception critical for adaptation to situations. We are mimetic to this model when we adapt not as a hero who coerces situations towards a result but as a thief who pockets what can be made from it. The weak place serves to open us to what is in the air. We feel through our pores which way the wind blows. We turn with the wind; trimmers.

An opportunity requires a cold-snake sense that we call intuition and that reveals the daimon of a situation. The daimon of a place in antiquity supposedly revealed what the place was good for, its special quality and dangers. The daimon was thought to be a serpent, a *familiaris* of the place. To know a situation one needs to sense what lurks in it.

These deeper aspects of awareness give to opportunism a different value. By connecting opportunity with the snake of Hermes, the local snake of the hero cult, and the snake *familiaris* who lives in our neuro-vegetative reactions of fear and greed (below the mind and the will), we see that puer opportunism is also an *instinctual adaptation to psychic realities.* The shiftiness and suddenness is a correspondence between inner genius (complex) and outer daimon (situation), snake speaking with snake through the holes in normalcy. This is the opportunism that the genius of Spanish literature has captured in the genre of the picaresque.

VII

Again we are approaching shadow psychology. What is "shadow" when we stand in it rather than against it? How do the twilight regions of the serpent look when the threshold is imagined as a doorway and not as a censor—where consciousness itself slithers, slips its skin, and speaks with a forked tongue?

First of all, loss dreams would look different from this shadow psychology. The motifs of cheating, robbing, and stealing would indicate a gain for the underworld at the expense of Old Ego up top. It is no longer able to hold its own. It's losing its bag. Its senex accumulations are being taken by the little people. Robbery redistributes the wealth, transferring values to the unknown *daimones,* the oppressed and repressed forces in the forest. As Old Ego feels impoverished, deeper, darker values begin to be felt, so that even in our outrage we sense new things uprising. For the Hood is a Robin, harbinger of a new season in our red breast.

Second, "cases" and "symptoms," the very stuff of psychotherapy, betray in their etymologies (a word game that, too, belongs to Hermes) an occasional, opportunistic sense. *Casus, caere; Fall* (in German) refer to the accidental way things fall, how they lie, their situation. "Casualties" and "accidents" also go back to the same Latin root, *caere,* to fall. Where the senex systematizes these fallings with accident and casualty insurance, puer consciousness may move into each fall as a moment of meaning. Symptoms, too, from the Greek *symptoma,* refer to anything that has befallen one, a happenstance, a chance. Puer consciousness can hear case histories and symptoms from this accidental, casual perspective. A symptom can be read as a moment, as one kens the fall of the *I Ching* sticks, the thrown together dice. There is a meaningful pattern in the precision of a symptom itself, its picture, its timing, its immediate effects. Then a case is not only an abnormality, nor is a symptom merely a disorder. They are opportunities.

Hermetic puer as psychopompos! Puer psychotherapy—not psychotherapy of the puer, but *by* the puer! We seem a long way now from opportunism, yet we have had to go to the end of an affliction in order to recover the spirit moving in it. And so, we have found that opportunism is itself an opportunity when it is imagined from within the same puer consciousness that is afflicted by it. As healing emerges from disease, or is the disease when imagined hermetically, so the psychopompos is the psychopathology itself when, as the alchemists say, it has been "touched by quicksilver."

The shadowy *Doppelgänger* brings a sense of ourselves as opportunists, cheats, weasels. At the same time, this duplicity in our consciousness—between what is promised and what is done, what is felt and what is shown, what is seen and what is said to have been seen—

brings awareness that at least two lives are being led at the same time. We are here and yet also not here at all, hidden. To focus on the opposites is to miss the opportunities, the Hermes whose presence is precisely in the *between*. Perhaps this has been the Hermes function of the puer all along: to double our awareness by returning a portion of it to the serpent who can move only by wriggling left and right at the same moment. Let us imagine Hermetic awareness less as a transcendent function that holds the opposites together, or overcomes them, and more as a consciousness that requires and even creates a betweenness in which to operate. This sort of awareness must wriggle out of moral oppositions. There is no space for the serpent when the world is set up as either black or white.

For Hermes, whose territory is in the borderlands where many currents live side by side, there is no compartment mentality. He can commit "perjury with the most guileless face;" the baby-faced little brother is also a bare-faced liar. Borders always have two sides and Hermes thrives in this between-world. When psychologists degrade the between into a schizoid gap or a psychopathic lacuna, they eliminate Hermes altogether from their considerations. Then analysts become therapeutic bridge-builders above the gorge, working at "the problem of opposites," rather than workers in the bottom land. If we stay closer to the serpent, by means of duplicity, a kind of in-between consciousness emerges, an awareness—not of opposites—but of relations, the filiation or brotherhood of differences. Consciousness sees parallels, analogies, likenings, family resemblances. Nothing is except *as* it is, in its relations, and these are presented as situations (rather than as opposites). This succession of situations, whether in life, in symptoms or in dreams, requires that each darkness be interpreted in its own light and by the standards it brings with it. Individuation not as tree, spiral, child or union; these paths gone. Instead, individuation as situational hermeneutics, opportunities for kairotic soul-making. It is the moments that are momentous, the pearls not their string.

Once we are able to revalue the soul's divisions in terms of the between, then, like Jung, we are recognizing Mercurius as center of the opus.[39] Then, too, we can understand the necessity of seeing in terms

---

39. See *CW*13:248; *CW*14:707–19.

of opposites: they are made for the sake of the between. They pull apart so as to give opportunity for mercurial space; they give *kairos* a chance. And usually, this space is no bigger than a tiny chink in the armor, a hole in the wall where grand visions do not fit. By seeing with the beady snake eyes of Mercurius, we make possible the appearance of Mercurius and of a hermetic significance in any situation. Puer consciousness may indeed act as psychopomp.

III
PUER IN MYTH AND LITERATURE

First published in 1979 in *Puer Papers* and emended for this edition.

Artemis and the Puer

THOMAS MOORE

Is it possible for that cold one
To pull me so
That I am mad with wanting?
I run toward her
As to one on intimate terms
With my own soul.
　　　　—Patricia Dietel, "Pothos"

I. ACTAION: ENCOUNTER WITH THE VIRGINAL PSYCHE

Actaion, one of those daring young men of myth, wanders deep into the woods and intrudes upon the virgin goddess, Artemis, as she is bathing. Ovid tells the story vividly:

Bath Time As Usual for Diana: & here comes
Cadmus's grandson! tired, straying, unsteady,
woods unknown; but he finds the grove! fate brings him;
enters cave: splashing fountains, naked nymphs!
they beat their breasts: "Man!" loud outcry
fills entire woods: they surround Diana, covering
her body with theirs

but the tall goddess towers over others
by a neck! seen undressed, Diana's face
goes scarlet dawn, sky color when
clouds deflect sun; her troops crowd round:
she, sideways, looks back, wishing
she had arrows ready: instead throws water,
soaks virile face, wets his hair, adds

to water-vengeance words promising disaster:
"Now say you saw me undressed!
if you can!"

no more threats: she sprouts old stag
antlers on his wet head, expands neck, points
his ears, lengthens arms & legs, spots on body;
& adds fear: hero flees surprised at his own speed

he sees, in water, head antlered & starts to say,
"Oh dear!" but no word comes; groans
only;[1]

This simple but intriguing mythic figure has given rise over the centuries to a variety of interpretations. Robert Graves, for example, mentions a Euhemerist version according to which Actaeon was thought to be an Arcadian gentleman so addicted to hunting that the expense of keeping a pack of hounds ate him up.[2] But fortunately myth reaches deeper springs of imagination, and we find Actaion himself hounding the minds of mythographers like Apollodorus, Callimachus, Nonnos, and Ovid; painters like Veronese, Tintoretto, and Titian; and poets such as Shelley, Oscar Wilde, and Robinson Jeffers. Their representations of the image, even the earliest of them, suggest directions for an archetypal exploration.

Actaion, a mythic image of youth full of innocence, daring, and idealism, suggests a style of consciousness, a special spirit, and a psychological pattern in many ways typical of the general puer attitude. But he also reflects a sensibility and a pathology peculiar to him alone. We may inquire, then, into the particular manner in which puer psychology is presented in the character and fate of Actaion.

THE FAMILY TREE

In mythology, genealogy is a story in itself. Families of even the plainest figures have skeletons in their closets, secrets that shed light on numerous episodes in the mythological lives of family members. Actae-

---

1. *Ovid's Metamorphoses,* translated by Charles Boer (Thompson, Conn.: Spring Publications, 2024 [1989]), Book 3.

2. Robert Graves, *The White Goddess: A Historical Grammar of Poetic Myth* (New York: Farrar, Straus, and Giroux, 1966), 12.

on's family tree is exceptionally revealing, presenting a larger context within which his own fate originates and unfolds.

Cadmus

Actaion's grandfather was Cadmus, founder of the ill-fated city Thebes. Cadmus was the regal, aggressive paterfamilias whose line was destined for tragedy: Semele's Dionysus, Agave's Pentheus, Ino's Palaimon, Autonoe's Actaion, and even Laius's Oedipus. The history of Thebes begins with inhuman struggle and forboding mystery. Cadmus kills the great dragon and plants its teeth in the earth. The chthonic beast had been protecting the spring called Areia, after Ares, god of warfare and violence, and associated with Ge or Demeter, the goddess of earth. From this strange sowing come forth armed men who fight among themselves, killing each other off until only five remain, and with these Cadmus builds his city.

Deep in Actaion's blood, therefore, stirs this fantasy of fighting violence with violence and raising a new race seeded in the moist " ground" of Ares and bred in a heroic battle with the earth goddess.[3] The masculine strain in this "family" of fantasies originates with the *spartoi,* the sown men, and the martial attitude of solving problems with force. Cadmus himself tamed the influence of Ares in his life by marrying Harmonia, daughter of Ares and Aphrodite;[4] but we find in his lineage tragic attempts to maintain balance in the service of civilization. Euripides's Pentheus offers a striking example of the Theban king suspicious and heroically defensive in face of the feminine, awkward in his struggle to maintain senex rule, and finally overwhelmed and annihilated.

Such an aggressive struggle to maintain the structures of civilization, whether within a society, a family, or an individual, may bring to

---

3. Richard Broxton Onians, *The Origins of European Thought: About the Body, the Mind, the Soul, the World, Time, and Fate* (Cambridge: Cambridge University Press, 1951), 233. Onians discusses the *spartoi* with reference to the ancient understanding that the head and mouth house the moist soul and are themselves sources of fertility. The teeth of the dragon or serpent are therefore seeds.

4. For a less imaginative account of the Cadmus-Harmonia relationship, see Lewis Richard Farnell, *The Cults of the Greek States,* 3 vols. (Oxford: At the Clarendon Press, 1896), 2:623. Karl Kerényi describes Harmonia within the context of Apollo's lyre, which produces a harmony in the tension of strings: *The Gods of the Greeks,* translated by Norman Cameron (London: Thames and Hudson, 1974), 148–49.

the surface a puer desire to flee the arena of Ares and Aphrodite, and Harmonia too, in search of the virginal, untouched country of Artemis. We see this pattern at work socially in that our national "founding fathers" not only create a political climate where productivity can flourish and traditional values and desires can be realized, they also set limits and impose structures which they feel impelled to defend with force. And, like Cadmus, in order to build their cities they engage in combat with the earth mother. In response, an attitude of agrarian romanticism arises—a counterculture—and young Actaions move to the hills and streams and resuscitate religions of nature. In families, fathers play out their daydreams of royal rule and plant in their sons a longing for the freedom to be untamed. And in the individual, as well, a reigning Cadmus heroism and kingliness may become so overbearing as to generate a puer *wanderlust,* so that the Actaion fantasy leads one away from one's own ego patterns.

Aristaius

Puer longing and wandering may also be set in motion by another, more gentle, senex style. Actaion's father, Aristaius, son of Apollo and the Artemis-like Cyrene, was known as "the best god of all."[5] Brought up by centaurs in the cave of Chiron, an excellent school, he learned to heal and prophesy, and he was respected and sought after as a benefactor to human society. It was said that he freed Sardinia of wild birds, but more commonly he was recognized as a guardian of herds, a position which resembles that of a dog who watches over domesticated animals and protects them from threatening beasts. Aristaius was also the founder of beekeeping, having invented the beehive. We will soon see the importance of bees in the imagery surrounding this puer pattern. Finally, not unrelated to the bees, it was Aristaius who beckoned the cool winds when the hottest days of summer arrived—the time we and the ancients call "dog-days."

Like Cadmus, Aristaius tamed, organized, protected, and preserved culture, but he did it in his own gentle, beneficent way. His home was not in the city amid the complexities of rule and defense, but rather on the farm. His is a spirit closer to nature, knowing the winds and familiar

---

5. Kerényi, *The Gods of the Greeks,* 142.

with the industrious work of bees; nevertheless, in true senex fashion he builds fences, domesticates animals, and directs his energies toward a harmony of nature and human life. But even this moderate civilizing sensibility fathers the puer desire to wander. "Don't fence me in" is an Actaion wish that turns the soul away from even the most kindly and beneficial movements of culture and the civilized, well-taught ego. Whereas in mythology overbearing fathers instigate rebellion in their sons (Ouranos and Kronos) and guiding, instructing fathers breed a reaction of disobedience and excess (Helios and Phaethon, Daedalus and Icarus), Aristaius, a creative and sensitive architect of culture, gives rise to a son who sports and hunts and deserts the cultivated farm for the wild woods.

Actaion reflects that common boyish desire to get out of the house and explore the marvels of nature, not in adult scenic tours or in movies and slide shows, but close at hand. Boys and tomboys wandering through fields and farmlands, investigating the odd faces and manners of animals, feeling the strangeness of uncharted paths and wild vegetation—these common childhood delights reveal that special puer curiosity, an affection and movement of the soul toward the unknown aimed at sheer absorption in the vision. In these innocent contemplative faces there is no trace of pragmatic motive or of the egoistic leering typical in more "mature" forms of curiosity. A moment's reflection marks a new direction in experience. Whether the soul discovers the inimitable untamed delicacy of a new-born calf or beholds the flush of an unfamiliar development in the virginal psyche, the usual rush of busy time slows and idles, a deep and inexpressible curiosity is somewhat satisfied, and the atmosphere rather ominously signals arrival at a crossroads, an initiation.

Like a boy let loose in the fields, Actaion wanders "with uncertain step" through the forest, and it is important to notice that it is his wandering, his aimlessness, that leads him to the grove of Artemis. Senex styles of curiosity, desire, and movement cannot uncover Diana, nature in her pristine condition. Measurement, research designs, statistical analyses, and other senex methods may uncover what they are looking for (often what they already know) but they do not come across Diana—unless the researcher takes Actaion's deviant path, but then he would be a wanderer too. The passage from Ovid makes it clear, as does the tradition of Actaion interpretation, that the young man's intrusion was the work of fate. In Titian's painting of Diana surprised by Actaion, for example, the goddess is given all the properties of Fortuna, goddess of fortune.[6] One cannot decide consciously to find the virginal retreats of the macrocosm or microcosm; they are accessible only to the wandering puer whose discovery is chance, even error.

Dionysus

One further central figure in the family of Cadmus, Actaion's cousin Dionysus, plays a major role in this drama. Kerényi emphasizes the importance of Dionysus by pointing out that the bull, prominent in Cadmus's history, prefigures the bull-nature of Dionysus.[7] The peculiar nature and proclivities of Dionysus permeate this lineage, and Actaion is no exception. Remarkable correspondences and coincidences strengthen the Dionysian connection. For example, Pentheus, another cousin, resists for a while the tempting invitation to participate in Dionysian worship. In the end, however, he succumbs to a violent reversal in which he becomes a double to Dionysus and is attacked and torn apart by the maddened women.

Significantly, Pentheus met his fate on Mount Cithaeron, the very same mountain where Actaion came upon Artemis. In *The Bacchae*, Euripides alludes several times to this parallel between Pentheus and Actaion, noting in particular the similarities between the Dionysian women and Actaion's dogs. We must, of course, keep in mind differences between the two as well. Pentheus felt the deathly Dionysian side of life as a consequence of his excessively masculine, senex efforts to maintain rigid control of his kingdom—psychologically, a spartan endeavor to keep ego king, supported by will power and tough, rigid rationality. Actaion, on the other hand, moves into the Dionysian scenario after innocent, youthful wandering.

There is no doubt that in the end, the god here, with his corresponding pathology, or *impact upon the soul*, is Dionysus. In Nonnos, the story

---

6. Marie Tanner, "Chance and Coincidence in Titian's *Diana and Actaeon*," *The Art Bulletin* 56, no. 4 (1974): 535–50. Among the many studies of Actaion among art critics and historians, Tanner's is exceptional for providing insight into Renaissance iconography.

7. Karl Kerényi, *Dionysos: Archetypal Image of Indestructible Life*, translated by Ralph Manheim (Princeton, N.J.: Princeton University Press, 1976), 26.

of Actaion is part of his Dionysian tales, and a recently explicated fragment from the Oxyrinchus Papyri suggests that the Dionysian context of the Actaion image is ancient, as old as Hesiod.[8] Therefore, we see deep in the Actaion pattern two deities, Artemis and Dionysus, working together to produce this particular puer fate.

Let us recall the character of Dionysian dismemberment. Kerényi describes Dionysus as "indestructible life." Though dismembered, scattered, filled with death, nevertheless in Dionysus life endures. For Nietzsche, champion and model of Dionysian sensibility, the Dionysian way is to say "yes" to life in all its ecstasy and pain—"the will to life rejoicing over its own inexhaustibility even to the very sacrifice of its highest types,…the eternal joy of becoming *beyond all terror and pity.*"[9] In Walter Otto's words: "With him [Dionysus] appears the unfathomable mystery of life and death cemented together into a single entity,"[10] In the context of Dionysus, there is no moralistic or psychologistic choice of life over death, pleasure over pain, or wholeness over dismemberment. Dionysus does not rise triumphant over death, rather he lives as he dies. Therefore, the end of Actaion, a Dionysian enactment, is not tragic in the usual sense, eliciting pity and repulsion, but rather in the original sense of the *sparagmos,* the ritual rending of the goat, where the feeling of terror is in the tearing of ego. Actaion is not punished moralistically for having trespassed on sacred ground, he simply enters upon his essential fate, his necessity. The sporting youth wandering in the forest of the soul, stumbles upon nature, inner nature perhaps, in her most naked and washed purity, and of necessity his nature is turned around. Formerly a hunter, cultured and educated, though dallying on the borders between the light and the dark, the raw and the cooked, the farm and the forest, he is now turned into the hunted one, himself raw, dark, forested, and horned

These relatives of Actaion and the gossip concerning his elders form not just the backdrop but the ground itself of his story. These "relations"—

---

8. A. Casanova, "Il mito di Atteone nel Catalogo esideo," *Rivista di Filologia e di Istruzione Classica* 97 (1969): 31–46.

9. *Twilight of the Idols,* in *The Portable Nietzsche,* edited and translated by Walter Kaufmann (New York: The Viking Press, 1968), 562.

10. Walter F. Otto, *Dionysus: Myth and Cult,* translated by Robert B. Palmer (Bloomington: Indiana University Press, 1965), 201.

Cadmus, Aristaius, Pentheus, and Dionysus—provide both contexts and contrasts, the *metier* for this puzzling drama of the horned boy.

ARTEMIS AND DIONYSUS

The terrible death-dealing side of pure nature is revealed in the mythic image of Artemis, who was widely recognized in the ancient world as a manifestation of the Earth Mother and as *"potnia therōn,"* Lady of the Beasts. In her mythic adventures she is often hard and cruel, as when she kills the young Orion with her scorpion after he has accidentally touched her. In later representations, when she is related to or identified with Hecate, Artemis can be seen as the dark side of the moon—that aspect of pure nature that is wild, dangerous and unpredictable. One does not wander too far into the untamed wilderness of nature or of the soul without risk. In the case of Actaion we find Artemis's deadly nature revealed once again, but this time we see the relationship which exists between contact with untamed nature and Dionysian falling apart.

According to Nonnos, the dogs change their allegiance at a cue from Artemis; at her nod they are maddened and pursue their former master. As we will see in another context, Artemis has the power to "uncivilize," to return things to their earlier forms. In the dark, deep interior where Artemis rules, one cannot trust impulses and instincts which in a more cultivated world serve their master. In Ovid, the dogs are referred to explicitly as the "servants" of Actaion, but with only a nod from Artemis they become mad, lose their training, domestication, and loyalty; wild again, they no longer serve human purposes. The civilized instincts of intuition, curiosity, premonition, longing, and ambition—feelings the puer mentality may assume will serve his plans and ideals—may cease tracking the wild beasts of nature and turn on their master, attacking the ego, surprised in puer innocence, tearing it apart with the ferocity of Dionysian maenads.

Nonnos is more explicit than Ovid in showing the two sides of Actaion's fate: his innocent curiosity and his subsequent painful transformation. In Nonnos, he appears to his father as a ghost in a dream, where we see a psychologizing and deepening of his puer idealism. He relates how mercilessly *he* is now hounded with feelings of regret and remorse. "Father," he laments, "if you had only kept me unversed in hunting." "If only I had loved a mortal girl." He even resents the character of his death: "Would that a scorpion had killed Actaion with a sharp sting!" "Remorse, literally to be bitten or stung, well expresses the reversal by which the daring hunter becomes the lamenting hunted—bitten by his own dogs and stung by his bees of innocence. Puer sensibility is susceptible to the bite and sting of Dionysian deepening. Dionysus, a lord of death, gives life its depth dimension precisely through sensations of being scattered and dismembered. Unsuspecting puer innocence—carefree sauntering into some new experience—turns into regret and remorse. It takes innocence to enter some virginal territory; yet that boyishness sets us up to be "stung," a colloquial image for the pain of innocence betrayed.

We see a similar reversal in psychology itself. Modern man has put his trust in domesticated language, the tame jargon of textbook psychology, the hounds of his introspection. These, too, at the overpowering will of the goddess of inner nature, have come to dog him. Only rarely does a psychological wanderer acknowledge polytheistically the Dionysian reality: *any true entry into the unknown interior, the forest of the psyche, entails a reversal, a breaking up of the mentality that entered the woods.* One becomes as unpredictable and mysterious as that which one hunted. In physics, the observer is to be taken into consideration when reporting an observation, but in psychology, more radically, the observer *becomes* that which he observes. Psychological creativity is not simply a talent one brings to psychological investigation, like a dog on a leash; one's soul itself is affected in the process of introspection.[11] We who start out as skillful hunters, enthusiastically and confidently in search of firm knowledge about the psyche, become mysterious and elusive ourselves. Drawn toward mystery with the illusion of conquering, we soon become as mysterious and untamed as that we sought to overcome.

Even outside academies and consulting rooms, popular attention to psychology and introspection destroys the unconsciousness of psychological innocence. Modern psychological awareness has not made life simple and carefree; on the contrary, we are hounded by questions, doubts, remorse, and confusion. The Actaion reversal appears, for example, in popular curiosity about dreams. People often bring a naive enthusiasm to the study of dreams, prepared for a pleasant excursion

---

11. James Hillman, *The Myth of Analysis: Three Essays in Archetypal Psychology* (New York: Harper Torchbooks, 1978), Part One: "On Psychological Creativity."

in this curious but unfamiliar territory. They do not recognize the awe-
some power of this untamed, inhuman world, literally filled with beasts
and unknown dangers. Eventually, if they truly wander, like Actaion
with eyes open, they will feel themselves turned into prey, hounded
and lacerated by the dogs of this wilderness. One glimpses the soul in
unusual purity by looking into dreams and in other forms of psychological reflection. Here Artemis may be caught unawares—but Dionysus
has his part to play as well.

James Dickey's *Deliverance* depicts the Actaion image in a modern setting, vividly showing innocence and terror inescapably joined
in a puer wandering into the woods.[12] In the novel, Lewis is especially
Actaion-like: an expert archer, bored with his job, uneasy amid talk
about sex, and obsessed with the desire for immortality.[13] The four men
want to "break the pattern" in which they find themselves, and so they
go "off the beaten path," leaving civilization for the mysterious woods.
"In there," as they speak of the country cut off from civilization, they discover the brutality and indifference of nature, especially the merciless
power of the river, which Dickey describes as "some supernatural force
of primal energy." Of course, they also behold their own capacity for
murder, and in the struggle to survive, old values are torn to shreds. Ed,
the narrator, imagistically demonstrates that he, the hunter, is also the
hunted, when he shoots a fatal arrow at a suspected enemy and simultaneously forces another arrow through his own flesh. Tracking down his
victim he "could not tell," he says, "which was my blood and which was
his."[14] The Dionysian factor is revealed in the irrational discovery that
physical pain can be "luxurious." To affirm the Dionysian is to recognize
and appreciate the place of pain and death in life, and to tolerate the full
range from death to life and from pain to ecstasy, including the wounding in which one is "delivered" from the flat ennui of numbing conformity to cultural and familial expectations.

---

12. James Dickey, *Deliverance* (Boston: Houghton Mifflin Co., 1970). Set against the
background of the Actaion myth, many elements in *Deliverance* are highlighted and
amplified, though Dickey's fiction is not as closely and explicitly related to the myth
as other literature is.

13. Ibid., 9. Like Actaion, Lewis chooses the immortal over the natural and mortal;
he is led into a quest for the soul in nature.

14. Ibid., 196.

Another literary source which brings the Actaion image into modern life is Robinson Jeffers's "Science."

> Man, introverted man, having crossed
> In passage and but a little with the nature of things
>   this latter century
> Has begot giants; but being taken up
> Like a maniac with self-love and inward
>   conflicts cannot manage his hybrids.
> Being used to deal with edgeless dreams,
> Now he's bred knives on nature turns them also inward:
>   they have thirsty points though.
> His mind forebodes his own destruction;
> Actæon who saw the goddess naked among leaves
>   and his hounds tore him.
> A little knowledge, a pebble from the shingle,
> A drop from the oceans: who would have dreamed
>   this infinitely little too much?[15]

The scientist peers through his microscope and his telescope like Actaion gazing at Artemis from the tall oak tree. Whatever his intentions and motivations, and whatever "servants" he brings with him in the form of method, instrumentation, or symbolic language, once he has *seen* the unknown his nature is transformed. There is no going back. A mere drop from the oceans scatters the mind that dared take even a passing glance at that which is holy because it is pure and uncultivated. Science, though in recent years shocked by some of its monstrous creations and cautious in the face of public scrutiny, nevertheless generally considers its motives irreproachable, its methods trustworthy, and its productions safe; yet every move into virginal nature carries with it the threat of disintegration. This is not to judge science moralistically, but rather to gain a perspective on science through the mythic image of Actaion. Scientists tend to tout their innocence and purity—"pure science"—like true Actaions, and like him they often admit their regrets and remorse too late. The image of Actaion in myth brings into focus the dark side of innocent exploration and investigation.

---

15. *The Selected Poetry of Robinson Jeffers* (New York: Random House, 1937), 173.

A scientist is like Actaion—innocent and yet threatened—in his research, speculation, and theorizing. It is not a question here of nature's revenge for man's heroic attack on the earth and its natural progeny, the developer's frenzied bulldozing of all standing vegetation. Gilgamesh heroically defeats Humbaba and devastates the cedar, but Actaion quietly and swiftly travels the woods with little trace, armed with bow and arrow, an image of his erotic pull into the depths of nature rather than an instrument of subjugation. Actaions, therefore, are not punished for outright crimes against nature; rather, they are deeply affected by their visions, by their very identification with the pristine qualities of the virginal.

HORNS OF SPIRIT

Let us return to that striking image of Actaion making contact with Artemis. Ovid reminds us that Artemis is the tall goddess; she stands too much above her companions to be curtained by their bodies. Like the mountains where in ancient Greek religion she was to be found, Artemis focuses attention upward and her posture is vertical—Artemis Orthia, the "upright," worshipped thus in Sparta.[16] Actaion's name, too, may suggest mountain[17] or coastal peak.[18] In the figures of both Artemis and Actaion, therefore, we find an upward spiritual tendency, typical of the puer and of the goddess who is the patroness of youth.

The tall, upright Artemis responds to Actaion's intrusion by throwing water on his head, causing horns to sprout. Once again we have to resist the temptation to read this moralistically as punishment and instead explore the significance of the action. Actaion is not simply made into a beast, though he clearly loses his human appearance and his capacity for human expression. He becomes a particular beast, a stag, whose outstanding characteristic is his rising, branching, pointed horns.

In myth and iconography, Artemis has many points of contact with deer and their horns. Pausanias (6.22) informs us that the goddess was

---

16. For a discussion of several suggested interpretations of the "upright" Artemis, see H. J. Rose, "The Cult of Artemis Orthia," in *The Sanctuary of Artemis Orthia at Sparta*, edited by R. M. Dawkins (London: Macmillan and Co., 1929), 403-4.

17. Jacques Bonnet, *Artémis d'Ephése et la légende des sept dormants* (Paris: Libraire Orientaliste Paul Geuthner, 1977), 40 n. 3.

18. Casanova, "Il mito di Atteone nel Catalogo esideo," 45.

worshipped as Artemis Elephiaia (*elaphos*, deer). In the Callimachus's "Hymn to Artemis" (3.103), she goes out and finds deer whose horns "shine gold," puts golden bridles on them and harnesses them to her vehicle. In the story of Iphigeneia, too, the deer is prominent. Her name means "she who governs births with power" and was probably a title of Artemis herself.[19] According to the famous tale, Iphigeneia, daughter of Agamemnon, was to be sacrificed to Artemis as substitute for a deer "with its antlers sprouting and dappled hide,"[20] but Artemis rescued her at the last moment and re-substituted a deer.

The deer not only accompanies Artemis as huntress and Lady of the Forest, the antlers, too, represent the intense spirituality of this virgin goddess. Onians explains that in classical times horns were understood to be an outgrowth of the brain and therefore manifested soul and fertility, elements thought to be contained in the head.[21] He also mentions the practice of covering the heads of the dead with gold, and then the related practice of gilding horns, like the Minoan horns of consecration and similar horns on the altar at Delos and in Hebrew worship.[22] The gold seems to have witnessed to both psyche and immortality, while its brilliance, like the shafts of Apollo, graphically conveyed the light of spirit.

As Actaion was transformed from human to beast, he began to feel the weight of this horn of spirit on his head, another sensation of Actaion consciousness: *an excessive burden of spirit.* Awareness of the horns gradually growing and then weighing down the head and shoulders is the feeling of heavy idealism, spiritual ambition, and extreme sublimation in the Freudian sense. Dickey says of Lewis in *Deliverance* that the burden of his own "laborious immortality too heavy to bear" tempted

---

19. Karl Kerényi, *The Heroes of the Greeks,* translated by H. J. Rose (London: Thames and Hudson), 331.

20. Ibid., 132.

21. Onians sketches an etymological relationship between brain (cerebrum), fertility (*cerus*), and horn (*cornu*). He also mentions a connection between the horn of plenty and the river god Acheloos, a connection which might help us understand the importance of the river in *Deliverance*. Finally, he adds a reference to Homer's observation that dreams which are fulfilled issue through "gates made of horn" (*Odyssey* 19.562–67); see Onians, *The Origins of European Thought*, 233–44.

22. Ibid., 237. See 1 Kings 1:50.

him to get rid of it in an accident.[23] Actaion consciousness dehumanizes not by exposing low bestial potentialities but by revealing a grotesque excess of spirit. In Nonnos, Actaion tells his father (and us) that if we wish to make an accurate image of him we should show him with the body of a stag and the face of a human. We must not lose sight of the *grotesque* nature of his fate.

Horns of spirituality appear in other contexts as well. One of the most well-known "horned men" is Moses, horned as he comes down from the mountain after having seen Yahweh, a visage epitomized by Michelangelo.[24] Jesus, too, is an Actaion figure, raised on a cross or tree, torn to pieces, and crowned with thorns that focus unbearable pain and heaviness on his head. In the *Ovid Moralisé,* attributed to Philip de Vitry, Jesus is identified with Actaion, crucified after beholding a vision of the Trinity. In hagiography, Saints Hubert and Eustace trace the Actaion pattern, first beholding a grace-filled vision of Jesus crucified, the cross appearing between the horns of a stag, then finding their lives destroyed and finally martyred. Dürer placed many Actaion elements in his etching of St. Eustace's vision, but Pisanello's version even more strikingly reveals the fantastic and spiritually intense tone of the image.[25] Shamans as well wear horns on their heads when engaged in their spiritual practices.[26] The horns of Actaion appear not only on the young men who fill our scientific laboratories and psychologists' offices, but also on those youthful heads meditating in ashrams and zendos, intent on achieving spiritual heights. As their horns grow their natures change; they appear too much in the spirit to be human. They find it difficult or impossible to express their thoughts in human language—their insights are "ineffable" and silence is golden; often, too,

---

23. Dickey, *Deliverance,* 9.

24. Exodus 34:30. The Hebrew *qaran* (קָרַן), to be radiant, was misread as *qeren* (קֶרֶן), horn, hence the Vulgate translation: "his face was horned."

25. Pisanello's work is often cited for the realistic detail with which the animals of the forest are portrayed, but the fantastic nature of the painting highlights the dreamlike appearance of the crucifix among the horns. The same vision, only this time granted to St. Placidas, may be seen among the stained-glass windows of Notre Dame de Paris.

26. Mircea Eliade, *Shamanism: Archaic Techniques of Ecstasy,* translated by Willard R. Trask (Princeton, N.J.: Princeton University Press, 1972), 155 and 462.

Pisanello
The Vision of Saint Eustace, c. 1438–42
Egg tempera on wood
The National Gallery, London

beneath the placid veneer of peace and tranquility, they feel the teeth of the "Hound of Heaven" in perfectionism, scrupulosity, and unattainable purity.

The horns are also, obviously, sexual. Actaion is excessively masculine in his spiritual ambition. Even today we talk about "stag parties" and going someplace "stag," signifying complete decontamination from the feminine. Avoidance of the feminine might also appear as chastity or celibacy—the virginal psyche may be encountered through sexual virginity. Young religious seminarians and monastic novices offer a concrete image of Actaion consciousness with their obvious concern for spirit, their idealism, and their removal from the entanglements of sex. Like lovely deer in the woods, those pueri may be immensely attractive, and yet lack a certain human complexity.

Part of the pathology found in the Actaion image is the sense of impotence arising from exaggerated attention to spirit. Horns are the source of fertility and potency as well as spirit, but, in the case of Actaion, tradition imagines the horns as signs of inadequacy. To be "actaioned" or "horned" has long meant to be revealed and reviled as sexually impotent.[27] The cuckolded husband has horns on his head, sometimes made with a gesture of the fingers, signifying that his "horn" has to be supplemented. Therefore, in the Actaion puer pattern, extreme potency in the realm of spirit is accompanied by impotence in the lower parts. In Freudian fashion we might imagine that fertility and potency are "displaced upward," "horniness" sublimated from the genitals to the head.[28] Actaions may lack the earthiness, warmth, and eros that is given by "lower" nature; they seem psychologically top-heavy.

The Artemesian Baptism

Artemis, virgin goddess of pure nature, embarrassed and angered by the intrusion of human eyes at the moment when she is purest and most naked, sprinkles Actaion's head with water, an action that begins his transformation into a stag. Artemis's ire reflects the resistance of nature, whether inner or outer, to the work of human consciousness. The virginal psyche and the cultivated soul are basically incompatible, precluding each other; one must give way to the other. Often the fantasies and impulses of the uncultivated psyche, those blinding and confusing movements of the soul, are tamed by rational paradigms and cultural forms. But nature and the unbroken stirrings of the psyche may sometimes take command and dissolve human learning and understanding. Raw, irrational feelings may seize consciousness and produce the sensation of utter terror and confusion which Actaion feels.

Artemis, by nature a goddess of purity, is absolutely undefiled as she stands deep in the woods, naked, and in her bath. She is like Hera and other goddesses who renew their virginity in an annual bath.[29] And like

---

27. See Onians, *The Origins of European Thought*, 242–44.

28. Ibid., 243 n. 6. Stags' horns grow every year for sexual contest, but when stags are castrated, their horns do not grow fully.

29. Karl Kerényi, *Zeus and Hera: Archetypal Image of Father, Husband, and Wife*, translated by Christopher Holme (Princeton, N.J.: Princeton University Press, 1975), 119 and 131. Kerényi also mentions the ritual practice of "binding" Artemis, as Hera was bound, to protect against her dangerous aspect (164). See also Joseph Campbell,

Hera Artemis was imagined to be the new moon rising from the bath of purification.[30] Jung pointed to several images connecting Artemis's lunar nature with Actaion. He describes a parable from the Museum Hermeticum, the cover of which pictures Artemis and Actaion: A prince sees Diana bathing, joins her, and is pulled down into the water. Their souls appear above the water and announce that they will not return to "bodies so polluted."[31] Jung also shows the similarity between Actaion's encounter with Artemis and the image of Apollo surprising Coronis, the black crow-maiden, the new moon, as she is bathing in Lake Boibeis:[32] alchemically, Coronis represents the phase of *putrefactio*. (Incidentally, Jung mentions a further aspect of horn imagery, noting that the stag renews his horns annually and therefore serves as still another image of lunar death and renewal.)

Rafael López-Pedraza describes baptism as an acceptance of being connected to the god whose child one is.[33] Actaion's baptism on the head identifies him with the dark moon of Artemis, shows the dissolution of culture and learning, and marks the appearance of the horns of "headiness" and extreme spirituality.[34] This baptism signals a new perspective, cleansed of stale and borrowed learning and enculturation. More deeply, it may be a baptism into pristine, archetypal vision—an entry into the virginal psyche. Giordano Bruno suggests this interpretation of Actaion's vision in his Heroic Frenzies where he applies the persistent Renaissance neoplatonic focus on the psychological transparency of things, as opposed to a crass, concrete, materialistic perspective. Actaion's dogs, he says, are "thoughts bent on divine things, who

---

The Masks of God: Occidental Mythology (New York: Viking Press, 1970), 476.

30. Bonnet, *Artémis d'Ephése*, 81.

31. C. G. Jung, *CW* 14: 144.

32. Ibid., 157 n. 336. On Coronis, see also Karl Kerényi, *Asklepios: Archetypal Image of the Physician's Existence*, translated by Ralph Manheim (New York: Pantheon Books, 1959), 93ff.

33. Rafael López-Pedraza, *Hermes and His Children* (Zurich and New York: Spring Publications, 1977).

34. Onians quotes Democritus who claims that horns are an outgrowth of moisture in the head: "The horns grow forth, watered by the abundant moisture. The moisture, being continuous and flowing in, thrusts out the parts in front of it and the emerging liquid outside the body becomes hard, the air congealing it and turning it to horn"; *The Origins of European Thought*, 237.

"devour this Actaion and make him dead to the vulgar, free from the fleshly prison."[35] Puer wandering away from "tried and true" assumptions and values may lead deep into an immaculate imagery, the region of the archai, images underlying surface events but so unfamiliar as to be unusually powerful and disturbing. When Actaions explore unknown fantasies, not like the hero but like the innocent wanderer, they may see things hidden from others, but they may also feel the disintegration of old values and may not recognize themselves, so affected are they by what they have seen. Artemis splashes water on the face of consciousness, and the soul wakes to a fresh perspective.

In the 1960s, especially, we saw vivid biographical images of Actaions turning to drugs and drug rituals with spiritual motives, or establishment types flying off to the mountains of India. These youthful idealists demonstrated the self-destructive aspect of the puer: to be torn apart by their own spiritual visions, to have their life-styles, education, and plans "go to the dogs." The parents of these pueri, like Actaion's mother and father in Nonnos's story, searched for the children they used to know but kept passing them by, not recognizing them in their new shapes. Artemis drives consciousness back and away from developed, modern forms; back to long hair, beads, beards, and simple clothing; back to unprocessed foods and solar energy. In Nonnos, Actaion tells his father to look for his bow and quiver, unless Artemis has already changed them back into their native materials.

Dog Days and Bee Stings

The entire complicated picture of Actaion consciousness is given in a secondary set of images focused around that small animal emblem of virginity, the bee. Bees are not alien to the cult and iconography of Artemis. Bees and deer, for example, appear commonly on the coins of Ephesus, and the priestess at the Artemesion of Ephesus was called Melissa (bee).[36] According to Porphyry, the ancients called Artemis "Melitodes" or "honey-like,"[37] and in the version of the Actaion myth known at Corinth, his father's name was Melissos.[38] In *Hippolytus*, the bee alone

---

35. Tanner, "Chance and Coincidence," 549

36. Bonnet, *Artémis d'Ephése*, 34

37. Porphyry, *On the Cave of the Nymphs* 18.

38. Wilhelm Heinrich Roscher, *Ausführliches Lexikon der griechischen und römischen Mythologie* (Leipzig: B.G. Teubner, 1884–90), under "Aktaion."

is allowed to roam the meadow of Artemis, representing that wisdom of nature that furthers itself without violation. There is wisdom, form, and productivity in nature even when untouched by human intention, and this is part of the archetypal vision granted in Actaion consciousness.

Kerényi supplies additional information concerning bees that brings us back to a consideration of Aristaius and Dionysus.[39]

Before the advent of the wine god in Greece, the people were not without an intoxicating drink. They would mix honey and water, heat it up in the sun, and enjoy a spirited drink called mead. According to an Orphic story, Kronos was drunk on mead when Zeus castrated him. Pliny's home-style recipe for mead brings this concoction into the mythical realm of Actaion. The first step is to mix rain water, called "heavenly water," with honey in the proportion two to one. The mixture should then stand in the sun for forty days during the time of the early rising of Sirius, the time of the greatest heat. Literally, Pliny's direction reads: "let it remain in the sun at the rising of the dog."[40] For Sirius is the dog-star, rising early in the morning during the hottest days of summer. Roscher's lexicon in effect reduces the Actaion image to this astronomical aspect; however, we may see in it a further elaboration of factors already considered.

Bees are known for the sweet honey they provide and also for their sting. In the words of Kerényi: "The bees offered men the essential sweetness of pure existence—the existence of infants in the womb."[41] We find in bees, therefore, a reflection of Artemis's purity and her office of caring for women in childbirth, as well as her identification with dawn, eternally young, patroness of both the early hours of day and the first years of animal life.[42] In the modern cult of "natural" foods, in which purity and freshness are revered, honey is high on the list of favored foods. It is a cult of Artemis! This natural purity Aristaius domesticated, becoming the first beekeeper. Figuratively, beekeepers are those who bring human structures to this gentle apian wisdom of nature and of the psyche, like the psychologist-engineer who monitors and charts

---

39. For a rather extensive discussion of bees and mead, see Kerényi, *Dionysos*, 31–43.

40. Ibid., 37. Pliny, *Natural History* 14.113; see Bonnet, *Artémis d'Ephése*, 34.

41. Kerényi, *Dionysos*, 31. See also James Hillman's commentary in Gopi Krishna, *Kundalini, The Evolutionary Energy in Man* (Berkeley: Shambhala, 1971), 236.

42. Bonnet, *Artémis d'Ephése*, 70.

brain waves and skin temperature fluctuations, or the guru who tries to organize subtle impulses of the soul. But the son of Aristaius, a typical puer, prefers to visit the queen bee in the wild.[43] He is associated with another aspect of honey—its sting.

Honey and water exposed to the dog-star weather become mead, an intoxicating drink prefiguring the wine of Dionysus. The fermentation of mead like that of wine demonstrates, says Kerényi, that life is indestructible in fermentation, that is, even in decay.[44] It is the Dionysian mystery, the continuation, or better, the intensification, of life from the purity of honey and the grape to their destruction, dissolution, and transformation as mead and wine. The spirit of the puer, Actaion, is first like the purest honey-drawn to the undefiled and uncultivated, attracted by an immaculate imagery, by movements of the psyche not yet identified, labeled and enculturated. But once having seen the virginal quality of psyche, he is exposed to the dogs, the dogs of the sky, under whose biting influence he is lacerated and dismembered-fermented. Psyche takes on bite, maturity, and substance as the cultural forms formerly tacked onto the puer spirit dissolve and break apart.

Plato acknowledged two gifts granted by the season of the dog days: fruit and Dionysian joy (*Laws* 8.844d). It is a season, from the beginning of July to mid-August, when flowers bloom and bees are hard at their honey-making, and it is also the time for fermenting mead and wine—two sides of Actaion and two deities, Artemis and Dionysus. Mid-August was a festival time dedicated to Artemis, as later it was dedicated to the virgin of the Christian tradition, a virgin who had her own story of a horned beast, the unicorn, lured to her round garden to be killed by her hunters.[45] Whether imagined as thoughts which hound the heart (or hart—a pun long exploited in Actaion imagery) or as alchemical heat which matures the lofty fantasies of the puer, the dogs intensify the torment of betrayed innocence.

---

43. I am not suggesting any serious attention to the image of the "queen bee"; her gender was discovered only in recent timed.

44. Kerényi, *Dionysos*, 38.

45. Similar imagery appears in the biblical Song of Songs: "I hear my Beloved. See how he comes leaping on the mountains, bounding over the hills. My Beloved is like a gazelle, like a young stag" (2: 8–9). "She is a garden enclosed, my sister, my promised bride; a garden enclosed, a sealed fountain" (4:12).

Titian
Diana and Actaion, 1556–69
Oil on canvas
National Galleries of Scotland, Edinburgh

As Actaion wanders too close to naked Artemis, he is like a moth attracted to the light and extinguished by the heat of the lamp. Light as well as heat plays a role in this drama of metaphorical physics. Kerényi tentatively identifies Pindar's reference to the dog star as "pure light of high summer" with Dionysus. Dionysus is Sirius. Kerényi then notes a fifth-century vase painting showing a child-god emerging from the thigh of Zeus. The child is identified as *dios phos,* the light of Zeus. Vineyards are the gift of this star and of this god. The vitalizing power of fermentation is Dionysus's work: the dissolution of grapes into wine, and the wine's intoxicating dismemberment of social patterns and ego control. Even before Dionysus came to Greece, Orion's dog was known to have discovered wine, and Orion's dog was Sirius, that remarkable light in the summer sky.

The other light in that sky, the one heavenly body we have not mentioned in this astronomical excursus, is Artemis herself, the moon, rising at dawn in company with Dionysus-Sirius. Perhaps Titian's image of Diana and Actaion best reveals the mystery of Artemis's lunar nature. We see a crescent diadem in her hair and immediately behind her a black attendant, her double, her other side. In her, Actaion beholds the honey and the mead, the light and the dark. Lunar light is not as devastating as that of the sun, but the moon has its own kind of destructiveness. The dark moon, like Dionysus, is born in its death. Actaion spies the lunar Artemis in her stark purity, the moon precisely in its death. Her fullness is white but her freshness is black—Titian's double Diana. The dark moon is the avenging, cruel Artemis, close to Hekate, the underworld, and *their* dogs. In fifteenth-century Tarot decks, we see the moon's moisture falling, maddening the dogs. Diana's water of renewal brings horns of torturing madness to Actaion's head.

The Voyeur

The moon bright and dark, honey pure and potent, and the mythic image idyllic and tragic—these oppositions demonstrate the subtle ambiguities and paradoxes associated with the Actaion pattern. One further similar facet of this boyishness of the psyche appears in an obvious part of the myth we have not yet considered but which deserves at least a brief mention. Actaion enjoys a long look at that beautiful nymph-like maidenly goddess at her toilet. Nonnos pictures the young man high in a tall oak tree, taking in "the whole body of the archeress bathing; and gazing greedily on the goddess that none may see, he surveyed inch by inch the holy body of the unwedded virgin close at hand." Among other things, Actaion is an *innocent voyeur.*

Scoptophilia, taking pleasure in looking at certain things, is part of the Actaion manner. But as in so many psychological patterns, sexual behavior and interest intensifies and concretizes a broader concern. The Actaion puer may well feel drawn to the fascinations of the literal voyeur, but that tendency is only a signal of a more pervasive habit of watching life from a distance. One senses in Actaions a reverence for the virginal not only as life uncontaminated by society's rules and interpretations, as ideas not tried and tested, and as styles of relationship and expression not conforming to social standards, but also as a perspective not penetrated with insight, knowledge, and deep feeling.[46] Actaion consciousness keeps its distance and height and shows as well an element of narcissism—attention turning back on itself. It is not surprising, of course, that Actaion and Narcissus would have something in common, both pueri enjoying visual contemplation in the hidden hollows of nature. But whereas Narcissus consciousness becomes absorbed in the images formed in imagination and daydreams, the Actaion tendency is to allow external events to stimulate and sustain fantasy. This subtle interplay between the external world and private fantasy, and between sexual curiosity and a broader "hunt" is brought out delicately in Robbe-Grillet's novel *Le Voyeur.*

In the novel, Mathias's world has little to do with the people and events around him, except that they continually feed his paranoia and his sexual desire. The kingdom of his private fantasies is secret and set apart, as he makes no genuine contact with the many characters he meets and casts in his inner scenarios. He is out of touch with the concrete. *Reality hounds him.* Similarly, puer fantasy continually creates scenes and images based upon a modicum of experience. People become intriguing, worthy of observation, study, and thought because of all the themes they suggest, not because of their inherent value. The world of social intercourse is left behind by the puer who moves deeper into the woods of his fantasy, and the pain of his pathology begins when he has become no longer a visitor in that inhuman world, but an inhabitant.

The ultimate focus of this puer voyeurism is fantasy, though not all voyeurism is so contemplative and internal. The parallel images of Nonnos's Actaion and Euripides's Pentheus high in their respective oak trees, taking in the womanly spectacle, lead us to imagine two kinds of voyeurism: senex and puer. Both involve delight in watching the goddess and the dancers from a distance, but they originate in different styles of consciousness and focus on different conditions of the feminine. Senex voyeuristic desire appears as a compulsive attraction to behold the wild, savage feminine so incompatible with senex concern for order and control. Senex consciousness, enjoying a pornography of raw, unimagined sex, seems especially lured by exposure of the uncul-

---

46. A description suggested by James Hillman.

tivated, unrepressed side of feminine nature. Senex voyeurs like blood, mutilation and grotesque violence in their forbidden visions. Puer sensibility, on the contrary, comes upon the feminine as if by accident, in his wandering away from senex structures. His delight is in the pure, virginal side of the feminine. He likes his pornography soft and suggestive, a tease for his own fantasy. The longing, the hunt, the desire, and the distance from the object are essential to the puer experience, his *pothos*. He is not satisfied with conquest or acting out his fantasy. He wants to keep his visions pure, titillating though they may be.

Jung suggests that the voyeur looks at the world as at a circus, chiefly because he does not see the struggles of the world taking place within himself—he projects shadow outwardly.[47] Purity is indeed a problem for the newly baptized, especially for one who has been sprinkled on the head by Artemis. Fantasy is so much more exciting than "reality" that the puer is more at home in fantasy than in an embodied world. Cleanminded Actaions, furthermore, do not see the sexual side of their fascinations, the inescapable shadow factor in their voyeurism. Such voyeuristic purity or innocent voyeurism may be seen in young men and women "born again" in Christ or Krishna, lasciviously detained in a forest of purity, looking at the rest of the world as a circus of unredeemed monstrosities, yet unaware of the horns on their own heads making them no less grotesque. Or, Actaion may appear in the intense, impatient face of a social reformer, infatuated with his cause and chained by his dream of a perfect society. These Actaions are "horny" in the spirit—Casanovas lusting after untarnished ideals.

Voyeurism is classified as a perversion; it is deviant behavior. To become pleasurably absorbed in looking without touching, to tarry inwardly when any normal person would rush outwardly into action, is off that "beaten path"—*de via*. Yet, as Giordano Bruno lamented: "Very few are the Actaions to whom destiny gives the power to contemplate Diana naked."[48] As for any archetypal pattern, a simple normative attitude is impossible and undesirable. Senex types, who perhaps know from experience the dangers and subtle traps in innocent wandering and looking, scold young voyeurs. Yet, in spite of the dangers and the unavoidable dismemberment that follows such innocence, Actaions are

---

47. C. G. Jung, "Marginal Notes on Wittels: 'Die sexuelle Not,'" in *CW*18.
48. Tanner, "Chance and Coincidence," 49.

rewarded with new visions and fresh perspectives. Peeping Tom enjoys his glimpse of Lady Godiva, a vision of the feminine secret veiled to those who prefer not to let their eyes wander.

II. HIPPOLYTUS: THE YOUNG MAN AND HIS HORSE

> His top half felt all afloat in a starry firmament of ideals and young voices singing; the rest of his self was heavily sunk in a swamp where it must, eventually, drown.
> —John Updike, *The Centaur*

Prominent among the animals which roam the psyche in dreams and fantasy and stir the soul with obsessions, phobias, and fascinations is the horse. Young people especially are notorious for forming close attachments and unnerving fears regarding horses. Children's books and films reflect the young person's love for horses, as in *National Velvet, Black Beauty: The Autobiography of a Horse,* and C.S. Lewis's *The Horse and His Boy.* Freud's famous analysis of Little Hans, the five-year old boy with a phobia for horses, is only one of a number of psychological studies dealing with horses and youth. Peter Shaffer's play, *Equus,* won numerous awards and drew thousands of people to watch an imaginal horse-god race and bolt within the soul of a young man. Finally, perhaps most mysterious and intriguing of all, Euripides's *Hippolytus* depicts a young man trampled to death by his own horses, betrayed by the animals he grooms in utter innocence.

Obsessed with Freud's repressed Id and dominated by a ubiquitous moralism, Hippolytus's analysts have declared that the young man's death is due to rebellious passions. It has been said, in fact, that Hippolytus is the most abnormally repressed individual in all of Greek tragedy.[49] The horse then becomes an emblem for powerful passion, and the subtle problems occasioned by the "horsiness" of youth are passed over. D.H. Lawrence is among the few to argue against those who would see the horse as passion; he writes:

> In modern symbolism, the Horse is supposed to stand for the passions. Passions be blowed. What does the Centaur stand for,

---

49. D. W. Lucas, "Hippolytus," *Classical Quarterly* 40, nos. 3–4 (July 1946): 69.

Chiron or any other of that quondam four-footed gentry? Sense!
Horse-sense!...Horse-sense, I tell you. That's the Centaur. That's
the blue Horse of the ancient Mediterranean, before the pale Gal-
ilean or the extra-pale German or Nordic gentleman conquered.
First of all, Sense, Good Sense, Sound Sense, Horse Sense.[50]

Lawrence's horse is a "horse of a different color," a spirit intense and
vibrant, yet lucid and transparent—quite different from blinding,
opaque passion.[51] "It would be a terrible thing if the horse in us died for
ever," warns Lawrence.[52]

Poets and playwrights rewriting *Hippolytus,* and classical scholars
analyzing it, have regularly given only scant attention to the horse; yet
the young man's name is "horse"—*hippo.* Literally, "hippolytus" means
"horse-loosed," although Ovid translates the name as *furis diremptus
equorum*—overwhelmed by the furies of horses (*Fasti* 3.265). Horse is
of the essence of this youth, or, to put it another way, to have a horsey
nature is to dally with the unfortunate fate of Hippolytus. Hippolytus
is an image for a puer pattern of consciousness in which this particular beast is let loose, an example of the pathological outcome of ram-
pant horse power. Just as, in the presence of an actual horse, one feels
both the exciting power and threatening force that encircles and therefore inflects the animal's beauty and grace, so the horse of the psyche
exhibits both promise and threat. Both sides of this psychic beastliness
require insight so that we may see mytho-logically some rewarding yet
deeply disturbing powers of the puer attitude.

AMAZONIAN SELF-SUFFICIENCY

Hippolytus is not the only mythological figure, of course, to have horse
in his name and story. Hippe, for example, was the daughter of Chiron, the learned and respected centaur.[53] Hippodameia, the "tamer of
horses," was the prize in a great horse race that attracted the attention

---

50. *The Collected Letters of D.H, Lawrence,* edited by Harry T. Moore, 2 vols. (London:
Heinemanns, 1962), 2: 769.

51. See Adolf Portmann, "Color Sense and the Meaning of Color from a Biologist's
Point of View," in *Color Symbolism: The Eranos Lectures,* edited by Klaus Ottmann
(Putnam, Conn.: Spring Publications, 2005)

52. *The Collected Letters of D.H, Lawrence,* 2: 769.

53. For her story, see Kerényi, *The Heroes of the Greeks,* 70ff.

of Poseidon and Artemis, two deities intimately involved with the fate of Hippolytus.[54] "Hippo" is also commonly found in the names of Amazons. Hippolyte, in fact, is the name sometimes given to the Amazon mother of Hippolytus.[55]

Hippolytus, therefore, inherited some of his horse nature from his mother; for Amazons were known as lovers of horses. Hippolytus was occasionally described as an "Amazonian man," and this close relation to Amazons leads us further into the specific qualities of the horse. Amazons were shy with men, avoided them as much as possible, and especially resisted heroes like Theseus, Hippolytus's father. Two months a year they would have sexual relations with men in darkness, then they would sacrifice to Ares and the virgin Artemis. They would cripple the legs of their boys and would burn off one of their own breasts.[56] They would have nothing to do with men and marriage, but they put every effort into grooming their horses and waging war.[57]

We can see this Amazonian tendency in Hippolytus: turning away from the opposite sex, he directs his attention and desire towards his horses. The movement away from sexuality seems correlated with a movement toward the horse. In *The Cretan Woman*, Robinson Jeffers's modern version of the myth, the young man's love of horses is connected with his obvious homosexuality; and when *Equus* is acted on stage with male actors playing the roles of horses, their equine heads and hooves mere transparent, suggestive outlines, the homosexual tone of Alan's physical attention to the "horses" is inescapable. But it would be a mistake to understand this homosexual factor only literally and clinically. Here, like the horse itself, homosexuality is a metaphor. Turning attention to the horses implies not merely aversion to heterosexuality but disinterest in heterogeneity itself, in intercourse in the broadest sense. Concern for one's own sex suggests attention toward oneself.

---

54. Ibid., 62ff.

55. Ibid., 240. She is also called Antiope.

56. For a critical review of this mythologem and for further information on Amazons, see Carol Schreier Rupprecht, "The Martial Maid and the Challenge of Androgyny," *Spring: An Annual of Archetypal Psychology and Jungian Thought* (1974): 269–93.

57. For more details concerning Amazons as well as some psychological commentary, including a theory of "Artemistic eros," see René Malamud, "The Amazon Problem," *Spring: An Annual of Archetypal Psychology and Jungian Thought* (1971): 1–21.

This conflict between attention to self and demands for involvement with the outside world lies at the heart of Euripides drama and is represented in the difficult relationship between Artemis and Aphrodite. These goddesses are more than mere allegorical personifications of physical chastity and sexuality. They personify the depth and power of profound qualities of soul, felt and imagined in bodily sexuality and bodily virginity, but far transcending these factors.

THE VIRGINAL PSYCHE

Artemis is the huntress, often depicted in art with her tunic tucked up, roaming the woods and mountains, staying in remote places, surrounded by animal and vegetative life of the wilderness. Walter Otto describes her as nature itself—virginal, free, brilliant, wild, pure, and uncanny, remote and untouched, "a teeming concourse of elements, flora and fauna, life unnumbered."[58] Artemis is virgin nature: the pristine forest, the unassaulted mountain, the unseen stream. She is remote, far away from the human civilized world. "Seldom it is that Artemis goes down to the town, says Callimachus in his hymn to Artemis.[59] This goddess is not only "out of touch" with the human world, she is also untouchable, as the story of Orion demonstrates. Hunting one day with Artemis, Orion accidentally touched her clothing, and she, in a rage, sent a scorpion after him.

We may also imagine Artemis as the divinity of inner nature, goddess of those remote places of the psyche not yet given cultural form, as yet unnamed and untamed. We might encounter her in an actual walk through a quiet forest, sensing inwardly the emotions and fantasies stimulated by remoteness from civilization. Or, we might find her in the woods of the psyche itself, in those unfamiliar regions shadowed, tangled, dank and thick with vines, dead leaves, and underbrush. This terrain, difficult for human passage, is the psychological world of Artemis.

As a virgin, Artemis also suggests that capacity of the psyche to serve as an intact vessel of containment. The unbroken sexual membrane suggests other images of enclosure: the "garden enclosed" of the Song

---

58. Walter F. Otto, *The Homeric Gods,* translated by Moses Hadas (New York: Pantheon Books, 1954), 80–81.

59. *Hymns of Callimachus,* translated by A. W. Mair (New York: Putnam's Sons, 1921), 61.

of Solomon (4:12); "Les Baricades Mistérieuses" of the French com-
poser François Couperin;[60] the garland of flowers Hippolytus weaves
for his deity. More than thirty years ago, John Layard sketched a notion
of psychological virginity by contrasting images of Eve and of the Virgin
Mary.[61] Eve, he said, mothers the creations of the material world, while
Mary is the mother of our spiritual and psychological creations. With
Eve, imagination flows out into the world of matter, putting our fantasies into production. With Mary, our fantasies are contained; nothing
comes in and nothing goes out. We do not contaminate our thoughts,
feelings, and imaginings with introjections—expectations, standards,
and assumptions, usually moralistic, absorbed from the outside world.
Nor do we "act out" our fantasies, unaware, in the world around. The virginal psyche does not too soon put its contents to the yoke of culture. Its
moment is one of retreat and reflection. Though there is much activity
and movement, like the hunts of Diana this all takes place in the dark
of the forest, unseen by the civilized world, perhaps unnoticed by consciousness itself

Layard acknowledges his debt to M. Esther Harding, who describes
psychological virginity as an aspect of the psychology of women. We
need not restrict Harding's observations to the experience of women
as she describes how the virginal psyche might be manifest in a social
world. "As virgin," she writes, woman "belongs to herself alone, she is
one-in-herself."[62] This woman is motivated not by social convention or
approval but by faithfulness to herself. She does not identify herself
in reaction to a man or even to introjections from outside. "Woman is
what she is because that is what she is," says Harding in a tautology
that might be expected in a reflecting, mirror-like closed chamber of
psyche. Not responding to the outside world, or to that world internal-
ized, the virginal psyche manifests itself in untried and perhaps impossible wishes, in emotions not yet channeled and timed "properly," in
endless plans and schemes that have no hope of being actualized. In

---

60. Couperin saw a parallel between musical suspension—unbroken und unre-
solved harmonies—and the physical barrier of virginity.

61. John Layard, *The Virgin Archetype* (New York and Zurich: Spring Publications,
1972).

62. M. Esther Harding, *Woman's Mysteries: Ancient and Modern* (New York: G. P. Putnam's Sons, 1971), 103.

the virginal psyche, the world absorbed by the senses fails to serve as a standard and limit.

These qualities of Artemis as goddess of the virginal psyche—deep interiority, pristine freshness, imaginal containment, and freedom from external contamination—support puer psychology, itself a movement inward away from pragmatism and heroism toward imagination. When Hippolytus turns away from Phaedra in favor of his horses we may see a partiality toward the horse of the psyche, that which gives vitality and vigor to imagination and fantasy. The image of the horse Pegasus carrying Bellerophon high into the sky, serving as a vehicle for his soaring ambition to hear the conversations of the gods, demonstrates the empowering function of the horse in the puer pattern. People in whom this young man of the psyche breathes and moves not only exhibit an imagination of novelty and freshness, they also charge the atmosphere with their energy and nervous impatience—their horsiness—and, as we shall see, they suffer a corresponding pathology.

PUER AND VIRGIN

Artemis's patronage of youthful spirit is attested in archaic ritual and myth. She was called upon devoutly to protect women in childbirth, not as the goddess of birth itself, but of mothering and the young.[63] Whatever is coming to be and is not yet mature is under the care of this virgin goddess. In Greece young girls nine years of age were consecrated to her,[64] and young men, too, prayed for her protection.[65] The very virginal intactness of the psyche protects what is immature and unripe; Artemis takes care of the puer, for the young man is an image for the defenselessness and vulnerability of incipient developments in the psyche. Whenever new movements of the soul come to life, stir, and press upon consciousness, puer may constellate. One is then close to virgin soil, filled perhaps with the spirit of adventure, excited, nervous, and unsteady— like a colt on shaky legs, eager to run but awkward and unpredictable.

As the mythic images clearly demonstrate, Artemis is never herself a horse; nor, obviously, is she the puer. Yet all three are intimately con-

---

63. Malamud, "The Amazon Problem," 11.
64. Kérenyi, *The Gods of the Greeks*, 145.
65. Otto, *The Homeric Gods*, 88.

nected. The puer is that youthful movement in the psyche that requires a context of virginal containment and gives attention to its own energy and drive, grooming this horsiness for its own sake, lacking any senex goals and purposes. The puer and the virgin are mutually supportive: puer spiritual ambition, imagination, and flightiness represent a particular manner in which the virginal psyche presents itself; and conversely, the virginal incubation of psychic contents fosters puer's continuing fascination with the imaginal realm.

The boy, his horse, and the goddess also converge in a penchant for speed and swiftness. "Winged speed, haste—even the short cut—are imperative," says James Hillman in his description of puer consciousness.[66] There is no attachment, no "odyssey of experience." In a poem by Crinagoras of Mytilene, a young man begs Artemis to "lead him straight to the season of gray hairs."[67] For the puer, there is youth and old age, with nothing in between. Like Phaethon, Bellerophon, and Icarus, the puer strives for vertical flight. His feet are not on the ground. He has little patience for development, for working things out. Puer wants things done immediately, and his impatient idealism finds the sage counsel of the senex establishment an anchor and a weight. As the street pueri like to say: "It's a drag!"

Restless and nervous, the puer "chomps at the bit," ever ready to move on to something new. Movement itself seems more satisfying than endeavor or accomplishment. So Hippolytus runs his horses, as does Alan Strang in *Equus,* and as does each youthful spirit who races the engine of his Trans-Am or speeds his Harley-Davidson along a clear stretch of freeway.

The followers of Artemis, like the goddess herself, were also known for their speed. Atalanta, a famous if not altogether successful runner, is pictured in mythology and art with long stride and hair flowing; and Daphne, on the run, flees the advances of Apollo in an attempt to maintain her virginity. For virgins like Daphne, movement and flight is a desperate attempt to avoid intercourse. Virgin fantasy and imagination remain tree, uncontaminated and unpenetrated by a mascu-

---

66. James Hillman, "Senex and Puer: An Aspect of the Historical and Psychological Present," in this volume.

67. Otto, *The Homeric Gods,* 88.

line world, such as Apollo's insistence on enlightened consciousness, the senex concern for order and discipline, and the heroic efforts to put imagination to work in a pragmatic context. The virginal puer runs away from hard work and careful thought, not simply because of the effort required—in the right project the puer shows immense energy and strength—but because he does not want to be "tied down" to senex or heroic programs. He wishes to be free of the responsibilities of any "marriage" to a world of structure and demand. Along with his impatience, his desire to be a "free spirit" keeps him moving, like a cowboy in countless westerns roaming from town to town, never tempted by a picket-fenced homestead or a wife and family. In order to remain a virgin, the puer must keep moving, and for that purpose he exercises his horses regularly.

In modern popular imagery the young man is also shown lovingly grooming his hair with all the pleasure and absorption that Hippolytus brings to his horses. The physical vibrancy of the puer is part of his horsiness, as when weightlifting and jogging are judged in the mirror rather than in the wrestling ring. The homosexual tone associated with hair-grooming and cosmetic weightlifting is also part of the Artemisian world. The youthful followers of Artemis are often pictured with subtle hermaphroditic qualities. The Amazons, for example, by mutilating themselves and their sons activate their own masculinity and their sons' femininity.[68] The result is a sense of self-sufficiency and self-containment. As Hillman says, "There is therefore no need for relationship or woman, unless it be some magical puella or some mother figure who can admiringly reflect and not disturb this exclusive hermaphroditic unity of oneself with one's archetypal essence."[69] There is, as Harding suggested, faithfulness to oneself.

The unisex character of Artemisian hermaphroditism appears in images of the Goddess and in her cult. She herself is shown as a young huntress in the dress of a young man. Of Atalanta, a minor reflection of Artemis, Ovid writes: "...a face you'd call really girl's/in a boy, boyish in girl."[70] Kerényi informs us that when men performed the kordax

---

68. Malamud, "The Amazon Problem," 14.
69. Hillman, "Senex and Puer."
70. *Metamorphoses, Book* 8 (trans. Charles Boer).

dance in honor of Artemis, they made exaggerated female movements, and when women danced they wore artificial phalluses.[71] It is in this spirit of self-containment that Hippolytus turns his back on Phaedra to groom his horses.

As Hippolytus tends the horses in his care, he tends the horse within himself as well. Turning toward one's own horse, one finds an inner vitality either unavailable outside or restrained by external coercions. Alan Strang feels his own spirit shackled by the "chinkle-chankle"—the bit and reins that hold and curb his horse power. He mocks the so-called civilized world where virginal thought has been replaced by inane lilting advertising ditties. Buffeted by this culture, he finds vitality in *Equus*.

In "Roan Stallion," Robinson Jeffers tells a similar story of the discovery of horse power. California, a young woman dominated by an authoritarian, money-hungry, despicable husband, recovers her virgin sense of self in all its wild spirit through the stallion. To this day, in the body politic of the United States, California represents the puer spirit on its high horse. It is widely known as a state at odds with the rest of the country, a home for idealists, for social and psychological experimenters, and for fast living. Jeffers offers a rationale for such a puer spirit of rebellion: "Humanity is the mould to break away from, the crust to break through, the coal to break into fire, / The atom to be split."[72] As the oppressed woman, California, rides the stallion (like Alan, at night) she feels the energy of her recovered horse spirit: "She feeling between her thighs the labor of the great engine, the running muscles, the hard swiftness, / She riding the savage and exultant strength of the world."[73] Imagination is sparked by the spiritedness of the horse—one's own inner vitality and power. Aricia, a slave girl in Racine's version of *Hippolytus*, admits: "To fasten my dominion on a force as nervous as a never-harnessed horse—this stirs me, this enflames me."[74] Puer consciousness finds life and energy in an inner power, so unbroken and

---

71. Kerényi, *The Gods of the Greeks,* 149. See also G. Dickins, "Terracotta Masks," in *The Sanctuary of Artemis Orthia,* 172–73.

72. *The Selected Poetry of Robinson Jeffers,* 149.

73. Ibid., 152.

74. Jean Racine, *Phaedra,* translated by Robert Lowell, in *Phaedra and Hippolytus: Myth and Dramatic Form,* edited by James L. Sanderson and Irwin Gopnik (Boston: Houghton Mifflin Company, 1966), 127.

untried as to give a sensation of nervous and restless unease, but capable of breaking through the human moulds of learning and habit.

OF HORSES AND BULLS

We might get a clearer idea of the character and function of the imaginal horse by comparing it to another animal that appears in *Hippolytus*—the bull. The puer, with his horse, contends like a picador with the bull. Horse and bull are antagonists. So, what is said here about the bull, an animal so important in the fantasy life of the Mediterranean, is but a partial, biased view, the perspective of the young contesting horseman.

One of the most dramatic moments in Euripides's *Hippolytus* occurs when the nurse is trying to pry out from Phaedra the cause of her sickness. Phaedra tries to resist disclosure but the nurse is cunning. Finally, Phaedra gives in with an oblique remark about her mother. The allusion does not pass by the nurse. She responds: "The bull! You mean her lust for the bull? What do you mean?" Phaedra replies: "My misery began with them. It is no new thing."[75]

Pasiphae, wife of Minos, was the woman who fell in love with the bull Poseidon had given Minos for sacrifice. The unfortunate union of the Cretan woman and the bull brought forth the monstrous minotaur, a creature with the body of a man and the head of a bull. In the first part of *Hippolytus*, the conflict is set between the Cretan woman's daughter and the Amazon's son—the ancestry of the bull against the ancestry of the horse. Faced with an intense Artemis-puer alliance, Aphrodite mobilizes her powers of erotic compulsion, deception, and seductiveness with the purpose of luring puer to his destruction in his own fanaticism. Ultimately, it is she who conjures up the bull from the sea.

The bull, whose horns are seen in the nourishing crescent moon, seeds mother earth. It is his spirit and power that daily inseminate this modern world of material delights. Psychologically, he is that masculine, animal power that fertilizes and empowers attitudes of materialism and naturalism. The bull is the consort of all that is material, pragmatic, earthly, fixed, and natural. He is also, according to myth, the destructive force in service of the governing goddess, a function we see in the story of Gilgamesh when Ishtar sends her bull to punish Gil-

---

75. Euripides, *Hippolytus* (translated by Philip Vellacott), in ibid., 22.

gamesh for offending her. Therefore, while bullish brute power and natural instinct and spirit are important for survival, they are also dangerous. When nature, whether cosmic or personal, is offended or violated, it can avenge itself in cosmic or personal disaster.

In the image of the minotaur, bullishness has seized the head, the faculties of understanding and intention. This is quite the reverse of the centaur, in whom human intention—the human head—is served by the instinctive power of the horse body. In the minotaur, intention is bullish-pragmatic, unimaginative, concerned more for survival than cultural achievement, directed toward satisfaction of instinct and physical comfort. And to all of these earthly, dense purposes, human effort is bound. Socially, youthful, puer ideas and imagination are sacrificed regularly to this bullishness, just as in Crete young men and women were sent into the Minotaur's labyrinth to be consumed.

The bull's head is also a source of suffering, the pain and torture of the weight of animality and material sexuality burdening consciousness. Amid exhilaration in developing the land, increasing profits, and expanding "creature comforts"; and amid the satisfactions of "scoring" in the pasture of quick, physical attachments, this bullish potency depresses the spirit, hides the expressiveness of the individual human countenance, and creates a self-image of beastliness and insensitivity. In Picasso's minotaur etchings and especially in his "Guernica," the bull's head is monstrous and threatening, overpowering the shrieking, wounded horse; but in earlier representations in art, the minotaur reveals his own suffering and betrays a heavy self-consciousness of his own beastliness.

Yet the spirit inherent in the mother's material world, the Earth-Mother's realm of nature and survival consciousness, can be liberated, as is shown in the intricate Perseus myth. Poseidon, immediate source of the bull that made Hippolytus's horses bolt, is a consort of the earth goddess, a role mentioned in the Linear B tablets from Pylos.[76] But Poseidon himself is a horse. He had mated with the terrible mother Medusa, herself a horse, and when her head was severed by the sword of Perseus, she gave birth to both horse and puer: Pegasus, the flying horse whose spirited kick caused a spring to gush forth and thereafter

---

76. Campbell, *The Masks of God,* 47.

to inspire poets, and Bellerophon (Chrysaor), the spiritually ambitious young man. The horse's kick activates imagination and supports youthful spirit with power and loft. The muscle of the horse, unlike that of the bull, raises consciousness above the literal concerns of the mother's bullish practicality, and rather than depress spirit, the horse fills consciousness with restless energy and spiritedness.

Bovine pragmatism can also be contrasted with equine playfulness. The horses of the puer race rather than work, and this is an Artemisian trait too. Artemis herself is at home at the hunt, and her nymphs are always to be found racing or dancing. Within horse-sense there is an appreciation for horse-play. While the productive members of society are hard at work producing a comfortable world for us, the pueri are "horsing around, creating works of art or playing with words and ideas, dreaming up visions of idealistic worlds, and finding their *raison d'etre* in sports and athletics.

THE HORSE'S KICK

While the rhythmic pounding of horses hooves may be exciting at the race track, that same powerful kick can also be frightening. That same horsepower that activates imagination also threatens cultural and personal structures. It is not only the racing and dancing horse that kicks, but also the bucking bronco who refuses to be saddled with human intentions. From a senex point of view this horse-spiritedness is felt to be evil, as Alan Strang's mother complains: "I only know he was my little Alan, and then the Devil came."[77] When Freud tried to fathom the horse phobia in a friend's child, he saw an Oedipal fright stimulated by the obvious, visible sexuality of the horse. Jung was intrigued by Freud's analysis of Little Hans, but for him the sexual aspect was only a secondary factor. More significant to Jung was the rhythm and action of the horse's legs.[78] Freud himself mentions that Little Hans was particularly afraid when horses would paw their feet on the ground and was terrified one day when a horse fell and kicked *his* feet around.[79] The lit-

---

77. Peter Schaffer, *Equus,* edited by Adrian Burke (Harrow: Longman, 1993), 63.

78. C. G. Jung, *CW*5: 370.

79. Sigmund Freud, "Analysis of a Phobia in a Five-Year-Old Boy," in *Collected Papers,* translated by Alix and James Strachey, 5 vols. (New York: Basic Books, 1959) 3:195.

tle boy was also frightened once when he saw his father in bed with his mother kicking his feet around. It is the power and movement of the horse, its activation, that is frightening. Puer idealism and lofty ambition seem attractive and harmless in themselves, but the bucking, kicking energy that activates them can appear menacing—all that power ready for action but still awkward and nervous.

Those powerful legs of the horse can be more than menacing-they can either carry off their rider "at a mad gallop," as Jung says in his discussion of the etymology of "nightmare," or they can tread or trample people around them.[80] A young woman related a dream in which several young people were saved from flooding lowlands by a horse that brought them up the side of a mountain; later that same horse broke out of his corral and trampled to death all the youths but one, who was kicked to safety high on a fence. The strength of the horse rescues youthful consciousness from the flooding of emotionalism and materialism, but it threatens destruction as well. To quote Lawrence once again: "Horse, horse, when you kick your heels you shatter an enclosure every time."[81] The horse spirit will not be checked by the corrals of conscious intention or cultural forms. The kick of the psyche's horse breaks through these human partitions, manifested in the actual kicking rage of a young person resisting conformity to adult regulations, or in the painful inner sensation of having one's ego structures trampled.

MONOTHEISTIC WORSHIP OF THE VIRGIN

This particular equine pathology of the puer originates in his tendency toward a peculiar monotheism, a single-mindedness so virtuous and appealing on the surface that its potential for destructiveness easily remains hidden and overlooked. The attitude of daring typical of puer consciousness slips easily into an air of extreme self-sufficiency and then into an overbearing sense of pride and purity. Even the puer Narcissus, according to Ovid, experienced his protective virginal membrane as a hard shell of haughtiness (*dura superbia*). That intense pride and purity of the puer not only distances him further from ordinary human intercourse, it also leads him toward a reckless toying with dan-

---

80. CW 5: 370.
81. *The Collected Letters of D.H. Lawrence*, 768.

gerous borders. The puer may overestimate his strength (Phaethon), soar too high (Icarus and Bellerophon), or, in the case of Hippolytus, venture to the edge of Aphrodite's realm. Hippolytus leaves the green woods of Artemis in order to run his horses on the beach—and there he must confront the consequences of his headstrong allegiance to a single goddess.

Like the virgin forest, the beach is also an image of virginity. Jeffers has Hippolytus say to a friend: "Or shall we race/Our horses along the shore, where the careful waves/Comb the sand clean and smooth?"[82] In *Equus*, Alan enjoys his first intimate encounter with a horse on a beach. But the virginal sand lies dangerously close to the waters of Aphrodite, the very sea that threatens Phaedra with "shipwreck."[83] The danger, however, is not the threat of being overwhelmed by Aphrodite herself; as Euripides shows clearly, the problem is a hyperactivation of the puer's own horse spirit. The horses get out of hand, they run amuck. Hippolytus gets tangled in the reins Haughtily facing an ocean of passion with utter disregard for its claims upon him, the puer succumbs to his own inner spiritedness. A "high-minded" puer may be exclusively devoted to some intellectual or spiritual discipline, feel genuinely uninterested in sex and love and other concerns of Aphrodite, and experience no real struggle with passion; yet he may eventually feel betrayed and abused by his own purity. That drive toward spirit and pristine fantasy can madden, confuse, and disorient consciousness.

While mating with Poseidon's bull can create a depressive burden of materialism, that is, the emergence of a Minotauric mentality, when that same bullish power of nature rises into the purview of virgin puer consciousness, the result may be a manic stampede of thoughts and emotions. Aphrodite will not be staved off indefinitely. When avoided, unacknowledged, repressed, and reviled in an attitude of purity and superiority, she sends the bull, the full force of nature and bodily reality to frighten and menace the very spirit and energy one had trained to be pure. One's own sexual and earthy powers loom like a monster from the depths.

82. Robinson Jeffers, *The Cretan Woman*, in *Phaedra and Hippolytus: Myth and Dramatic Form*,178.

83. Charles P. Segal, The Tragedy of the *Hippolytus*: The Waters of Ocean and the Untouched Meadow," *Harvard Studies in Classical Philology* 70 (1965): 117–69.

The puer locked in his sanctimonious monotheism is not attacked from without, he is trampled from within his own pattern of consciousness. In *Hippolytus*, this monotheistic character of the virgin puer is demonstrated in the young man's proud purity and in his hatred for women. Hippolytus presents to Artemis a garland of flowers from a virginal meadow where only bees work; the meadow is open only to those modest from birth and is barred to the vulgar. He shouts a tirade against women whom he sees as a source of impurity, concluding: "I hate women, I'll never quell that loathing. Some say I'm insatiably hostile-but women are insatiably lewd. Either convert them to chaste decency or allow me to stomp on their sex till I'm dead."[84] When Hippolytus explicitly refuses to acknowledge Aphrodite, a servant gives him a warning that contains a solution to his pain: "My son, each god makes a claim on us which we may pay only in the god's coin—this is inescapable fact."[85] But, like the saints of legend, in the presence of Aphroditic "temptation" the puer becomes only further entrenched in his monotheism.

A puer attitude is often quite attractive and engaging in its idealism, youthfulness, spirit, dedication, and physical vibrancy. But these potentialities in Hippolytus are overshadowed by his narrow-mindedness and blindness, his insensitivity, misogyny, and haughtiness—all occasioned by his uncompromising monotheism. Even the goddesses he worships and ignores respectively acknowledge the possibility of polytheism. In the play's opening lines, Aphrodite tells the audience plainly that it is not the young man's worship of Artemis that draws forth her ire: "Such a friendship between human and god is a remarkable event— I would not deny him this happiness. I have no reason to. It's purely his offenses against me which I resent and will punish—today."[86] And at the end, Artemis reminds Theseus: "Since we gods have agreed not to frustrate each other's cherished purpose, we always stand aside."[87] Though conflict, ambiguity, and paradox are inescapable in any polytheistic consciousness, one may worship at the altars of both goddesses with-

---

84. Euripides, *Hippolytus*, translated by Robert Bragg (New York and London: Oxford University Press, 1973), 48.

85. Ibid., 22.

86. Ibid., 18.

87. Ibid., 79.

out any inner contradiction. In the sphere of sexuality, for example, for some a merely moderate sex life might rip open their delicately sealed interiority, while for others an active sex life poses no threat to psychological virginity. Or, virginity, like Artemis herself, might be imagined as a lunar phenomenon, with phases of waxing and waning, fullness and void. There may be a period when one's moon is full, so to speak, and it overflows, as in Norman O. Brown's notion of "erotic exuberance"—an eroticization of the world rooted in overflowing love toward one's own interiority.[88] One may have simultaneously a sense of purity and of promiscuity, an appreciation for untouched nature and for sensual pleasure, and a desire to be involved which is at the same time coupled with reserve.[89]

The problem Hippolytus has with Aphrodite, however, is not simply an enticement to love but specifically an invitation to love with his stepmother. James Hillman has observed that the puer has to deal with the seduction of matter, indeed seduction into incest.[90] In this sexual metaphor, the high-flying imagination and spiritedness of puer psychology is threatened by absorption into material forms and purposes. Phaedra herself saw that her passion for Hippolytus might be a repetition of her mother's love for the bull—that enticement toward materialism. Puer imagination needs body and therefore may gain by giving reverence to Aphrodite, but he must be cautious of the attraction of the mother and her bull. The puer may become literally fascinated with the physical curiosities and delights of sexuality, or in a broader sense he may be lured into fantasies of the mother's productivity. How many young puer authors, for example, commit incest by turning their talents to advertising copy, producing those jingles Alan mocks, selling their virgin souls to bullish markets?

Finally, in order to remain truly polytheistic, we might recall other gods and further possibilities. Hippolytus presents problems peculiar to the Aphrodite-Artemis conflict frequent and fundamental in puer psychology, but it does not offer the only mythic image of puer, horse,

---

88. Norman O. Brown, *Life Against Death* (New York: Vintage Books, 1959), 50.

89. A description I owe to James Hillman.

90. James Hillman, "The Great Mother, Her Son, Her Hero, and the Puer," in *UE*3: *Senex & Puer,*

and goddess. Athene, for example, is also particularly important in this regard since mastery of the horse is her prerogative.[91] In the thirteenth *Olympiad,* Pindar tells how Athene appeared to Bellerophon in a dream and gave him the golden bridle with which he could charm Pegasus: "The child of Zeus, whose sword is lightning,/ In her own hands brought him the golden charm/That tames the savage spirit."[92] In Greek, this bridle is called *pharmikon*—a charm or magic potion. We usually think of political, military, or intellectual elements in the wisdom or cunning (*metis*) of Athene, but here we are reminded that she can weave into the fabric of the polis a certain degree of magic and enchantment.[93]

Even in the ordinary, mundane, and normal dimensions of life a goddess is at work. Athene is a goddess associated with intellect, commerce, crafts, justice and judgment. She would seem to personify a realm quite rational and orderly. Whether we see her as the goddess presiding over her allotted realm, the city, or analogously over the ego, she would appear to arrange all things in a reasonable manner. But Pindar reminds us, in the passage quoted, that Athene also has recourse to dream and magic. Though charms and magic potions are more properly Medea's technology—witch's brew—they are also available to the more ordinary, surface concerns of Athene. With this recourse to the charm, Athene can tame the puer's horse, not breaking the animal's spirit altogether, but at least allowing the puer to hold the reins with some confidence. The horse Pegasus carries Bellerophon aloft after the animal has been bridled

Literally, the city in fact can embrace within it the groves of Artemis, putting a charmed rein on the wild. The city park is certainly not a virgin forest, but some of the forest of Artemis may be brought into the city as a meeting of the two goddesses, Athene and Artemis. Psychologically, the ego can acknowledge the raw and the untouched, tam-

---

91. Marcel Detienne, "Athene and the Mastery of the Horse," *History of Religions* 11, no. 2 (1971): 61–86. On Athene, see also Karl Kerényi, *Athene: Virgin and Mother in Greek Religion,* translated by Murray Stein (Putnam, Conn.: Spring Publications, 2008).

92. Pindar, *The Odes and Selected Fragments,* translated by G.S. Conway and Richard Stoneman, edited by Richard Stoneman (London: J.M. Dent, 1997), 86–87.

93. James Hillman, "On Athene, Ananke, and the Necessity of Abnormal Psychology," in *UE6.*

ing it not through intellectual cleverness or brute strength, but with a more magical intuition and imagination. Ordinary surface bridles will not check the horse within—bridles such as moralism, legalism, and repression. What will keep the horse from bolting is the golden charm given in dreams, in imagination—something beyond the power of ego alone to fabricate.

Athene is not a solution to the problem of Hippolytus, but her intriguing connection to the horse and puer suggests that in genuine polytheism conflict can never be reduced to simple dualism, dialectic, or two-horned dilemma. A polytheistic perspective always opens out onto increased complexity and additional possibilities.

RESURRECTION

There can be no final word about the young man and his horse because they have an uncanny habit of coming to life again and again. In legend, Hippolytus is restored to life and established in the grove at Nemi, a phenomenon that intrigued Frazer in the opening pages of *The Golden Bough*. Later, we hear of Christian saints named Hippolytus who were martyred on August thirteenth, the time of the Catholic festival of the Assumption of the Virgin, and a day dedicated to Artemis as well. Not surprisingly, these saints named Hippolytus were martyred by horses trampling them to death. In the words of Frazer, St. Hippolytus "is no other than the Greek hero of the same name, who, after dying twice over as a heathen sinner, has been happily resuscitated as a Christian saint.[94]

As we have seen, puer resurrects because resurrection in the psyche is puer. Always there is something incipient, some new theme or movement, and that beginning is itself psyche's puer. As Jung said, puer is "never anything but an anticipation of something desired and hoped for."[95] The horse accompanies that resurrecting puer as the power and vitality behind or under it. In the dream recounted in which the horse saved people from the flood but then crushed them, one boy was saved, kicked high to safety by the horse. The horse raises the puer, carries it high, and if necessary kicks it to safety. Puer fantasy is sustained and brought back to life by that nervous energy and boundless power

---

94. James G. Frazer, *The Golden Bough*, abbr. ed. (New York: Macmillan, 1922), 6.
95. C. G. Jung, *CW*5: 392.

found in the horse. In another dream told by a woman waking from a period of unconsciousness, the horse signals resurrection: Two boys are lying in the snow. One is dead. The other is caressing him affection-ately. For a moment the dead boy's head becomes a horse's head, then it fades back into the boy's face. The dead boy comes back to life, and then it is springtime.

First published in James Baird, *Ishmael: A Study of the Symbolic Mode in Primitivism* (Baltimore: The Johns Hopkins University Press, 1956) and emended for this edition.

Puer Aeternus:
The Figure of Innocence in Melville

JAMES BAIRD

In the sense of Jung's theory, an *archetype of transformation* is a theme (the snake, as one example, which marks the passing over of a commonly shared collective, without imagistic identity, from the areas of the unconscious to the areas of the conscious, wherein the collective is expressed in typical images. Jung's examples of such archetypes are extensive. In beginning a discussion of puer aeternus, the eternal youth, it will be useful to review some of these examples with specific reference to Melville. The archetypal richness of his work should be suggested, at least, even though it is certainly not my intention to offer a study of all the archetypal materials present in this art.

Melville may be thoroughly studied through Jung, of course, if one wishes to examine archetypes without attention to the nature of the unique symbol of the artist. I shall first quote some of Jung's examples, and then invite attention to some forms and incidents in Melville's work which may be studied in relation to Jung's distinctions. Jung writes:

> The birds and mammals are various forms of the sanguine instincts, whereas the serpent, the saurians, and monsters personify primordial, cold-blooded animal nature, and, as adversaries of warm-blooded, emotional nature with its panic excitement, are anticipations of everything divinely pre-eminent. Cave and sea refer to the unconscious state with its darkness and secrecy...Fire is emotional excitement or sudden bursts of impulse...Weapons and instruments represent the will.
>
> To the intermediate symbols belong...hanging, soaring, or swimming. Here, too, the tree has its place, or transformation into a tree, and represents rootedness, repose, growth, and a spreading

forth in the upper regions of air and light, as also the union of sky and earth.

The hero and the *puer aeternus* may appear as themes throughout the whole process.[1]

My choice of themes from Jung's categories is deliberately limited, since I wish only to propose figures and episodes from Melville which appear promising for study. Melville's albatross of *Moby-Dick,* in the footnote to the chapter on whiteness (LII),[2] shows such a bird-archetype as an anticipation of the "divinely pre-eminent." (So, too, does the albatross of Coleridge's *Ancient Mariner* show the same "divinity.'") Melville's obsession with the serpent appears at various points in his work in the form of the anaconda (to be discussed in a later chapter on imagery); and the sanguine instincts of mammals contending with the primordial, cold-blooded nature of the serpent may be seen in an obsessive image in *Redburn* (XX) of the whale swallowing Jonah "like an anaconda, when it swallows an elk and leaves the antlers sticking out of its mouth." Numerous descriptions of the sea, particularly those appearing in *Moby-Dick,* will provide examples of the "dark and secretive" unconscious. Ahab's address to the corposants (*Moby-Dick,* CXIX) and the fire of the try-works (XCVI) signify excitement and impulse. Ahab's will is represented by the harpoons. Billy Budd's hanging, Pip's descent through the primeval waters (*Moby-Dick,* XCIII), White-Jacket's fall from the yard-arm into the sea (*White-Jacket,* XCII) all suggest Jung's intermediate symbols of hanging and swimming. The tree and its relation to the Christian cross will be interpreted in a chapter to follow. At this point Melville's notice of the tree tattooed upon the back of the mysterious Marnoo of *Typee* (XVIII) may represent rootedness, repose, light (and the union of nature and man). These examples suggest the archetypal character of Melville's symbolistic expression. But it is the archetype of puer aeternus which presides over all of them. For it is the image of tattooed Polynesian and of innocent youth-outcast in the civilization of the Christian West, made one, which authorizes the symbols of sacrament displayed in Melville's primitivism.

---

1. C. G. Jung, *The Integration of the Personality,* translated by Stanley Dell (London: Kegan Paul, Trench, Trubner & Co, 1946), 93–94.

2. Roman numerals refer to chapter titles throughout the essay unless otherwise indicated.

Puer aeternus as Melville's full symbol is the emblem of corporate-ness, of communion with and in God. There can be no doubt of his obsession with sacrament, for he himself describes it in a confession to Hawthorne. As I shall presently show, the symbolic content of *puer aeternus* is the ideality of fraternal love between men, wherein the identity of one is discovered in the identity of the other. Melville's symbol is made of two disparate elements: the ideality of Polynesian friendship and the ideality of Christian communion in the Eucharist. It is perfectly clear in Melville's symbol that the inherited Christian ideality, no longer able of itself to command faith in a doctrinal reality, is brought to life in a new form by the addition of Polynesian reference. When this act occurs in Melville's art, it is perfectly clear, again, that the new sacramental symbol expresses a new reality: it means that the absolute self is relinquished to fraternal love and that the emphasis upon the self-act of Christ's suffering is exchanged for emphasis upon Christ as the innocent man among men. Despite Melville's professed resistance to Emerson's major theory, in this act he comes closer to Emersonian insistence upon Christ in the world, as a man, than any other American author.

Melville's concept of his relationship with Hawthorne is sacramental. Hawthorne has written to Melville his letter on *Moby-Dick* (November, 1851), that lost letter which every student of American letters would reclaim before any other American literary document, if he could. And Melville replies:

> Whence come you, Hawthorne? By what right do you drink from my flagon of life? And when I put it to my lips—lo, they are yours and not mine. I feel that the Godhead is broken up like the bread at the Supper, and that we are the pieces. Hence this infinite fraternity of feeling.[3]

The confession speaks for itself, and I shall not labor it. Melville's reference to feeling here must be understood for what it means. The fraternity of feeling offered to Hawthorne is the fraternity of selfless innocence, not the fraternity of men wrested from evil by the suffering of God. Melville brings to Hawthorne the feeling of Polynesian friendship, *tayo*, the

---

3. Eleanor Melville Metcalf, *Herman Melville: Cycle and Epicyle* (Cambridge, Mass.: Harvard University Press, 1953), 129.

same feeling which shapes the full symbol of Billy Budd, both innocent Tahitian and Christ, made one. Billy is the apotheosis of *puer aeternus.*

1. TAYO

Melville's ideality of selfless acceptance is expressed in *tayo.* This Polynesian word means friend or friendship, but it names a relationship which Melville and other travelers in the Pacific have seen as uniquely Oriental. Its equal is not to be found in the West. The custom of *tayo* is one man's acceptance of another man as his equal sharer. In the bond between the two, what one possesses, the other possesses; what success one has, the other shares; what adversity one encounters, the other must bear. This relationship usually comes about in early youth, and it may continue through the lifetimes of the two so bound together. The marriage of each will normally follow, and the rearing of the children; but these extensions of experience only widen the area of mutual responsibility in the bond which has been established. The ideality represented in *tayo* is distinctly Oriental. In it appears a union of two persons similar to that denoted by the sacrament of marriage in the Christian world. Ignorance of the meaning of *tayo* will, of course, permit vulgar errors in interpretation. Melville's confession to Hawthorne is no more than an expression of Melville's feeling about devotion between men as the release of self into selflessness. One may extend this fact by saying that he had the sense of men's love represented by Christ and the apostles. Or the sense may be Chinese, as it is described by Saint-Denys: "Perfect solidarity, mutual support, the sharing of both good and bad fortune between friends joined by a sort of marriage; such is the germ of strong cohesion which from the earliest times has possessed the Chinese race. In modifying the form of the pact, the centuries have not altered its essence."[4] But this sense in Melville, whatever parallels may be found for it, was a sense developed through his Polynesian experience and through his quest for sacrament, the feeling of oneness in communion. Hawthorne could scarcely have known the origin of Melville's offering, which he could not accept with an equal fervor (for some have said, and perhaps rightly, that Hawthorne's decision to go to his consular appointment in Liverpool may have been to some degree influenced by

---

4. "L'art poétique et la prosodie chez les chinois," in *Poésies de l'Epoque des Thang,* translated by Marquis d'Hervey-Saint-Denys (Paris: Amyot, 1862), xxix,

a desire to escape Melville's intensity). The origin of Melville's ideality, as this took shape through his natural talent for friendship, was what he had seen and felt of Polynesian *tayo*. (When the prototypes of Polynesian culture are recalled, then this custom would seem to derive from the far Orient.)

Melville's definition of *tayo* appears in *Omoo* (XXXIX). He relates that the arrival of his ship at Tahiti brought to the sailors troops of "tayos" eager to form an alliance after the national custom, and to do our slightest bidding." He remarks that the annals of the islands preserve the histories of many "Damon and Pythias" friendships; and he speaks of Polynesian hospitality in the extension of *tayo* to the first white visitors reaching the islands. Then he turns to a description of the youth who was his faithful friend while he was ashore at Papeete.[5] But *tayo* is not new to him here. He has already acquired the sense of it in Typee Valley. His account of his friendship with Kory-Kory and other men of the tribe and his description of the mysterious youth Marnoo (*Typee*, XVIII) show his earliest interest in the nature of Polynesian fraternity. It is abundantly clear, furthermore, that in his experience among the people of Nukuhiva he had already begun to think of that union in fraternal love which reaches its highest expression in the "marriage" of Queequeg and Ishmael in *Moby-Dick*.

The literature of primitivism shows frequent examples of thematic relationship between the *puer aeternus* and the friend. This archetype of fraternal love is a clear distinction of primitivism through the last century. Even in the work of authors in whom religious sensibility has no importance, the theme is present and potentially capable of what Melville does with it. The first of English "primitive" novels, Thomas Hope's *Anastasius* (acquired by Melville in 1849),[6] presents Spiridion, the childhood friend of the hero. Anastasius alternates between wishing to worship at the Christian altar with Spiridion and wishing to assert his freedom as a visitor in Islam. The love of Spiridion is ideal

---

5. In the following chapter of *Omoo* (XL), Melville presents another *tayo*, one Kooloo, who is an opposite ot Poky. Kooloo professes great friendship in order to cajole gifts from the sailors; he is quite faithless. Melville's play with the theme at this point means little when the significance of *tayo* elsewhere in his work is considered.

6. See Herman Melville, *Journal up the Straits, October 11, 1856 – May 5, 1857,* edited by Raymond Weaver (New York: Cooper Square Publishers, 1971), 19 n. 2.

and selfless: "To see me wise, to see me happy, and that through his exertions; nay, to sacrifice, if necessary, his own repose and felicity on this globe to mine, became the only bliss Spiridion aspired to on this earth!"[7] Here *puer aeternus* as archetype follows the familiar theme: the youthful wanderer completes his identification of self in the friend, even though Hope's achievement amounts only to a representational token of sentiment. Another example may be found in the narrative of Jack London's adventurer David Grief. This crude and tedious hero-voyager in Polynesia is admired by Mauriri, a native youth of the island of Fuatino, who makes complete the Polynesian voyage of the narrative as David's faithful *tayo*.[8]

The friend as he is presented in these widely separated accounts does not reach the status of the true life-symbol. In the art of Melville a different resolution of the archetype takes place. The voyager and the friend tend constantly toward symbolic union; and the evidence of this tendency is apparent in the prefigurations of Melville's early work. The full symbol of the mature art is to be made of two elements: the ideality of Polynesian *tayo*, and the thematic figure, on the other hand, of the solitary voyager who may be described here as the "sailor savage," to use Melville's term from the image employed in the discussion of seamen carving the likeness of God (*Moby-Dick*, LVII). The sailor savage is the "receiver" of *tayo* extended; and in Melville's final symbol, Billy Budd, the dichotomy is removed altogether as Billy himself becomes both wanderer and Polynesian friend.

It is obvious to every reader of Melville that the theme of the search for union in friendship is projected through nearly all his work. *Israel Potter, The Confidence Man*, and some of the stories should perhaps be excluded, since friendship in these pieces is not centrally encountered. But even here the theme of the voyager in solitary pursuit of reality through communion with his fellow beings continues. The other works are all in varying degrees concerned with the same theme. A review of the relationships of Ishmael, which may be adjudged as expressions of reality through communion, will be of interest here. They are found in these patterns: in *Typee*, Tom—Toby, Kory-Kory, Marnoo; in *Omoo*, Paul—

---

7. Thomas Hope, *Anastasius*, 2 vols. (London: Richard Bentley, 1836), 2: 350–62.

8. Jack London, *A Son of the Sun* (Garden City, N.Y.: Doubleday, Page & Company, 1912), 88.

Dr. Long Ghost, Poky, Shorty; in *Mardi,* Taji—Jarl; in *Redburn,* Welling-borough—Larry, Carlo; in *White-Jacket,* White-Jacket—Jack Chase; in *Moby-Dick,* Ishmael—Queequeg; in *Pierre,* Pierre—Charlie Millthorpe; in *Clarel,* Clarel—Rolfe, and the Lyonese. In each instance, the pattern is of primary importance; in some of its uses it is essential in the structures of the works. When these patterns are studied for what they mean in the area of Melville's feeling as he described it to Hawthorne, they present the central fact of his primitivistic tendency: reality may be expressed through symbols of existential meaning which represent fraternal union.

Puer aeternus governs the pattern of the communal relationship. It becomes the avatar of reincarnation from the Orient when the themes of *tayo* and the innocent sailor savage meet in Billy Budd; and the prefigurations of both *tayo* and sailor point ineluctably to what is to come. The imagistic foundation of Melville's feeling for *tayo* is encountered very early in his work. The prototype of the Polynesian friend is Marnoo, the mysterious visitor to the valley of the Taipis.[9] Marnoo contributes to the symbol of fraternal love, as this fills the emptiness of Ishmael's I-You relationship with God. Marnoo as prototype and Marnoo transposed into Queequeg, for instance, mean feeling toward fraternal relationship. Furthermore, the sensuous character of images describing Marnoo tells us quite directly that impressive physical beauty, actually seen by the eye, orders the artistic form in which *tayo* is to be initially represented. The contention that the eye has seen the things that are abstracted by the imagination into symbols is equal, in my analysis of primitivism, to a law of the symbolistic process.

Marnoo (*Typee,* XVIII) arrives upon the scene quite suddenly. Young Tom fears that the stranger may persuade the inhabitants of the valley to do him harm, so great is Marnoo's obvious popularity in the community. But Tom is immediately seized with amazement at the beauty of the youth. His form has a matchless symmetry, his limbs are beautifully modeled; his beardless cheeks suggest the face of Apollo and are of a feminine softness; his hair, a rich curling brown, twines about

---

9. To Richard Chase belongs the distinction of having first recognized the symbolic importance of Marnoo. Chase sees in him Melville's first sketch of the hero-voyager, the man who accepts "the psychological and cultural sustenance of life"; *Herman Melville: A Critical Study* (New York: The Macmillan Company, 1949), 4.

his temples and his neck in close ringlets; and over his body spreads a richly profuse pattern of tattooing, the spine traced with the "diamond-checkered shaft" of the " artu" tree. The tattooing is of the brightest blue, contrasting with the light olive color of the skin; and over the loins Marnoo wears a slight girdle of white tapa. The visitor engages the inhabitants of the valley with his startling charm; and then he approaches Tom and asks questions of the youth. In his conversation with Marnoo, Tom learns that Marnoo is *tabu.* No one can harm him, since his person is held sacred by all the tribes of the Marquesas. Marnoo has been abroad, to Sydney, as cabin boy to the captain of a trading vessel; hence his knowledge of English. We are not told when he became *tabu* or why he enjoys this sacred distinction. In his brief meeting with Marnoo, Tom is fascinated. For here is Melville's first encounter with Polynesian masculine beauty, displayed in color, grace, and unstudied charm, which suggests the store of images acquired through observation and a totally receptive sensuous nature. Marnoo's tattooing seems, at this point, to pass into the symbol of the Tree of Life; his *tabu* protects him from harm; the white girdle becomes a representational mark of primitive innocence. Since he receives more attention than any other character of *Typee,* that is, attention revealing physical attributes, it may be proposed that his tattooing is prototypic for the tattooing of Queequeg, and his tabu a prefiguration of the freedom and innocence of such a figure as Jack Chase, who serves aboard an instrument of evil and suffering, the warship *Neversink* in White-Jacket. Jack Chase is, in turn, prototypic for Billy Budd.) The white girdle of Marnoo passes into the symbolism of whiteness surrounding the figure of Billy. Already one sees in Melville's ideality of *tayo,* as he thinks of Marnoo's excellence, the vision of manly and youthful friendship as a manifestation of God.[10]

Tayo has received in the *South-Sea Idyls* of Charles Warren Stoddard the same notice which Melville gives it, save that Stoddard's symbol of ideality does not pass from the area of description into the area of the sacramental symbol, as Melville's is to do in *Billy Budd.* Stoddard's *tayo* is Kána-Anà in the story "Chumming with a Savage." The same archetypal

---

10. Thirty years after the composition of *Typee,* Melville seems to recall the beauty of Marnoo and the significance of *tayo* in a scene of *Clarel.* See his description of the young Lyonese Jew (Part IV, Sec, XXVI, "The Prodigal").

theme of *puer aeternus* governs again. The meaning of *tayo* is embodied in images expressing physical grace and beauty, which in turn reflect innocence and purity. The voyager lands at an unnamed island (Maui in the Hawaiian group?) and joins a native community where people do not know "that it is one of the Thirty-nine Articles of Civilization to bully one's way through the world."[11] His "fellow barbarians" hate civilization as much as the visitor and are "quite as idolatrous and indolent as I ever aspire to be." In this new vale of Typee, Kána-Anà is the faithful friend. Stoddard describes him with almost the same intensity which Melville feels for Marnoo. "His sleek figure, supple and graceful in repose, was the embodiment of free, untrammelled youth. You who are brought up under cover know nothing of its luxuriousness."[12] The effect of sensuous experience appears here in luxuriousness. But how really important is the distinguishing absence of tattooing! Melville's attention to this art of adornment has already been reviewed as one of the major consequences of his Polynesian voyage. Tattooing serves him so indispensably in his later symbolism that one may almost say it represents in his sensibility the total ideality of *tayo,* as well as the mystery of God in man.

---

11. Charles Warren Stoddard, *South-Sea Idyls* (Boston: James R. Osgood and Company, 1873), 63.

12. Ibid., 33. For an account of *tayo* in the narratives of Louis Becke, see "Te-bari, the Outlaw" in *The Call of the South* (London: John Milne, 1908), 191–202. The author is accompanied for two years by the faithful Susuega-le-moni from Tanumamanono in Samoa

I have omitted Robert Dean Frisbie from my discussion of the lineage of Ishmael (IV) because I do not find his studies of Oceanic life—excellent as they are—symbolistic in the expression defined. Furthermore, I consider him less authoritative than Louis Becke in his readings of the Polynesian personality. He is more clearly related to the art of Nordhoff and Hall than to that of Melville and his successors. Nonetheless, I must call attention to Frisbie's description of Polynesian friendship in *Mr. Moonlight's Island* (1939) as the most informative and accurate account in American literature. Frisbie uses the relationship of two native youths of Danger Kland, George and Toa, as a theme of the narrative. He contends justly that the love conventions of Oceania are governed by *tabus,* George and Toa are united in *tayo.* Thus it is George's duty to separate Toa from his amatory relationship with one young woman of the community so that he may know the " salutary adventure of promiscuity" among many women (100–101). Later, in the chapter "Birth on a Coral Atoll," a child is born of Toa's adventure with the first woman of his experience, and it becomes the office of George, as the equal sharer in friendship, to support the mother in labor and to assist in the delivery of Toa's child.

2. THE SAILOR SAVAGE

The prefiguration of *puer aeternus* as the sailor savage begins with Melville as Tom of *Typee,* the same savage who is to be named Ishmael in the first sentence of *Moby-Dick.* The ideality of *tayo* provides the first element of the sacramental symbol that Ishmael makes of his archetypal theme. The second element is provided by the sailor savage whom Ishmael meets. He is the "savage of Christendom, as Marnoo and his Polynesian brothers are the savages of the uncivilized (i.e., the non-Christian) world. The sailor savage is called by Melville the Handsome Sailor, as this epithet is given to Billy Budd. The first of the handsome sailors encountered as the friends of Ishmael is, of course, Toby of *Typee.* This character (Richard T. Greene, Melville's shipmate on the *Acushnet*) is described by Tom (as Ishmael) in an image which is the most usual of all Melville's conditions of the hero. "He was one of that class of rovers you sometimes meet at sea, who never reveal their origin, never allude to home, and go on rambling over the world as if pursued by some mysterious fate they cannot possibly elude."[13] Toby is "slightly made"; his dark complexion is matched by the dark locks clustering about his temples and the darker shade in his large black eyes (V). Melville's description suggests the symbol to come as he interprets Toby's voyage, the first voyage of the Handsome Sailor, as the journey of the unknown wanderer. One is at once impressed with the symbolistic tendency: to divorce the wanderer from the knowledge of his origin, to make his meaning as a human being general rather than specific. It is this general reference which Toby ever afterward possesses in Melville's recollection. Thus Toby is transposed to the poetry of *John Marr and Other Sailors* (1888) where he becomes Ned Bunn.[14] Ned's poem appears in the "Minor Sea Pieces" published with "John Marr":

> Ned, for our Pantheistic ports:—
> Marquesas and glenned isles that be
> Authentic Edens in a Pagan sea.

---

13. Herman Melville, *Typee: A Peep at Polynesian Life* (New York: Wiley and Putnam; London: John Murray, 1846), 38.

14. See Howard P. Vincent's notes in *Collected Poems of Herman Melville* (Chicago: Packard and Company, 1947), 472.

Now Melville turns back to the sailor savage of *Typee*. In these "glenned isles" and " authentic Edens," this savage was free of bondage to the laws of the Christian pilgrimage. Like Marnoo, he was *tabu*; he was safe; no one could harm him. These lines of "John Marr" show Melville's own recognition of union between the Ishmael-voyager and his sailor savage companion:

> Twined we were, entwined, then riven,
> Ever to new embracements driven,
> Shifting gulf-weed of the main!
> And how if one here shift no more,
> Lodged by the flinging surge ashore?
> Nor less, as now, in eve's decline,
> Your shadowy fellowship is mine.
> Ye float around me, form and feature:—
> Tattooings, ear-rings, love-locks curled;
> Barbarians of man's simpler nature,
> Unworldly servers of the world.

(I have already disclaimed any concern with the disorders and encumbrances of Melville's verse.) The image of entwining here represents the symbolic fusion accomplished between Ishmael and shipmate.

The relation of the sailor savage to the sea influences Ishmael's devotion, beyond question. The archetypal significance of ocean as the element over which the voyager travels is that of timelessness—eternity. The sea is primitive and timeless; the ego is subsumed by the sea; and here man returns to his first objective in his atavistic longing for origins. All the major pilgrimages of Melville's books, save those of *Pierre, Israel Potter,* and *Clarel,* take place on water. The seaman becomes by association primitive and eternal like the sea beneath him. This feeling for the life of the mariner is, after all, the feeling of Conrad's artistic concept in his men of the sea, those, for instance, of *Typhoon,* and the feeling of O'Neill in his play *The Moon of the Caribbees.*

But to illustrate Melville's feeling here, Loti is particularly appropriate. *Pêcheur d'Islande* expresses the same feeling toward the sailor savage. Pierre Flottes offers a description of the *dénouement* of this novel which serves the study of Melville as well as that of Loti. Yann, as Loti's symbol from the archetype of *puer aeternus,* is the "savage" of the voyage (just as Melville's heroes all stem from the race of sea savages). Yann is lost in the end to the sea, after sea and woman (Gaud, who wishes to marry him) have contended for the possession of his love. Flottes considers the conclusion of *Pêcheur* a superior symbol. The drama of woman against sea is over, and Yann is wedded to the ocean "with her virgin and generative joys of force."[15] So it is, indeed, a symbol of arresting power. Throughout the novel we have seen the "savagery" of Yann, his sense of loss when he is ashore, his attainment of existential meaning when he is sustained upon water. The sea seems to give him his savage nature, for even in play his caress is often very near brutal violence.[16] His heart is a virgin region, difficult to govern, unknown.[17] Yann's brother, Sylvestre, tells Gaud that Yann has promised himself in marriage to the sea,[18] and on the appointed wedding night with Gaud (representing the ties of home, identification with the land) the wind roars to remind Yann of his betrothal to another.[19]

In my discussion of Loti in an earlier chapter, I suggested that *Pêcheur* stands closer to *Moby-Dick* than any other novel of its time. I had in mind particularly a similarity of artistic vision: the sea "with her virgin and generative joys." It is this mighty sea forming the nature of the man who sails upon her waters that brings these two books together. They are united in the archetype of *puer aeternus,* who is primitive like the sea over which he wanders. For as unknown aeons of life sprang from the mysteries of the sea's generation, in those darker depths, so the sailor savage who sails over the surface, the man who knows her upper and virgin joys, is man carrying in him all the time of human history. Loti, like Melville, thought of the tie, the "betrothal" of man to the sea as the oldest relationship of man to nature: civilized man is savage in his role as mariner.

Thus the theme of sailor savage is identified in Toby and in Ned Bunn; and nearly all the art that lies between the two shows this civilized savage again and again. When one proceeds to *Omoo,* he finds him in Dr. Long Ghost, Paul's companion ashore; he finds him, too, in

---

15. Pierre Flottes, *Le drame intérieur de Pierre Loti: Document inédits* (Paris: Le Courrier Littéraire, 1937), 111.

16. Pierre Loti, *Pêcheur d'Islande* (Paris: Calman Lévy, 1939), 13.

17. Ibid., 161.

18. Ibid., 72.

19. Ibid., 223.

Shorty, whom the two adventurers meet at Imeeo, near Papeete. Like Marnoo, Shorty is twenty-five. In his blond good looks and his radiant temperament, he is a prefiguration of Billy Budd, and he seems to reflect Jack Chase whom Melville, of course, had already known aboard the United States before he wrote *Omoo*. "His cheeks were dyed with the fine Saxon red, burned deeper from his roving life; his blue eye opened well, and a profusion of fair hair curled over a well shaped head."[20] Like Billy Budd, he sings at work. Shorty passes symbolically into honest Jarl of Mardi. Now the sailor savage becomes a Scotsman who was yet "an old Norseman to behold" (*Mardi*, III). The love that binds him to Taji becomes the symbol of universal love. Jarl's language is a universal "Lingua-Franca of the forecastle." "Ah, Jarl! an honest, earnest wight; so true and simple, that the secret operations of thy soul were more inscrutable than the subtle workings of Spinoza's" (III). And *Redburn*, following *Mardi*, replaces the excellent Jarl with Larry, an ordinary seaman aboard the *Highlander*. (Harry Bolton, Wellingborough's English companion in Liverpool and London, who signs on for the return voyage, must be excluded here. He is a youth of the land and its vices, not the savage of sea-going life.)

Before leaving *Redburn*, this summary must digress for an interpretation of Carlo, the unlettered Italian boy who travels aboard the Highlander on the return voyage to New York. Carlo is not a sailor; but he belongs with the company of the hero-voyagers. There is much here that prefigures Billy Budd, and much that recalls Marnoo. Melville's portrait is the most sensuous of his art after the description of Marnoo, and it deserves careful study for what it reveals of the obsessive image:

> The head was if anything small; and heaped with thick clusters of tendril curls, half overhanging the brows and delicate ears, it somehow reminded you of a classic vase, piled up with Falernian foliage.
>
> ...His whole figure was free, fine, and indolent; he was such a boy as might have ripened into life in a Neapolitan vineyard; such a boy as gypsies steal in infancy; such a boy as Murillo often painted, when he went among the poor and outcast, for subjects wherewith to captivate the eyes of rank and wealth;

---

20. Herman Melville, *Omoo: A Narrative of Adventured in the South Seas* (New York: Harper & Brothers; London: John Murray, 1847), 254.

such a boy, as only Andalusian beggars are, full of poetry, gushing from every rent.

Carlo was his name; a poor and friendless son of earth.[21]

Carlo is a musician. He had come ashore at Prince's Dock, Liverpool,
some months before, from a vessel bound in from Messina, carrying with him a hand organ; and with his music in the foggy streets of
the port he had collected enough to pay his passage over the Atlantic. Aboard the *Highlander* he entertains the passengers and earns his
board. The primitive excellence which he shows in every word and look
and gesture is approximate to the perfection of Marnoo, Jack Chase,
and Billy Budd.

But it is the obsessive image of Polynesian beauty which orders the
ideality expressed in Carlo. Melville describes his eyes as shining "with
a soft and spiritual radiance, like a moist star in a tropic sky," speaking
of "humility, deep-seated thoughtfulness, yet a careless endurance of all
the ills of life."[22] As the music of the organ is recalled, images of antiquity crowd upon Melville's mind, images of Saracens, Persians, of Greek
and Judaic myth. The tribute to Carlo continues:

> Play on, play on, Italian boy!...let me gaze fathoms down into thy
> fathomless eye;—'tis good as gazing down into the great South
> Sea, and seeing the dazzling rays of the dolphins there.[23]

These images of "moist star in a tropic sky" and of gazing through Polynesian waters at the dolphin illustrate Baudouin's subjacent affective
reality. Carlo is in part described for what he was; but he is in part
rendered in an image which Melville had acquired in waters adja-
cent to the Polynesian youth, as he was seen in Nukuhiva and Tahiti.
The image is the more striking when it is studied in its first form in
Typee, in a scene immediately preceding the appearance of Marnoo.
Young Tom, bathing with the "nymphs" of the valley, relates that they
swam like a "shoal of dolphins," tumbling him about and ducking him
(*Typee*, XVIII). This blending of imagistic experience is vitally related
to Melville's symbolistic process, in which the focal centers of oppos-

---

21. Herman Melville, *Redburn: His First Voyage* (New York: Harper & Brothers,
1849), 310.

22. Ibid.

23. Ibid., 313–14.

ing cultures are united in the concept. The sight of the innocent wanderer seems to invoke Polynesia immediately in the consciousness of Melville's art.

Thus, the same dolphin image appears in the description of Mortmain, the Swedish outcast of *Clarel*. Here the subject is a youth who was illicitly highborn and cast into the world with only wealth to sustain him. As the wanderer from society, he frequents the gray places of earth. Derwent, one of the pilgrims, offers consolation to Mortmain, "the dream of fair redemption": he tells of a wreck adrift which he once saw at sea, and of the rainbow cast over it from the spray of gamboling dolphin (*Clarel*, Part II, Sec. IV). The wreck represents Mortmain as the derelict of society, the dolphin the same "careless endurance" associated with Carlo. For it is Carlo who seems to be recalled in Melville's description of a Palm Sunday procession in *Clarel* (Part IV, Sec. XXXII), when the image is employed to describe a group of young singers, "a rainbow throng, like dolphins off Madeira." In the poem, "Jack Roy" (*John Marr and Other Sailors*, 1888), the dolphin image returns with the same evocative power. Melville recalls another wanderer gifted with the careless endurance, the complete acceptance of Carlo; and once again the unreasoned perfection of Polynesian innocence becomes Melville's ideality of the sea-going hero. Jack "vaults over life" like that "iridescent arch," the rainbow cast by the dolphin. The associations revealed in these instances show that the dolphin is an emblem of Polynesian life and that the contexts in which it appears invariably mean the life of innocence and acceptance in contrast to the civilized life of law, convention, vice, egocentricity, Prometheanism.

After *Redburn*, the prefigurations of Billy Budd become still more clear in the sailor savages of *White-Jacket*. The inimitable Jack Chase as a prototype for Billy Budd is known to every reader of Melville. The significance of Melville's dedication of his last work to this comrade has long since been recognized. Jack is a scholar, a reader of Byron, Shakespeare, and Homer, and an ardent admirer of Camoëns; he is a linguist; he is a skilled mariner in his post at the foretop; he is the perfect companion, "better than a hundred common mortals."[24] But most of all, he is the man of acceptance; like Jack Roy, he "vaults over" life. Ishmael

---

24. Herman Melville, *White-Jacket, or The World in a Man-of-War* (New York: Grove Press, 1956), 26.

on the *Neversink* finds him the master hero-wanderer. With him in the ship's company are two other youths, Peter and Frank, both known and admired by White-Jacket. Peter is a handsome lad of nineteen and a great favorite in his mess. He is flogged by the boatswain's mate for his "crime" of fighting on the gun-deck with John, a malignant rascal of the crew. The scene (XXXIII) prefigures Billy Budd's "crime" in striking down the malignant Claggart. Frank is another shipmate, a genial boy whom White-Jacket sometimes singled out for conversation, "a very handsome young fellow, with starry eyes, curly hair of a golden colour, and a bright, sunshiny complexion: he must have been the son of some goldsmith."[25] Billy Budd's physical attributes seem to take form from these images of Peter and Frank; his strength comes directly from Jack Chase just as his innocence, expressed in his singing, recalls the musical Carlo, and his Polynesian good humor, the ideality of *tayo*.

But for all Jack Chase's relationship to Billy Budd, who is really a younger and unlearned Jack, I do not think that Melville makes here as obvious a transfer as he does in creating Rolfe of *Clarel*. Rolfe is Clarel's companion, like the sailor savage, the man of perfect acceptance; and he is surrounded in Melville's description of him with the familiar images of Polynesia. He appears as the voyager into the waters of the tropics. He possesses a genial heart and an austere mind. He is a man given to study, but no "scholastic partisan." Clarel thinks of his union with Rolfe as the closing of two halves of an apple. These two natures are united under the sign of the tropics: "To him here first were brought together/ Exceptional natures, of a weather/Strange as the tropics with strange trees,/Strange birds, strange fishes, skies and seas."[26] The "weather" is the area of feeling in which the communion of friendship is realized. This, again, is the friendship offered by Melville to Hawthorne.

The last of Melville's sailor savages for notice here, the friend who is no sailor at all, has the meaning of sanity as clearly distinguished from insanity. He is Charlie Millthorpe, the friend of Pierre Glendinning. Charlie is the sanity of primitive acceptance; Pierre, the real son of Ahab in Melville's art, is insanity, the overreaching absolutist who finds

25. Ibid., 233.

26. Herman Melville, *Clarel: A Poem and Pilgrimage in the Holy Land*, edited by Walter E. Bezanson (New York: Hendricks House, 1960), 100.

his end in an indifferent God. Thus does Pierre burn his *mementi,* the memorials of his past life:

> Of old Greek times, before man's brain went into doting bondage, and bleached and beaten in Baconian fulling-mills, his four limbs lost their barbaric tan and beauty; when the round world was fresh, and rosy, and spicy, as a new-plucked apple;—all's wilted now!—in these bold times the great dead were not, turkey-like, dished in trenchers, and set down all garnished in the ground, to glut the damned Cyclop like a cannibal; but nobly envious Life cheated the glutton worm, and gloriously burned the corpse; so that the spirit up-pointed, and visibly forked to heaven![27]

These words are but Ahab's curses in another language: the oaths against life itself, the destruction of the quadrant, and that baleful wish for a bough of cherries before death comes to him under the furious lashings of the unconquerable God. How quietly Charlie Millthorpe, Pierre's friend of boyhood, he whose heart was "a far more excellent and angelical thing" than brain,[28] stands there opposite to this young Ahab. Not long before the end of his bitter quest Pierre reflects: "...the god that made [Charlie] Millthorpe was both a better and a greater than the god that made Napoleon or Byron.—Plus head, minus heart—...the heart's the preserving salt itself, and can keep sweet without the head."[29]

Heart, in this denunciation of head, means feeling distinguished from reason. *Tayo* and the sailor savage are Melville's prototypes of feeling. Each expresses an ideality made of the artist's experience, and each has its own store of images to describe the affective reality of that experience. It remains true, both in these prototypes and in the prefigurations of Billy Budd, that feeling (heart) governs with an undiminishing control; it is equally true that feeling controls in the master symbol, the avatar of Billy Budd. But some will say: this feeling is sentimental. So it may be to antagonists, if they are as well prepared to say that the sacraments of the Christian faith are the same. Whatever their judgments of sacrament may be, it happens that the elements of Billy Budd as a symbol are these provinces of feeling which have been described.

---

27. Herman Melville, *Pierre; or, The Ambiguities* (New York: Harper & Brothers, 1852), 269.

28. Ibid., 379.

29. Ibid., 436

3. BILLY BUDD

It cannot matter whether *Billy Budd,* the story, is the capstone of Melville's art or not. Various critics have advanced it as Melville's testament of acceptance, his resolution of the problem of good and evil; and as many others have found it less important than *Moby-Dick* in this respect. It is studied here not as a moral allegory (allegory representing the life of reason, the life of the head), but as a full achievement of the symbolistic imagination governed by feeling. As the archetype of the primordial whale becomes the avatar of God the unknowable in *Moby-Dick,* so the archetype of *puer aeternus* becomes in *Billy Budd* the avatar of God the knowable through the communion of fraternal love, innocent, free of self-consciousness, carelessly enduring. This avatar of Billy becomes sacrament in an art form when it is completed with the symbolic pole opposite to the state of innocence of *tayo* and the sailor savage. The new pole, represented in the execution of Billy by hanging from the main yardarm of the ship, is the crucifixion of Christ. Thus Billy becomes the symbol of sacrament in which the innocence of *tayo* and the innocence of the sailor savage (itself envisioned, as I have shown, through various Polynesian images associated with *tayo*) are unified with the innocence of Christ. The symbol takes the place of the Eucharist, even as it preserves the images of the cross in the yardarm and the fleece of the Lamb of God, the vestigial emblems of an orthodox symbolism. At the moment of his execution Billy Budd represents the body of God. But I wish again to emphasize that the element of Christ in the symbol represents Christ the innocent among men, not the suffering Christ of the cross. The agony in Gethsemane, the ascent of Calvary, the cries from the cross have no place here. These hours of the Passion represent Christ in the act of reason and hence in Promethean suffering, Christ the tragic hero. Melville's rejection of the tragic hero, whom he studies in *Moby-Dick* and in *Pierre,* prefigures the rejection that he makes here. He presents, instead, Christ as the innocent among men, Christ freed of that dogma in which the emphasis falls most heavily upon Christ crucified. Thus this avatar of Billy as sacrament, with its reference to the pagan Orient of unreasoning acceptance, is heretical from the orthodox Christian view. It equates the ideality of Polynesian friend and the hero-voyager with the ideality of Christ. The equation is formed in the private domain of the artist's feeling.

Melville's dedication of *Billy Budd* to Jack Chase must now be regarded as an ascription of the sacramental symbol to Ishmael's fellow voyager bound to him in fraternal love. Early in the story Melville recalls a native African sailor whom he once saw in the street of Prince's Dock, Liverpool. He was magnificent in his impressive stature and in his abounding good humor. As he strode along, each of his shipmates crowding around him rendered a spontaneous tribute to this "black pagod of a fellow—the tribute of pause and stare, and less frequent an exclamation." These sailors "showed that they took that sort of pride in the evoker...which the Assyrian priests doubtless showed for their grand sculptured Bull when the faithful prostrated themselves."[30] We thus approach Melville's symbol through this adoration of the faithful, these who are the lawless, innocent wanderers, the priests of an image of God. When Billy is about to come aboard the *Indomitable* from the *Rights-of-Man*, we learn that he has been made the object of the same priestly adoration by the men of the ship from which he is transferred. On the Indomitable Billy wins the same devotion. Every reader knows his excellence. As foundling, exile, outcast, sailor, he is the apotheosis of the sailor savage: he is an Englishman of pure Saxon strain, touched by a Greek sculptor with the look of Hercules; "noble descent was as evident in him as in a blood horse";[31] he might have passed for "a statue of young Adam before the Fall";[32] he is free of self-consciousness; he is illiterate, but he can sing; he is an "upright barbarian";[33] and "to deal in double meanings and insinuations of any sort is quite foreign to his nature."[34] "The sailor," remarks Melville later, "is frankness, the landsman is finesse."[35] The landsman's life is a chess game, which he plays out in tediousness and obliqueness by the light of a poor candle. Opposite to Billy's innocence and his barbaric perfection is the malevolence of Claggart with the finesse, the guile, and obliqueness of society. Once,

30. Herman Melville, *Billy Budd, Sailor (An Inside Narrative)*, edited by Harrison Hayford and Merton M. Sealts, Jr. (Chicago and London: The University of Chicago Press, 1962), 44.

31. Ibid., 52.

32. Ibid., 94.

33. Ibid., 52.

34. Ibid., 49.

35. Ibid., 86.

it will be remembered, he looked upon Billy as though he could have loved him, "but for fate and ban." But Claggart (even as sailor) is the player of the chess game, hating with all the passions of the civilized world the spectacle of frankness. The structure of the story need not be retraced once more. All the values that it presents are familiar. I am concerned only with the nature of Billy as the sacramental symbol. The meaning of Melville's sailor savage emerges from its early prefigurations to its apotheosis in Billy's death.

Billy does not understand the chaplain who would prepare him for death because he does not understand, in turn, the meaning of Christian suffering and the fear of death. As the sailor savage of careless endurance, he is unable to contemplate absolutism or Prometheanism. To Billy, God has one meaning—love; but as Melville presents him, the love he knows is the love of his fellow sailors, as primitive men, not the love of landsmen in Christian civilization. The cry "God bless Captain Vere" as Billy mounts the ladder and submits to the noose is not the cry of a stupid youth; it is a cry of unreasoning acceptance which reveals an ideality of complete selflessness. The Polynesian origin of Melville's concept is made known in the interview with the chaplain.

> If in vain the good chaplain sought to impress the young barbarian with ideas of death akin to those conveyed in the skull, dial, and crossbones of old tombstones; equally futile to all appearance where his efforts to bring home to him the thought of salvation and a Savior. Billy listened, but less out of awe or reverence, perhaps, than from a certain natural politeness...And this sailor way of taking clerical discourse is not wholly unlike the way in which the pioneer of Christianity, full of transcendent miracles, was received long ago on tropic isles by any superior *savage* so called—a Tahitian, say, of Captain Cook's time or shortly after that time.[36]

As the account of this scene with the chaplain moves on, it is Billy's indifference to death which establishes him as the true spiritual descendent of the Polynesian savage. "This sailor way of taking the discourse" is the way of the sailor savage, and the way of the innocent Polynesian. Thus the object of life is the pagan act of loving, not the doctrinal Chris-

---

36. Ibid., 121.

tian act of learning how to die in the sense of guilt and in suffering, and in answer to the preacher of redemption. By this one stroke Melville reveals his total feeling for the communion of man, and his scepticism toward doctrinal Christianity with its insistence upon absolute truth in the civilized world of Promethean anguish.

Thus Billy Budd, as the full symbol containing both Polynesian innocence and the original innocence of Christ in the world as man, hangs from the main yardarm in a new crucifixion. The civilized evil that raised him there and took his life is of God too, as Melville had already presented the all-encompassing unknowable God in the White Whale. But it is evil, the reasons for which man may not know. Billy does not question them. In the limits of man's feeling there is only the capacity to know God in his manifestation as fraternal love. Billy is an avatar, one reincarnation of a God of limitless aspect. In other forms this God may destroy the man who seeks him through reason. Captain Vere's bondage to the absolute of man-made law is the proof of another form of God; so is Claggart's evil, made by "fate and ban." At four o' clock in the morning, as the dawn breaks from the east, Billy blesses Captain Vere and selflessly yields to death. But this death is met indifferently by an innocence that has never felt the sickness of ego. "The vapoury fleece hanging low in the East, was shot through with a soft glory as of the fleece of the Lamb of God seen in a mystical vision; and simultaneously therewith, watched by the wedged mass of upturned faces, Billy ascended; and ascending, took the full rose of the dawn." The sacramental crucifixion and ascension are marked by a strange murmur among the men. "Whoever has heard the freshet-wave of a torrent suddenly swelled by pouring showers in *tropical* mountains, showers not shared by the plain; whoever has heard the first muffled murmur of its sloping advance through precipitous woods, may form some conception of the sound now heard."[37]

It was inevitable that Melville should have returned here to the Polynesian image. What we hear is the sound of water falling from mountain escarpments in the Marquesas or Tahiti, after a sudden inland shower. Thus the obsessive vision of Polynesia marks the last pages Melville wrote. His setting for the symbol of Billy in his crucifixion is attended

---

37. Ibid., 126; italics mine.

by the sound of grief and reverence in the murmurs of his shipmates who, through the image, become Polynesian worshippers, emblems of *tayo*. Even the scene of the worshippers, touched with the light of the sun in a sacramental ceremony, had been prefigured long ago in *Mardi*. The voyagers with whom Taji travels land on the isle of Serenia (CLXXX-VII). There one needs no temples, no shrines, no precepts; there only the love of Alma, the original Christ-Christ free of all dogma—is known. For Alma gave his laws to Mardi (Earth), not to Paradise; and in Serenia "reason no longer domineers." There the voyagers kneel before the old chieftain of Serenia, "and as the old man blessed them, the setting sun burst forth from mists, gilded the island round about, shed rays upon their heads, and went down in a glory—all the East radiant with red burnings, like an altar-fire." Melville had long ago visualized this last setting; only the sunset is exchanged for the dawn of Billy Budd's execution. For in this sacrament of an unsuffering youth, the symbol of Christ is made new again as Melville summons the ideality of Polynesian selflessness and the testament of innocence to the reality of man's communion in God.

First published in *Spring: An Annual of Archetypal Psychology and Jungian Thought* (1972) and emended for this edition.

On Finnegans Wake

THOMAS COWAN

The attention of Jungians might profitably be directed to the important work, *Finnegans Wake*.[1] My reluctance to undertake the job is practical. I do not now know enough about either Jung or Joyce, and feel I never shall. Besides, I stand somewhat in the shadow that Jungians and Joyceans cast on each other for I feel that I belong to both groups. The artist's natural antagonism toward psychotherapy has been examined at great length and explained more or less satisfactorily from the therapist's point of view, that is, in his own language and by his own methods. But the shadow which psychotherapy throws upon the artist is not explained by the artist. He deals with the matter in his own way. And he is not without weapons. And they can hurt severely.

Since Joyce lived in Zurich at critical stages in his life, it was natural that he should come into contact with Jung's work[2] and eventually with his personality. He accepted the work and used it extensively in his writings. The personalities (inevitably for Joyce but perhaps predictably for Jung as well) clashed. It may have been Mrs. McCormick's outrageous offer to continue to support Joyce financially—at a time when he

1. James Joyce, *Finnegans Wake* (New York: The Viking Press, 1967). Numbers appearing directly after quotations from the *Wake* are page numbers of the text, which are the same in the American and the British editions.

2. Joyce became acquainted with Jung's work as early as 1915–16 through Dr. Edoardo Weiss, the brother of Ottocaro Weiss, a student at the University of Zurich. Dr. Weiss was one of Freud's earliest disciples and the first psychoanalyst in Italy: "from his brother and from Dr. C.G. Jung, with whom he was also acquainted, Ottocaro Weiss had a knowledge of psychoanalysis which Joyce disparaged but found useful"; Richard Ellmann, *James Joyce* (New York: Oxford University Press, 1965), 405.

was utterly destitute and could find no teaching job—in exchange for an agreement on his part to submit to analysis by Jung that soured Joyce on Jungians.[3] He reacted to Mrs. McCormick's offer as though she had proposed lobotomy.

I must leave these matters of personality conflict to specialists for resolution. Joyce's life is well-documented in two full-scale biographies, in three volumes of letters[4] and in his largely autobiographical major works. Nothing comparable exists for Jung, so I suppose the question of the clash between artist and therapist as represented by these two dominant personalities must be examined in other ways. Perhaps the best that I can do is to exploit the advantages of an intermediary.

Jung and Joyce had complementary tasks. At the time that Jung was elaborating his theories of the nature of the psyche for science, Joyce was doing the same thing in literature. But, as I have already noted, contact between the two men was abrasive, and the half-hearted attempts of each to enter the other's realm of the spirit were abortive. Jung's ill-considered preface to the third German edition of *Ulysses* stung Joyce to the quick. Jung rewrote it as an article in 1932 and published it separately. He sent a copy to Joyce with a very flattering letter. In it, Jung says:

> The 40 pages of non-stop run in the end is a string of veritable peaches. I suppose the devil's grandmother knows so much about the psychology of women, I didn't.[5]

Joyce proudly showed his wife this tribute but she said of her husband, "He knows nothing at all about women."[6]

Despite his personal feeling against both Freud and Jung, Joyce used both without stint in *Ulysses* and in *Finnegans Wake*. Indeed, if Joyce

---

3. A more considerate account of this unfortunate episode, together with Joyce's belated tribute to Mrs. McCormick after her death is contained in Ellmann, *James Joyce*, 480-83. See also W. Walcott, "Carl Jung and James Joyce: A Narrative of Three Encounters," *Psychological Perspectives: A Quarterly Journal of Jungian Thought* 1, no. 1 (1970): 21-31. This article contains an account of the *Ulysses* episode as well as references to Jung's therapeutic treatment of Lucia and should be consulted for its parallel treatment of these and other aspects of the present paper.

4. Herbert Gorman, *James Joyce* (New York: Farrar and Rinehart, 1939); Ellmann, *James Joyce*, op. cit; *Letters of James Joyce*, 3 vols., edited by Stuart Gilbert and Richard Ellmann (New York: The Viking Press, 1957-66).

5. Ellmann, *James Joyce*, 641-42.

6. Ibid., 642.

had not accepted such gifts from the famous people he quarreled with, one has the feeling that he would have had much less to say. Therefore, his bad joke about "Doctor Tweedledeedum of Vienna, who is not to be confused with Doctor Tweedledeedee of Zurich," was sour grapes. The oblique point of the joke is that everyone knew the famous men to whom he was referring.

There is a recent book, not orthodox Freudian, but devoted to sex symbolism in the *Wake*. It is called *Eternal Geomater: The Sexual Symbolism of Finnegans Wake.*[7] There is nothing comparable that I know of on Jungian influence on the *Wake*. And this is understandable. The whole work is Jungian. Moreover, Joyce studied Jung's work, and consciously used his insights in writing the *Wake*. James Atherton, the distinguished author of *The Books at the Wakes*[8] said in another place: "Certainly Joyce read with interest everything Jung wrote."[9] Two other Joyce scholars, Kain and Magalaner, "suggest that the psychological level in the *Wake* is based on the work of Jung."[10]

Indeed, the first effort at a total explication of the book drew so heavily on Jungian structural analysis that critics felt that the work as a contemporary novel was all but submerged. I refer to *A Skeleton Key to* Finnegans Wake by Joseph Campbell and Henry Morton Robinson.[11] The *Key* appeared in 1944, just five years after the publication of the *Wake*, and set the canon of interpretation so firmly in mythological terms that subsequent readers find it difficult to get beyond the limits of that first study.

So much for these "Wakers," all of whom acknowledge Jung's influence on the *Wake*. What of Jungians? It seems to me that they steer clear of the *Wake* for the soundest pragmatic reason in the world: *The book is known to be unreadable.* Acknowledging this impossibility, I am never-

---

7. Margaret Solomon, *Eternal Geomater: The Sexual Universe of* Finnegans Wake (Carbondale and Edwardsville: Southern Illinois Universty Press, 1969).

8. James S. Atherton, *The Books at the Wake: A Study of Literary Allusions in James Joyce's* Finnegans Wake (New York: The Viking Press, 1960).

9. James S. Atherton, "The Identity of the Sleeper," *A Wake Newslitter: Studies in James Joyce's* Finnegans Wake, n.s. 4, no. 5 (October 1967): 84.

10. Atherton, *Books at the Wake*, 37, citing Richard M. Kain and Marvin Magalaner, *Joyce, the Man, the Work, the Reputation* (New York: New York University Press, 1956), 219. See also Hugh Kenner, *Dublin's Joyce* (London: Chatto & Windus, 1955).

11. New York: Harcourt, Brace and Company, 1944

theless going to try to show Jungians why the *Wake* ought to be read by them nevertheless. But first a few words about the difficulties.

The *Wake* is a newly created myth; Jungians seem to prefer old established ones. The material is northern European; Classical Greece and Rome figure hardly at all. Eastern religions and mythologies do figure, especially the Egyptian *Book of the Dead*, but these are minor structural elements. The languages of the *Wake* are English, Irish and Scandinavian, not Latin, Greek, French, Italian, or modern German, except as these are used as adornments. I hasten to add that the *Wake* itself really is written in English, despite many rumors to the contrary. All other languages including Irish are made to serve Joyce's explosive new English dialect. But the use of other languages, especially Irish, is a formidable obstacle to a reasonably easy reading of the text by those trained in continental cultural modes. It is not an accident that Jung himself reacted so violently to a first reading of *Ulysses.*

Language aside, the actual materials used are distressingly heterogeneous. A formidable pile of scraps of learning looted from all the major works of literature, art, drama, newspapers, books of reference, dictionaries, comic strips, children's fairy tales, popular songs: anything and everything in or out of the normal range of a novelist's materials.

Add to these the fact that everything that ever happened to Joyce, to his wife, his children, his extended family-everything existing in Dublin or in its history—all of Ireland and its real mythological past—anything English, anything Scandinavian, everything Irish, all these and a lot more are normal Wake materials. To balance this phantasmagoria, readers of the Wake are offered a set of very carefully done exegetical helps, unique perhaps to any modern work of literature.[12]

---

12. These are: *A Skeleton Key to Finnegans Wake* by Campbell and Robinson; *A Reader's Guide to* Finnegans Wake by William York Tindall (New York: Farrar, Straus and Giroux, 1969); *A Concordance to* Finnegans Wake by Clive Hart (Minneapolis: University of Minnesota Press, 1963); *A Second Census of* Finnegans Wake: *An Index of the Characters and Their Role* by Adaline Glasheen (Evanston, Ill.: Northwestern University Press, 1963); *The Books at the Wake* by James Atherton; *A Gaelic Lexicon for* Finnegans Wake *and Glossary for Joyce's Other Works* by Brendan O Hehir (Berkeley and Los Angeles: University of California Press, 1967); *Scandinavian Elements of* Finnegans Wake by Dounia Bunis Christiani (Evanston, Ill.: Northwestern University Press, 1965); *A Lexicon of the German in Finnegans Wake* by Helmut Bonheim (Berkeley and Los Angeles: University of California Press, 1967); *Song in the Works of James Joyce*

Heterogeneous as they are, materials are not the prime difficulty with the Wake. Joyce felt forced to create an entirely new English idiom to accommodate his purposes. All normal literary forms are broken up and then pieced together in the rigorous new Joycean canon. Nothing in the new amalgam is accidental, except of course the truly accidental; nothing is out of place. The huge juggernaut, a nightmare of dream discourse, rolls inexorably on its predetermined course.

I. ARCHETYPAL IDEAS AND THEMES

With all these difficulties in the way, why should a student of Jung bother with the outrageous mess? Well, to begin with, consider this: *Finnegans Wake is the only wholly synchronistic work in modern literature. Everything in it happens at once.* From the first word in the book until the last, all the action goes on at the same time. Joyce specifically accepts and uses space-time relativity. All events occur in a past-present-future frame of reference. Although the work is active, dynamic, moving, it has neither beginning nor end. The last word in the book is the word "the"; the first word is "riverrun." The sentence containing both words begins at the end of the book and ends at its beginning. The work is an *uroborus,* a snake with its tale in its mouth, the most lively symbol of synchronicity imaginable. In addition to creating this stupendous monomyth of synchronicity, Joyce knew about Jung's ideas on the subject, knew about them and used them.

Next, the *Wake* is a huge *mandala.* It goes round and round in twenty-four hours, imitating the rotation of the earth:

> ...in *Finnegans Wake,* as we should expect of an essentially archetypal book, though all these patterns [of Joyce's former books] and

by Matthew J.C. Hodgart and Mabel P. Worthington (New York: Columbia University Press, 1959); the biographies mentioned above; the three volumes of letters mentioned above. These are the working tools of a serious reader of the *Wake.* In addition, Jungians would find Hart's *Structure and Motif in* Finnegans Wake most interesting. There is a small periodical known as *A Wake Newslitter,* which appears six times a year. It is devoted exclusively to specialist studies of the *Wake. The James Joyce Quarterly* contains articles on the *Wake.* There is a complete bibliography of Joyce's writings in vol. 2 of the *Letters.* A complete set of Joyce manuscripts is in the British Museum. *A First-Draft Version of* Finnegans Wake, edited by David Hayman (Austin: University of Texas Press, 1963) contains much information about the manuscripts that are collated in a first draft of the entire book.

more are subsumed, the underlying structure is simpler, even if surface details sometimes tend to obscure it. The two main spatial configurations governing its shape are those which have always had pre-eminence in western symbology—the circle and the cross, together with their combination in a three dimensional figure consisting of two circles intersecting on the surface of a sphere. The importance that Joyce attached to these structural symbols may be judged from the fact that he assigned the mandala symbol ⊗ to the key passage in I.6 dealing with the pattern of cycles in *Finnegans Wake* (question 9).

The symbol of the circular universe with its timeless centre is also found in the figure of the Buddhist *mandala* which is of such importance to Jung…[Joyce's] use of it to designate a passage dealing with the structure of *Finnegans Wake* suggests that in one structural sense the whole of the book forms a *mandala*.[13]

The *Wake* is a *dream,* indeed a dream within a dream within a dream according to a most authoritative student of the book.[14] We should call it rather a work of the *active imagination* but what Joyce was imagining was dream, myth, and reality, the whole nightlife of the soul. And that Joyce accepted the modern notion of continuous dreaming is shown by the fact that the time span of the book is one full day of twenty-four hours.

I have mentioned that *Finnegans Wake* is wholly archetypal, consciously designed as such (But O felicitous culpability, sweet bad cess to you for an archetypt!" 263.28), as well as a novel about a socially submerged family in a Dublin suburb. What archetypes does it constellate? All of them that I ever heard of. In addition to the major archetype that the book itself represents (synchronistic uroborus-mandala), each of the characters in it and all their relations with one another are treated in archetypal fashion. The Father is symbolic of all fathers; the mother is a river; the warring twin sons are Cain and Abel, Esau and Jacob, Horus and Seth, as well as numerous more modern pairs. Any and every set of warring brothers known to history is apt to find its way into the *Wake*. Needless to say the *Wake* is itself a rich resurrection myth, and por-

---

13. Clive Hart, *Structure and Motif in* Finnegans Wake (Evanston, Ill.: Northwestern University Press, 1962), 110, 77.

14. Ibid., ch. 3.

trayed as such. The daughter of the family is a double-girl, in love with her mirror image. I think it unnecessary to elaborate further on the archetypal nature of the *Wake*. This subject can best be pursued in the course of its reading.

The *Wake* is the Bible of Joyce's self-created religion. It appears that Joyce was seriously offering it as a companion to all the great books of religion of the world, not merely their successor in time but their rival in doctrine:

> I have already suggested that the basic axiom underlying *Finnegans Wake* is that the artist is the God of his creation. Joyce seems to have gone a step farther than that and considered that the work on which he was engaged was itself a new sacred book.[15]

Students of the psychology of religion should welcome the opportunity to study this most serious attempt at a religious literature since Blake, whom Joyce profoundly admired and I believe sought to copy.

The *Wake* is a vast exercise in individuation. It was the final and complete statement of the experience and the aspirations of a profoundly gifted artist. I do not feel competent to say anything more about this aspect of Joyce's crowning literary work. It is at once too personal and entirely too vast a subject. I leave the rest to potential Jungian readers of the work.

So much for generalities. I feel I should now call attention to specific matters of Jungian interest that have come to my notice. This will be a mere sampling of topics.

On Synchronicity: "The first four paragraphs are the suspended tick of time between a cycle just past and one about to begin. They are in effect an overture, resonant with all the themes of *Finnegans Wake*."[16] But this is only an example. All other full episodes in the Wake contain themselves in themselves in the same fashion. The *Wake* is an eternal monad. Nothing ever happens. Everything happened before and will happen again (*Finnegans Wake!*).

Anna Livia Plurabelle: The wife-daughter-mother of the tale. A rich mythology covers her activities as woman the cleaner-upper, the river bearing away the filth of civilization (196–216). Women clean up. Perhaps

---

15. Atherton, *Books at the Wake*, 169.
16. Campbell and Robinson, *A Skeleton Key*, 15.

this is more important for the continuance of the race than even procreation, which takes place anyway and is under the supervision of powerful gods. But as cleaner-upper, woman is tested to the limit of her conscious being. Modern woman is fighting like a demon to lighten or to get rid of this immemorial social burden. Read what Anna Livia Plurabelle does about it in the Last Monologue.

ALP is the *Wake*'s anima. ("Anama anamaba anamabapa" 267.F4). Her name is consciously recognized and chosen as Anima (Anyma). Her Last Monologue (Book IV) is the death of the soul as a Woman. She flows out as the river Liffey to meet her ancestral Father the Sea, and in so doing gives up all her earthly concerns. The beauty of the passage is overwhelming. It can be read without too much trouble from 626.34 to the end. It is of course the man's anima that is evoked. It is not the female soul, but the masculine soul of both man and woman.

Anna Livia Plurabelle is a man's account of a certain kind of woman. Her description occupies a fair share of the novel and she is best known from the tales told of her by the Washerwomen at the Ford who go up and down the River washing whatever they come upon. As they wash, they talk about Anna Livia (196-216). ALP as Pandora is the horrible Mother also. She had one hundred and eleven children and her presents to them out of her bag are sometimes quite hair-raising. For example, to one of her soldier sons, Chummy the Guardsman, she gave "a cartridge of cockaleekie soup" (gonorrhea) (210.7).

The Daughter: Isobel, Issy, Isolde, the romantic daughter in love with her mirror image is a reflection of Joyce's own schizophrenic daughter Lucia. The episode of Joyce's consultation with Jung about her condition and the unfavorable outcome of this encounter (which in any event took place too late to do any of the three of them any good) is told in other places.[17] I feel that anyone who is interested in the interrelation between narcissism and schizophrenia might profitably study Issy. Joyce himself lived through a crisis of the *femme inspiratrice* (Jung's diagnosis) only half-knowing what was going on, but certainly as the artist concerned and the father in question, totally incapable of doing anything about it *except to use it to the fullest extent possible in his novel.* Issy's story is a progress from self-love to brother-love regressively to father-incest and more generally to the love of aging men for young girls.

---

17. In Ellmann's biography, for the Joycean account.

Shem and Shaun are the twin brothers. Shem is Jewish, introvert and artist, guilt-ridden and in the grip of his *daimon*. (He is horrendously execrated in the Shem chapter, 169–195.) Shaun is extraverted, native Irish, innocent, natural sensualist as contrasted with Shem's knowing and hence perverse sexuality (403 *et seq.*). The introverted-extraverted aspects of the personality are exploited in Jungian fashion. Joyce knew of Jung's work on typology and explicit use is made in the Wake of the dynamism of type-opposition.

Animus-Anima: "Is the Co-Education of Animus and Anima Wholly Desirable?" (307.3), Joyce has the children at their Night Lessons ask Whether it is or not, Shem, the rascal, is intent on getting his innocent (?) brother Shaun to admit to a knowledge of the secrets of the Mother, all worked out as a lesson in Euclid, with the letters ALP at the three points of the female △.

Incest: The total Freudian family romance is present in the *Wake*. For a starter consider the nullity suit under canon law at 572.19–573.32.

Perversion: It is said that all forms of perversion known to man are extant in the *Wake*. I'm not very good at spotting them. The subject needs qualified expert attention.[18]

Obscenity-blasphemy: This subject involves Joyce's principled opposition to state and church. The artist's life-long quarrel with these major institutions is much more relaxed in the Wake than in *Ulysses*.

Joyce's Ribbing of Psychotherapy: It is quite rough, though Joyce does include himself as one of the practitioners (rather unconvincingly). A few examples:

> ...we grisly old Sykos who have done our unsmiling bit on alices, when they were yung and easily freudened, in the penumbra of the procuring room and what oracular compression we have had to apply to them! could (did we care to sell our feebought silence in camera) tell our very moistnostrilled one that father in such virgated contexts is not always that undemonstrative relative (often held up to our contumacy) who settles our hashbill for us and what an innocent allaboard's adverb such as Michaelly looks like can be suggestive of under the pudendascope, and,...egotum sabcunsciously senses upers the deprofundity of multimathematical immaterialities wherebejubers in the pancosmic urge

---

18. See Solomon's *Eternal Geomater.*

the allimanence of that which Itself is Itself Alone (hear, O hear, Caller Errin!) exteriorises on this ourherenow plane in disunited solod, likeward and gushious bodies with (science, say!) perilwhitened passionpanting pungnoplangent intuitions of reunited seldom (murky whey, abstrew adim!) in the higher-dimissional selfless Allself...(394.30-395.2)

As to individuation, Joyce's temperament was, on the conscious level, opposed to the process. The *Wake* is so collectivized that one must struggle hard to find anything individuated in the characters. Joyce's way of putting it is this: "Whence it is a slopperish matter, given the wet and low visibility (since in this scherzarade of one's thousand one nightinesses that sword of certainty which would identifide the body never falls) to idendifine the individuone" (51.3). Still, as I have said before, I believe that the *Wake* itself is Joyce's record of his own life-long painful journey toward individuation.

II. SENEX AND PUER

The senex and puer archetypal complementarity in the *Wake* is a subject of such massive proportions that it deserves a separate study. Much of the studies on this configuration could be directly annotated to the *Wake*. While traditional considerations dictate that the tension between the father and the sons take the form of the *Totem and Taboo* myth, and the Oedipal situation seems to most Wakers to be the proper paradigm, a "Jungian" approach reveals that the relation of the older man and the younger is so extensively ramified in the Wake that it needs a full-scale examination of it in terms of the senex-puer configuration.

In the Wake the negative senex is personified in the four horrible old men, Matt, Mark, Luke and Johnny, who represent the Four Master. Waves of Ireland, the Four Evangelists, four Judges of HCE's crime in the Park, and any old four "rememboring" the past. Nothing of the puer exists in them except the vaguely obscene reminiscences of their past sexual conquests, and their lurid interest in the activities of Tristan and Isolde as they cuckold King Mark (383 *et seq.*).

Senex and puer are constellated in the father, Humphrey Chimpden Earwicker and in his songs; in Shaun as priest, academic lecturer and impotent arouser of sexual passion; and in Shem, the eternally youthful creative artist. This syndrome occupies most of the action of the book.

Senex and Anima

A striking interplay of these archetypes appears in Anna's attempt to arouse her husband Humphrey from a typical senex depression:

> Well, old Humber was as glommen as grampus, with the tares at his thor and the buboes for ages and neither bowman nor shot abroad and bales allbrant on the crest of rockies and nera lamp in kitchen or church and giant's holes in Grafton's causeway and deathcap mushrooms round Funglus grave and the great tribune's barrow all darnels occumule, sittang sambre on his sett, drammen and dromen, usking queasy quizzers of his ruful continence—and holding doomsdag over hunselv, dreeing his weird, with his dander up, and his fringe combed over his eygs and droming on loft till the sight of the sternes, after zwarthy kowse and weedy broeks—You'd think all was dodo belonging to him how he durmed adranse in durance vaal (198.28–199.10).

> Shyr she's nearly as badher as him herself…Do you know she was calling bakvandets sals from all around, nyumba noo, chamba choo, to go in till him, her erring chief, and tickle the pontiff aisyoisy? Yssel that the limmat? (198.9)—Throwing all the neiss little whores in the world at him! To inny captured wench you wish of no matter what sex of pleissful ways two adda tammar a lizzi a lossie to hug and hab haven in Humpy's apron! (200.29).

But all of Anna's tricks failed. Not even his favorite dishes could rouse old Hump:

> and as rash as she'd russ with her peakload of vivers up on her sieve—my hardey Hek he'd kast them frome him, with a stour of scorn, as much as to say you sow and you sozh, and if he didn't peg the platteau at her tawe, believe you me, she was safe enough. (199.2)

Joyce's rich exploitation of the senex archetype in the character of Humphrey Chimpden Earwicker could be mapped onto Hillman's phenomenological amplification of the senex in "Senex and Puer" and in "On Senex Consciousness."[19]

---

19. James Hillman, "Senex and Puer: An Aspect of the Historical and Psychological Present," in this volume, and "On Senex Consciousness," *Spring: An Annual of Archetypal Psychology and Jungian Thought* (1970): 146–65 (reprinted in *UE3: Senex & Puer*).

HCE, like his still more deeply mythological prototype, Tim Finnegan, is a master-builder:

> Bygmester [Ibsen's 'Masterbuilder'] Finnegan, of the Stuttering Hand, freeman's maurer, lived in the broadest way immargin-able-before joshuan judges had given us numbers or Helviticus committed deuteronomy [T.S. Eliot stealing from *Ulysses* to produce "Wasteland" in Switzerland]...he would caligulate by multiplicables the alltitude and malltitude until he seesaw by neatlight of the liquor wheretwin [Shem and Shaun] 'twas born—a waalworth of a skyerscape of most eyeful hoyth entowerly—What then agentlike brought about—this municipal sin business? (4–5).

Compare Saturn as builder of cities.[20]

HCE, the English-Scandinavian, is an exile in Ireland. The sinful culture-builder (the original sin which God first committed in creating the world) is Saturn's other side. In the intervals between his resurrection, HCE lives in a mausoleum at the bottom of Lake Neagh, the traditional interim burial place of the old Celtic heroes. Joyce uses the imagery of the Egyptian Book of the Dead to illumine these episodes. In his deep sleep in these intervals HCE has all the negative Saturnine characteristics:

> His braynes coolt parritch, his pelt nassy, his heart's adrone, his bluid-streams acrawl, his puff but a piff, his extremities extremely so: Fenglass, Pawmbroke, Chilblaimend and Baldowl. Humph is in his doge. Words weigh no no more to him than raindrips to Rethfernhim. Which we all like. Rain. When we sleep. Drops. But wait until our sleeping. Drain. Sdops. (74.13–19)

The Puer

In the *Wake*, the puer is double. Indeed, in the *Wake* everything without exception generates its double. Shaun is the more or less conventionally recognized counterpart of the senex. He is his father all over again. He is the puer of the "and Son" mytheme. Since the entire action of Book III of the *Wake* (403–590), almost two hundred pages of densely packed material is devoted to Shaun's "puerity," it is impossible to sketch out the development, progressing backwards, from Shaun as a mature young man to the moment of his conception, in a short study. In general,

---

20. Hillman, "Senex and Puer," *et passim.*

Shaun reproduces the young man as consciously following in his father's footsteps but unconsciously preparing for his father's destruction. Shem, mother's boy and conscious rebel and iconoclast, unconsciously works to preserve his father's cultural values. The war between the sons recapitulates this clash of the opposites.

The two sides of the puer configuration are illustrated in Hillman; Shaun is the crippled, lame, castrated puer. Throughout the *Wake*, his domain is space. His movement is horizontal. He is a postman. Shem is Ikaros, the continuation of Stephen Daedalus in *Ulysses*. His movement is vertical and his dimension is time. Together they represent the space-time continuum of modern physics, and this contemporary constellation of the archetype is exploited in the Wake. The fairy tale entitled the Mookse and the Gripes begins: "Eins within a space and a wearywide space it wast ere wohned a Mookse." Says Hillman, "The puer cannot do with indirection, with timing and patience...And when it must rest or withdraw from the scene, then it seems to be 'stuck' in a timeless state, innocent of the passing years, out of tune with time." But this is true only of the space puer. Read the fairy tale of the Ondt and the Gracehoper (414–19):

> The Gracehoper was always jigging ajog, happy on akkant of his joyicity...What a zeit for the goths! vented the Ondt, who, not being a sommerfool, was thothfully making chilly spaces at hisphex affront of the icinglass of his windhame...The Ondt was a weltall fellow, raumybult and abelboobied [Abel to Shem's Cain]. He was sair sullemn and chairmanlooking when he was not making spaces in his psyche.

At the end, the Gracehoper satirizes the Ondt, "Your feats end enormous, your volumes immense—Your genus it's worldwide, your spacest sublime! But, Holy Saltmartin, why can't you beat time?" (419.5–8). Shem and Shaun as Cain and Abel, the two halves of the warring puer archetype, carry on their war throughout the entire book.

The third great fable in the *Wake*, that of the Prankquean (21 *et seq.*) should be annotated to Hillman's discussion of the relation of the puer to the great mother. In it, "we hear echoes of the festivals for Attis called *tristia and hilaria.*" In the Prankquean's tale (21–23), the boys are Tristopher and Hilary. The mother kidnaps Tristopher from his father who is Saturnizing in his castle "laying cold hands on himself." She takes the sad one to her four masters "for to tauch him his tickles and she convorted him to the onesure allgood and he became a luderman." Then she took Hilary to "her four larksical monitrix to touch him his tears and she provorted him to the onecertain allesecure and he became a tristian." Hilary becomes Larryhill. But Tristopher becomes Toughertrees. Throughout the *Wake*, Shem is a tree but Shaun is a stone. The vertical puer is matched with the horizontal one.

Puer And Relationship

Hillman speaks of the puer's lack of entangling relationships. The Puer fails at the critical moment of human involvement. In other words, as archetype he is true to himself. The Wake's pueri do relate, most intensely, to each other. Shem and Shaun describe elliptical orbits that touch at a point. As they draw near, their rivalry becomes more intense; as they recede from each other, tolerance grows. Shaun, the "and Son" puer is also related to his father; Shem, the mother's boy, to Anna Livia Plurabelle. *The point is that they cannot relate to their own generation properly.* Subsidiarily, they cannot relate to the older generation properly either—Shem to his father or Shaun to his mother.

The Puer as Messenger of the Divine

The *Wake* is a Letter, in fact, two Letters, but one will do. Anna Livia Plurabelle dictates the Letter (she cannot write), Shem the Penman writes it, Isobel ("Miss Sender," *absender*) misdirects it, Shaun the Postman undertakes to deliver it. It is sent to Humphrey, the culture builder. The Letter never reachers its destination: Who can read the *Wake*?

Senex-Puer Archetype Split

"Then," says Hillman, "we have a too-familiar pattern: action that does not know and knowledge that does not act, fanatic versus cynic, commonly formulated as youth and age." In the *Wake*, the split reaches down into the pueri. Shaun, father's son, is a cynic. His sermon (432 *et seq.*) to the twenty-nine girls is a parody of world-wise advice: "look before you leak, dears" (433.34). Shem's fanaticism is the main subject of the famous Shem Chapter (169 *et seq.*). Shaun execrates his brother as:

> Sniffer of carrion, premature gravedigger, seeker of the nest of evil in the bosom of a good word, you, who sleep at our vigil and fast for our feast, you, with your dislocated reason, have cutely foretold, a jophet in your own absence, by blind pouring upon

your many scalds and burns and blisters, impetiginous sore and pustules, by the auspices of that raven cloud, your shade, and by the auguries of rooks in parlament, death with every disaster, the dynamitisation of colleagues, the reducing of records to ashes, the levelling of all customs by blazes, the return of a lot of sweet-empered gunpowdered didst unto dust. (189–90)

Shem, the knower, cannot do; and Shaun, the man of action, is mindless. Yet, in another place, Joyce accepts the more traditional notion of the split as one between puer and senex: "If juness she saved! [si jeunesse savait...] Ah ho! And if yulone he pouved! The olold stoliolum!" (117.10).

Puer and Psyche

"The anima has the thread and knows the step-by-step dance that can lead through the labyrinth," writes Hillman. In the Wake the "Mime of Mick, Nick and the Maggies" (219 *et seq.*), the children's play, given every night, re-enacts the puer and psyche myth in a game of "Colors." Isobel unsuccessfully tries to get Shem to guess the color chosen. Her panto-mime, full of hints on the right answer, escapes him, for all his smartness.

Many other echoes of Hillman's study resonate in the *Wake*. HCE, the father, is deaf; Shaun the Post has "feet trouble." The night lessons of the children (260 *et seq.*) are under the aegis of Mercury. "Ainsoph (HCE), this upright one, with that noughty besighed him zeroine (ALP). To see in his horrorscup he is mehrkurios than saltz of sulphur" (261). Compare Hillman.

Finally—for now—this passage on Shaun. In the Mime, or children's nightly play-acting, the twenty-nine girls (Maenads to his Dionysus) sing the following hymn:

Enchainted, dear sweet Stainusless, young confessor, dearer dear-est, we herehear, aboutobloss, O coelicola, thee salutamt. Pattern of our unschoold, pageantmaster, deliverer of softmissives, round the world in forty mails, bag, belt and balmybeam, our barnaboy, our chepachap, with that pampipe in your putaway, gab borab, when you will be after doing all your sightseeing and soundhear-ing and smellsniffing and tastytasting and tenderumstouchings in all Daneygaul, send us, your adorables, thou overblaseed, a wise and letters play of all you can ceive, chief celtech chappy, from your holy post now you hast ascertained ceremonially our names. Unclean you are not. Outcaste thou are not. Leperstower,

the karman's loki, has not blanched at our pollution and your
intercourse at ninety legsplits does not defile. Untouchable is not
the scarecrown is on you. You are pure. You are pure. You are in
your puerity (237.11–25).